Taking Responsibility for Children

Studies in Childhood and Family in Canada

Studies in Childhood and Family in Canada is a multidisciplinary series devoted to new perspectives on these subjects as they evolve. The series features studies that focus on the intersections of age, class, race, gender, and region as they contribute to a Canadian understanding of childhood and family, both historically and currently.

Series Editor
Cynthia Comacchio
Department of History
Wilfrid Laurier University

Manuscripts to be sent to
Brian Henderson, Director
Wilfrid Laurier University Press
75 University Avenue West
Waterloo, Ontario, Canada N2L 3C5

TAKING RESPONSIBILITY FOR CHILDREN

Samantha Brennan
and Robert Noggle,
editors

WLU

Wilfrid Laurier University Press

This book has been published with the help of a grant from the Canadian Federation for the Humanities and Social Sciences, through the Aid to Scholarly Publications Programme, using funds provided by the Social Sciences and Humanities Research Council of Canada. We acknowledge the financial support of the Government of Canada through the Book Publishing Industry Development Program for our publishing activities.

Library and Archives Canada Cataloguing in Publication

     Taking responsibility for children / Samantha Brennan and Robert Noggle, editors.

(Studies in Childhood and Family in Canada)
Includes bibliographical references and index.
ISBN 978-1-55458-015-6

     1. Child rearing—Moral and ethical aspects. 2. Child rearing. 3. Parenting— Moral and ethical aspects. 4. Child welfare—Moral and ethical aspects. 5. Children's rights. I. Brennan, Samantha, 1964– II. Noggle, Robert, 1966– III. Series.

HQ767.9.T336 2007   305.23   C2007-901787-8

© 2007 Wilfrid Laurier University Press
Waterloo, Ontario, Canada
www.wlupress.wlu.ca

Cover photograph © 2006 R.W. Harwood. Cover and text design by P.J. Woodland.

∞

This book is printed on Ancient Forest Friendly paper (100% post-consumer recycled).

Printed in Canada

Every reasonable effort has been made to acquire permission for copyright material used in this text, and to acknowledge all such indebtedness accurately. Any errors and omissions called to the publisher's attention will be corrected in future printings.

CONTENTS

ACKNOWLEDGEMENTS

This book has been published with the help of a grant from the Canadian Federation for the Humanities and Social Sciences, through the Aid to Scholarly Publications Program, using funds provided by the Social Sciences and Humanities Research Council of Canada. We are grateful for this support.

We are also grateful for the support of the Social Sciences and Humanities Research Council of Canada for funding several workshops on ethics and children, which were held to meet, discuss, and improve the chapters of this volume. Samantha Brennan also acknowledges the support of the Social Sciences and Humanities Research Council of Canada for her strategic research grant, held between 1998–2001, "Children's Rights and Family Justice."

In addition, we wish to thank our universities, Central Michigan University (Noggle) and The University of Western Ontario (Brennan), for research support in various forms. Brennan also owes thanks to her colleagues in the ethics reading group at Western—Tracy Isaacs, Dennis Klimchuk, Michael Milde, Richard Bronaugh, and Robert Binkley—and to the graduate students who took part in her seminar on children's rights and family justice. Robert Noggle would like to express his gratitude for a sabbatical leave from Central Michigan University, part of which was used to complete some of the final editing of this book.

And, in keeping with the themes of this book, we both wish to acknowledge the love and support of our spouses and children.

Taking Responsibility for Children

ROBERT NOGGLE and
SAMANTHA BRENNAN

Children and the Questions They Raise

Children raise many questions. Some they raise themselves: "Mummy, why does the sun shine?" "Daddy, where does the rain come from?" Less direct, but surely just as important are the questions that arise not from children directly, but from the fact that no instruction book accompanies them to tell us how best to meet their needs and to prepare them for adulthood. New parents often face a bewildering array of sometimes conflicting advice about such issues as breastfeeding, toilet training, discipline, vaccinations, television viewing, daycare, and so on. The answers to these particular questions are often based on specific biological and psychological theories about the nature of children and childhood, about how children differ from adults, and about how children can best be prepared for their journey into and through adulthood. Our theories about the biological and psychological nature of children and childhood underlie general approaches to such practical issues as nutrition and health, socialization and character development, and education and psychological growth. These theories provide much of the practical know-how required for those who must take responsibility for children.

Psychological and biological theories about the nature of children and childhood address many of the day-to-day questions about children, but children also raise questions on a deeper, more philosophical level. These questions focus on the moral and ontological status of children and childhood: To what extent is the child "the same person as" her future adult self? To what extent (if any) should we regard the child's desires and decisions about her own future as binding on her future self? Is childhood best seen instrumentally, as a transient phase in the journey to adulthood and defined in terms of the lack of characteristics that define adulthood, or is childhood a stage of life that should be defined in its own terms, a stage possessing its own unique and valuable qualities to be enjoyed as goods in themselves? Is a child—even a very young one—a person in the same sense that an adult human being is a person? Is the moral status of the child the same as that of an adult person, and if not, how does it differ? What difference, if any, do the differences between children and adults make to their relative moral status? Do children have the same moral rights as adults? If so, then what, if anything, justifies the differences between how we treat them and how we treat other adults? If children have the same basic moral status as adults, then is parental authority over them justified, and if so, then how and to what extent? Should the child be seen as a full citizen of the state?

Answers to these more theoretical, philosophical questions about children have important practical implications. Understanding the moral and ontological status of children would help us to give and defend principled answers to some very practical questions facing parents and others who must take responsibility for children: Should certain freedoms that parents normally enjoy—such as the freedom to smoke in the home—be curtailed in order to benefit the child? To what extent (if any) do parents have the right to try to influence the child's present and future choices about religion, lifestyle, and world view? How much are parents obligated to do for their children? Do parents violate their moral obligations if they spend resources on their own interests (expensive vacations for themselves, for example) that could have been spent on in their child's interest (an expensive private education, for example)? When—if ever—does the parent's right to self-determination conflict with the child's right to sound and effective parenting? What responsibility does the state have for ensuring that children's needs are met? How much power should the state exercise in making sure that the parenting practices exercised on her are sound and effective? How intrusive should child protection agencies be in scrutinizing parenting for signs of abuse or neglect? Should the state regulate parenting and perhaps even license parents? How great a priority should the state place on funding public education? Should private schools and homeschooling be encouraged, discouraged, or perhaps even prohibited, and on what grounds? What limits, if any, can schools legitimately place on student privacy and free expression? Should children be allowed to "sue" or "divorce" their parents? Should interracial adoption be encouraged or discouraged? Should gays and lesbians be encouraged or even allowed to adopt? Is there any principled reason for thinking that the ideal number of parents is two? Is corporal punishment morally legitimate, and if so, under what circumstances?

The answers to questions like these will depend in large part on one's fundamental beliefs about the metaphysical and moral status of children and childhood. Of course, beliefs of these sorts have changed a great deal over the last several hundred years. For a very long time, the dominant view in Western culture was that the moral status of children was inferior to that of adults, and that, as a result, parents (and especially fathers) had something very much like property rights over children. With a few notable exceptions—such as John Locke and Jean Jacques Rousseau—the philosophers of previous centuries seemed reluctant to challenge this traditional attitude toward children. Indeed, in the pre-twentieth-century philosophical canon, there is distressingly little discussion of children that suggests, assumes, or argues for the view that children are already persons with the same basic moral status as other persons.[1]

This traditional Western conception of children as inferior (or perhaps only potential) persons over whom parents may exercise a hopefully benevolent, but, in any case, nearly absolute authority began to be challenged during the nineteenth century and was largely defeated during the early and middle parts of the twentieth century. Challenges to the traditional view came from many directions and took many forms: the end of the system of indentured servitude for poor children, legal reforms (including changes to custody law and the rise of child-protection laws), the rise of mandatory public education, new work in the psychology of child development, and progressive social movements that sought to overturn the traditional systems of power and prestige enjoyed by adult males of European ancestry. The last of these forces played a particularly important role in helping to make it untenable to think of any human person as a second-class citizen, much less as mere property. But while the political and social liberation of women and other oppressed groups clearly called for their being granted all of the rights and powers of adult males of European ancestry, it was less clear that this was an appropriate way to recognize the moral status of children as persons. Although some people did advocate a program of complete or nearly complete "child liberation," for the most part Western society has persisted in thinking that it is both necessary and proper to withhold from children some of the powers and privileges granted to adults.[2] This raises a fundamental question, of course: Is it really consistent to say that children are persons and yet to say that they may be treated in ways that would clearly be oppressive if directed at adults? This fundamental question forces us to grapple with the similarities and differences between children and adults; it challenges us to understand how human rights and basic human dignity are expressed in children, and how our families and social institutions can best respect and care for them.

It is perhaps a bit surprising to find that philosophers—who were well represented among the supporters and theorists of movements to end the oppression of women and those of non-European ancestry—have had far less to say about the more complex questions posed when we begin to ask whether and in what ways our current institutions and practices might be oppressing children. Indeed, between 1905 and 1950, barely any articles about the moral or political status of children appeared in any of the mainstream academic philosophical journals.[3] Over the next two decades, a small but growing trickle of philosophical articles appeared (most of which involved discussions of the proper methods and goals of education in a free society) that began to address the arguments for and the implications of according children the same moral status as other persons. Finally, starting in the 1970s, academic philosophers began to take seriously the important theoretical and practical issues surrounding childhood and to publish an increasing number of articles and books on these topics. Although they had a late start, philosophers have begun to take their rightful place in discussions about the nature and value of children and childhood, and to bring their own unique intellectual tools and conceptual resources to bear in an effort to answer fundamental moral and political questions about children and their relationship to parents and the rest of society.

The philosophers who address philosophical questions about children are also human beings—and often parents—and as such they have many of the same everyday, practical questions and public-policy questions about children that face everyone who must take responsibility for children. For this reason, much of the work that philosophers have done on children's issues has been motivated as much by practical concerns and questions as by philosophical ones. The hope of philosophers working in this area is that philosophical work can help us not only to answer abstract philosophical questions about children, childhood, and child-rearing, but that it might give us some guidance in approaching the more everyday, practical, and public-policy questions about children.

The chapters in this book reflect this mix of concern with the practical and the philosophical aspects of taking responsibility for children. They address such topics as the limits and extent of parental obligations, the nature and extent of the rights and entitlements of children, the responsibility of the state to protect children, the proper role and nature of public education in a liberal society, the best ways to ensure adequate child protection, the question of whether we should license parents, the conflicts over children's religious education, and questions about children's health.

All of the chapters share one fundamental assumption—that adults have responsibilities toward children. The disagreements arise when we ask what those responsibilities are and who has them. These disagreements center on two fundamental moral and political questions: What is required of those who take responsibility for children? Whose obligation is it to take this responsibility? This book primarily focuses on the first of these questions: each chapter traces out a particular idea about some aspect of what it means to take responsibility for children. Some chapters focus primarily on the responsibilities of parents toward children, while others focus primarily on what society and government must do to play their proper role in taking responsibility for children. Each chapter offers at least part of an answer to the question: What do we, as a society generally, and as parents in particular, owe to our children? As the various practical questions addressed by the chapters of this book make clear, each of the philosophers included here believes that developing and defending a morally and philosophically sound answer to this question will help us to know how we, as a society and as individual parents, should treat our children.

Philosophical Discussions of Taking Responsibility for Children

In "Raising Children: Who Is Responsible for What?" Colin Macleod addresses two main kinds of questions about what is involved in taking responsibility for children. The first concerns what entitlements children have. The second concerns who has the responsibility to provide these entitlements to children. The first question—what Macleod calls the "entitlement problem"—raises a further question about why children have whatever entitlements they have. Macleod assumes that the ground for children's entitlement claims is some form of equal consideration principle grounded in an impartialist theory of justice. He considers two main answers to the question of the extent of children's entitlements. What he calls the minimum provision thesis (MPT) claims that children are entitled to only enough resources and nurturing to ensure that they can have minimal decent lives. A more ambitious answer Macleod calls the egalitarian provision thesis (EPT), which claims that children are entitled to an upbringing that gives them prospects for development and happiness equal to those of other children of their generation. Macleod favours the EPT over the MPT on the basis of his sympathy for an egalitarian liberal theory of justice.

Next, Macleod turns his attention to the question of how to allocate responsibility for providing for children's entitlements (whatever one thinks that they are). After drawing a number of very useful distinctions among various kinds of responsibility that various actors might be thought to have, he turns to the grounds on which the various kinds of responsibility for meeting children's entitlements should be distributed. Macleod distinguishes two main kinds of grounds or criteria for determining who bears responsibility for meeting a given child's entitlements. What he calls "strategic" grounds or criteria are broadly consequentialist in nature, and focus on allocating responsibility in a way that makes it most likely that the entitlements of children will be met. What he calls "principled" criteria are more deontological in nature; they ground responsibility for children in terms of such norms as the assumption of responsibility involved in begetting children and duties of reciprocity borne by members of society for the economic, social, and cultural benefits that the next generation brings. Interestingly, Macleod notes that both sorts of considerations (even though they are based on very different moral theoretical grounds) often point in the same direction. Thus, the practice of giving parents primary responsibility for meeting the needs of children can be justified both in terms of efficiency (a strategic consideration) and in terms of the voluntary choice of the parents (a principled consideration). Perhaps more importantly, a secondary or supplementary responsibility on the part of society in general to help meet the entitlements of children (especially the financial costs of these entitlements) can also be justified on both kinds of grounds.

In "Parental Responsibility" Jan Narveson offers a provocative approach to answering questions about the moral obligations of those who take responsibility for children. He begins by posing a fundamental and startling question, asking "In what way, and why, are parents responsible for their children?" Narveson notes that what makes this question interesting, and often of very great practical importance, is that a de facto parent could disown responsibility, not only by denying that he (or she) is in fact a parent of this particular child, but more interestingly by denying that he has any duties to or about, or any responsibility for, the children in question. Such a parent strikes us being a bad parent, but are we justified in making this claim? Setting aside hard questions posed by parents who would give away their children (such as whether others in the community have a duty or obligation to raise the children), Narveson moves on to his central topic: the responsibilities parents have to those children they choose to raise and provide for. Narveson writes that one popular view is that parents have moral obligations to their children, to provide a high but hard-to-define level of benefits for them. After considering problems with this view, Narveson goes on to consider another, stronger but less popular view that parents owe the rest of us (that is, society at large) certain things regarding their children. Narveson's idea here rests on the observation that parents can impose risks on other people by virtue of their parental activities—adults, in particular, but probably others too. Parenting can constitute irresponsible behaviour. Thus, in this view, parents owe a duty to society to conduct their parenting activities so that their children do not grow up to be a net cost to the rest of us in the community. Narveson goes on to argue that today's parents generally know enough about child-rearing to avoid raising children who are moral monsters. Thus, he argues that even on the less popular route to deriving parental responsibilities, there are significant responsibilities involved in undertaking the task of parenting.

In "Children, Caregivers, Friends," Amy Mullin focuses on the most fundamental institution for taking responsibility for children—the parent–child relationship. Her analysis is centred on a comparison and contrast between the parent–child relationship on one hand and caring relationships among adults on the other. In this way, she addresses questions at the heart of much recent feminist ethical and political theory, in which a number of theorists claim that the mothering relationship should be seen as a paradigm or model for all ethically healthy relationships (and, in particular, that it should supplant the contractual model of such relationships). Mullin announces that her sympathies are (with some qualifications) with feminists who reject the mothering model as a paradigm for all moral relationships.

Mullin next turns to her comparison of the mothering relationship with adult relationships between friends. After a careful examination of the various forms of reciprocity that philosophers have taken to be the hallmark of friendship, she concludes that although friendships, like other genuine relationships, require some form of mutuality, it is misguided to claim that they always require quid pro quo reciprocity. Some adult relationships can involve non-reciprocated caregiving; and they can be healthy so long as they do not involve exploitation or paternalism. Thus, Mullin makes room for caretaking, even unreciprocated caretaking, in adult relationships, and in so doing she breaks down the dichotomy between supposedly reciprocal adult relationships and the parent–child relationship.

For Mullin, the difference between children and their caregivers on one hand and non-reciprocal adult relationships on the other seems to be that relationships between caretakers and children involve more inequality and dependency than adult relationships do. This dependency and inequality is of a certain sort—that which impedes the child's ability to judge what is in her own best interests. This kind of inequality and dependence—which characterizes childhood but not the kinds of vulnerability that can exist in non-reciprocal caring relationships between morally equal adults—is what justifies at least some paternalism toward children by their caretakers.

Mullin's conception of parenting involves mutuality even in the absence of full reciprocity, but she claims that children should be encouraged to display whatever forms of reciprocity toward their parents that they are capable of. It also involves spreading the work of child-rearing among networks of caregivers, rather than making only one or two parents responsible for it. Mullin suggests various ways that such networks would be good for both parents and children.

In "Parent Licensing and Responsibility for Children," Mark Vopat takes up the question of how the state should ensure adequate performance by those who take responsibility for children. In particular, he is concerned with the idea of parental licensing. His goal is to improve on the well-known proposals of Hugh LaFollette and Jack Westman. Vopat notes that LaFollette's proposal requires the development of extensive forms of psychological testing to determine which parents are likely to abuse children in the future. Vopat questions whether such testing is feasible, and whether the propensity for abuse and neglect is the right sort of thing for a psychological test to determine. Where LaFollette's proposal seems too stringent, Vopat argues that Westman's proposal is too lax. In particular, Westman seems reluctant to call for outright parental licensing, opting instead to defend tax and other incentives to encourage voluntary licensing. Vopat criticizes this proposal on the grounds of social justice, both for children and for parents, noting that such an incentive-based proposal would target disproportionately parents at the lower economic levels of society.

Vopat argues for an approach to licensing that is more minimal than the one advocated by LaFollette but more universal than the one advocated by Westman. He notes that his proposal, like others, is less radical than it may first seem, since we already to have de facto or implicit licens-

ing programs for foster and adoptive parents. As Vopat notes, those programs seem to be morally acceptable, at least in principle. Vopat examines the adoption criteria in both Canada and the United States, with the
intention of crafting his own proposal for universal parental licensing that
includes criteria and standards that society has already endorsed for adoptive parents. (This approach prevents him from adopting what he sees as
an unduly optimistic approach to psychological testing of the kind that
LaFollette proposes.) The minimalist proposal Vopat endorses is geared
not toward eliminating every case of bad parenting, nor to attempting to
speculate about future neglect or abuse by parents who show no obvious
danger signs at present. Rather, his proposal seeks only to ensure that parents are not abusing dangerous drugs, that they can provide economically
for the child, either through employment or through access to public welfare, that they meet minimal age and educational requirements, and that
they do not have a history of domestic violence or child abuse. His proposal
makes allowances for provisional licensing of parents who do not meet
all of these requirements, but with proper supervision of social service
workers.

Vopat ends his chapter with an examination of the main objections to
parent licensing proposals and argues that they are all unconvincing, especially when directed at a minimalistic but universal proposal of the kind
he favours.

The chapters by Macleod, Narveson, Mullin, and Vopat all focus on
broad issues about what it means to take responsibility for children. The
remaining chapters concern more specific moral and public-policy issues
that arise in the context of taking responsibility for children. In "Responsibility for Children's Rights: The Case for Restricting Parental Smoking,"
Samantha Brennan and Angela White ask whether those who take responsibility for children should be required to refrain from smoking around
them. They begin by examining the nature and content of the responsibilities that adult members of a society have towards children. In so doing,
they distinguish parental responsibilities from those of the state. They then
consider an often-neglected category of obligations to children: those that
apply to individual adults regardless of whether they are parents but are
separate from the responsibilities of the state. Based on the assumption that
children have rights, Brennan and White ask what responsibilities parents
have for children as right bearers or in some cases—depending on the
right—future rights bearers. Their goal is to determine what responsibilities we have for children when we begin with a fairly minimalist set of
moral commitments, such as those specified by rights against harm. The

first obligation we have is the direct duty not to infringe rights. The second kind of obligation that follows from the assumption of children's rights is the responsibility to educate children about their rights. Given that education is not enough to prevent children from being harmed, there is also a third category of obligation, a third-party moral responsibility to pay attention to infringements that occur. A final section puts these three kinds of obligation into practice through an examination of a controversial topic, the case of children's rights and second-hand smoke.

In "Political Liberalism and Moral Education: Reflections on *Mozert v. Hawkins*," Marc Ramsay examines the conflicts that arise between parents and the state when the state takes responsibility for children's education. Ramsay uses a 1987 US Federal Court case involving religion and the school system as a jumping off point for a discussion of fundamental questions about the limits of parental rights in a liberal society. The case of *Mozert v. Hawkins City Board of Education* is in some ways reminiscent of the much-discussed case of *Wisconsin v. Yoder*, in that it pits the child's rights to an education and the state's interest in providing that education against the parents' rights to religious freedom and their (alleged?) right to raise their children in whatever religion they choose. The parents objected to the use of elementary school texts that they said contained themes that contradicted the fundamentalist Christianity they were teaching their children. The main complaints of the parents focused on the positive portrayal of other religions or world views (such as Catholicism, feminism, humanism, and pacifism) that conflicted with their version of Christianity. (The parents' complaints are reminiscent of well-known claims by fundamentalists that the schools indoctrinate children in the "religion" of secular humanism.) A US District Court of Appeals overturned a lower court ruling allowing the children to be excused from the reading program. The appeals court decided, in effect, that the potential harm to the parents' religious rights were not great enough to outweigh the state's interest in providing a good education.

Next, Ramsay moves on to a discussion of the deeper issues in liberal political theory that this case raises. The case has formed something of a test case for two camps of liberal political theorists. Political liberals attempt to maintain strict neutrality among all reasonable world views, including those of their liberal fellow-travellers, the comprehensive, or autonomy liberals. This group of liberals endorses a particular and distinctively liberal world view that emphasizes critical reflection, the use of reason, and the value of personal autonomy. Although some political liberals have in fact endorsed the *Mozert* ruling, Ramsay argues that they can only do so by abandoning the neutrality that makes their view what it is. He defends this claim by examining various arguments for and against political liberalism. Autonomy liberalism encourages the same kind of critical inquiry that the curriculum in the *Mozert* case attempted to foster and to which the parents objected. Some philosophers have argued that political liberalism is consistent with the *Mozert* decision (and thus with the kind of curriculum that fosters tolerance and that may indeed encourage critical reflection). However, Ramsay argues that true neutrality of the kind political liberals favour would require deciding *Mozert* in favour of the parents. Ramsay's own sympathies lie with Will Kymlicka's moderate form of autonomy liberalism; although it is a form of comprehensive liberalism, he argues that it is far less parochial than political liberals claim.

In "Education in a Pluralistic Society: Implications of *Ross*," Karen Wendling approaches many of the same political issues about the state's obligation to take responsibility for the education of children that were raised in Ramsay's chapter. However, Wendling uses a Canadian court case as her point of departure for raising questions about the relationships between state and parental roles in taking responsibility for children's education. In particular, she examines *Ross v. New Brunswick School District No. 15*, a 1996 Supreme Court of Canada decision involving the education of children. In part 1, Wendling briefly summarizes the facts in the *Ross* decision, and discusses the Court's views on the political function of education in a free and democratic society. In part 2, she argues that the Court's reasoning can be applied to a broader range of educational cases. In part 3, she discusses some implications of *Ross* for education in a pluralistic liberal society.

According to the Supreme Court, education instills political values in children. This includes especially "equality with respect to the enjoyment of fundamental freedoms," which is an analytic requirement of political freedom. Wendling writes that these political values are important not only for students in public schools, however. They are "essential to a free and democratic society," and as such they must be taught to all children, regardless of the sorts of schools they attend. Currently provinces set requirements for curricula for children who are educated in private schools or who are home-schooled. According to Wendling, if the provinces have the power to mandate which skills ought to be taught to children, they also have the power to require that these skills include learning and practicing the values that underlie Canadian society. If a province does not currently require this, the relevant legislation should be changed on Wendling's analysis. Ideally, these changes should be made by legislatures; however, if

legislatures do not make appropriate changes to their education acts, perhaps because the issue is perceived to be too controversial, the courts
ought to "read in" the same political requirements for public and private
schools. Canadians have a stake in all children developing the appropriate
political values, not just those who attend public schools.

In the final chapter, Laura Purdy asks "Could There Be a Right Not to
Be Born an Octuplet?" The theme of this chapter is the question of whether
those who take responsibility for creating children have an obligation not
to create them in certain ways. Twice in recent years the bioethics sensation of the week has been the arrival of high-order multiple births, first the
McCaughey septuplets in Des Moines, Iowa, in 1997, then the Chukwa octuplets in Houston, Texas, in 1998. Each unleashed a storm of commentary,
some focusing on the miraculous nature of the events, some on the problems they represent. And, as is so often the case, both kinds mostly dealt
with short-term issues—the need for hundreds of diapers, the images of
babies on ventilators, and the expense. In part, perhaps because of media
formats that inhibit more in-depth exploration, and in part because of the
peculiar lack of sustained interest in children's issues, relatively little scholarly work has yet appeared on the subject. Laura Purdy addresses this issue
from the perspective of harm to the potential children. The harms addressed by Purdy include not just the physical harms and potential harms
that face all members of an octuplet pregnancy but also issues of parental
time and the challenge of raising eight children simultaneously. The main
focus of Purdy's chapter is moral responsibility. Canvassing various views
of who owes what to children, Purdy concludes that, morally speaking, we
ought to look unfavourably on octuplet pregnancies because of the harm
such pregnancies inflict on the children the octuplets become.

Although Purdy argues that parents have a moral responsibility to avoid
octuplet pregnancies, she does not favour making it illegal to enter into
them. Nevertheless, she argues that "it would be reasonable to protect
children from the dangers of being born of high order multiple pregnancies
by positing for them a right not to be born that way." She suggests that taking such a position "creates both individual responsibilities on the part of
those who would be parents, but also social responsibilities to create conditions for them to exercise their individual responsibilities."

The Role of Philosophy in Thinking about Children

At the present time, we lack a coherent, fully worked-out theory of childhood, and of the moral and political status of children. Such a theory would

give us a more solid foundation on which to make consistent, justifiable decisions about how to balance parental interests against children's rights. It would provide guidance for specific public-policy questions, such as those involving child custody, children's competence versus proxy decision-making in moral and legal contexts, moral education, and conflicts between parental rights (such as religious choice) and children's interests. Such a theory would integrate our deepest commitments to the value of children and empirical work on the cognitive and moral development of children to produce a conceptual framework that would allow our best science and our deepest moral values to guide policy-making with respect to children. So far, philosophers have yet to settle on such a theory. The chapters of this book can be seen as a snapshot of where we are on the way to developing one. Collectively, they provide a good view of where the philosophical community—and in particular the Canadian philosophical community—is in its grappling with the philosophical questions raised by the practical tasks of taking responsibility for children.

Notes

1 For a sampling of the views of some of the most prominent philosophers—from Socrates through John Rawls—see Susan M. Turner and Gareth B. Matthews, eds., *The Philosopher's Child: Critical Essays in the Western Tradition* (Rochester, NY: University of Rochester Press, 1998).

2 David Archard's *Children: Rights and Childhood* (London: Routledge, 1993) provides a useful intellectual history of attitudes toward children and childhood, as well as a critical survey of the debate over child liberation. In so doing he provides an overview of a truly vast literature on the history of the treatment of and attitudes toward children.

3 This and other claims in this paragraph are based on searches of the *Philosopher's Index* for the relevant years. The exact numbers of philosophical articles dealing with the moral status of children depends in part on how one counts several journals not currently recognized among the "standard" academic philosophical journals.

ONE

Raising Children:
Who Is Responsible for What?

COLIN M. MACLEOD

Introduction

Considerations of prudence and justice provide us with reasons to be concerned with the way children are raised. From a prudential point of view, it makes sense to ensure that children are raised to be self-reliant, productive members of society who can contribute to mutually beneficial forms of co-operation and interaction, and who are disposed to respect the rights of others. Poorly raised children are likely to impose undesirable costs on society, such as rights violations along with the costs of maintaining coercive enforcement mechanisms—police, courts, prisons, insurance—aimed at dealing with such problems. Considerations of justice provide even more compelling reasons to be concerned with the upbringing of children. Children have distinct interests that give rise to justice-based entitlements. Extending considerations of justice to children is partly a matter of ensuring that they are raised in a way that is respectful of their distinct justice-based entitlements. I shall assume in light of such considerations that we should accept the claim that every child is entitled to a decent upbringing. For the most part, I do not wish to explore the deep normative justification of this claim. Rather, I wish to examine how we should set about answering the two questions implied by the title of this chapter: (1) What sort of upbringing are children entitled to receive? (2) Who has responsibility for ensuring that children receive this upbringing? I suspect that crafting a satisfactory response to these questions may be more complex than is

1

sometimes assumed. Many discussions about rearing children focus on delineating the special responsibilities that parents have. This focus on parental duties is understandable, but it is potentially misleading insofar as it conveys the impression that responsibilities for raising children well lie almost exclusively with parents. The African proverb, "it takes a village to raise a child," reminds us that raising children is really a collective enterprise involving the coordinated efforts of many different people. In collective enterprises there are typically many different ways of allocating responsibility among agents for the achievement of ends. In the case of raising children, we need to know something about the appropriate objectives of raising children and who should assume responsibility for ensuring that these objectives are realized.

Let me state the dimensions of the problem somewhat more formally. First, there is the entitlement problem. Addressing this problem involves identifying the key components in a decent upbringing and the kinds of resources, opportunities, protections, and nurturing children are entitled to receive. Second, there is a responsibility allocation problem. Here the challenge is to determine who should be assigned responsibility for ensuring that the various entitlement claims of children are met. This problem is, to an important degree, distinct from the entitlement problem because, in many cases, merely specifying a child's entitlement is not sufficient to determine who has responsibility for ensuring its provision. For example, saying a child is entitled to nutritious food does not tell us who is responsible for providing food to the child. Sometimes, however, specification of an entitlement can uniquely determine the agent who has responsibility for ensuring the entitlement claim is met; for example, we might say that a child is entitled to the love of his/her parents. A solution to the entitlement problem will influence the solution to the allocation problem but it will not, typically, uniquely determine a solution. For most entitlements, there is a number of what might be termed "potential nurturing agents," that is, persons or institutions that could be assigned responsibility for meeting a given entitlement claim. The allocation problem consists in determining the criteria that should be used to determine which potential nurturing agents have responsibility for meeting which entitlement claims.

Implicit responses to both the entitlement and allocation problems are reflected in some common assumptions about child-rearing responsibilities. We tend to think that the degree of responsibility competent adult agents have (whether individually or collectively) for raising children is a function of the closeness of the relationship between children and adults. The factors that determine the overall closeness of the relationship between these potential nurturing agents and children are various, but they seem to include factors such as: (a) biological relatedness, (b) familial ties, (c) culture, (d) language, (e) nationality, (f) shared political institutions, and (g) geographical closeness. Thus we would typically suppose that I have a greater responsibility to ensure that my son is well fed than to ensure that a child in Peru is well fed. If we think children are entitled to religious instruction, we might say that the local Rabbi has a greater responsibility to ensure the spiritual well-being of Jewish children in the community than he has to ensure the spiritual well-being of non-Jewish children. We need not suppose, of course, that the existing allocation of child-rearing responsibilities is defensible. For example, the fact that mothers have traditionally been assigned primary responsibility for performing domestic labour essential to the well-being of children does not indicate that such a division of child-rearing responsibilities is correct. Indeed, there is good reason to believe that a gendered division of domestic child-rearing responsibilities is problematic.

I shall not try to articulate full responses to the entitlement and allocation problems. Rather, my aim is to examine more closely some of the issues that need to be addressed in developing satisfactory responses. Most of the analysis will address aspects of the allocation problem. Here I will propose some distinctions between different aspects of responsibility attribution, and I will suggest that there are two main kinds of considerations—strategic and principled—that are relevant to determining the allocation of responsibility. I begin, however, with some reflections on the entitlement problem.

The Extent and Grounds of Children's Entitlements

There are two main dimensions to the entitlement problem. First, there are questions concerning the normative grounds of children's entitlements. What factors determine the nature of children's moral status and the weight of their interests compared to other members of the moral community? Second, there is the finer problem of identifying the specific character and extent of children's entitlements. I will not say much about the first issue except that I assume that children are distinct but dependent and particularly vulnerable members of the moral community. Their interests cannot simply be subsumed under those of their parents or community. Children are entitled to consideration of their fundamental interests on an equal basis with mature members of the moral community. In short, I assume a broadly impartialist theory of justice in which the scope of moral concern is extended directly to children.

What does equal consideration of children's interests imply about their entitlements to nurture? One view can be termed the minimum provision thesis (MPT).[1] According to the MPT, all children have a basic entitlement to the kind of nurturing that is necessary to ensure that they are able to lead minimally decent lives as children and that they have a meaningful opportunity to lead minimally decent lives as adults. A rough approximation of what is involved in securing the conditions of a minimally decent life includes satisfaction of basic nutritional needs, access to adequate shelter and clothing, access to health care sufficient to secure normal biological development, provision of basic education, protection of security of the person, access to a living culture, and having affective attachments with members of family and/or community. The upbringing should also ensure basic development of moral powers—including the capacity to form and revise a conception of the good and a sense of justice. The specific entitlement claims entailed by the MPT are not very extensive. They fall well short of what would be required by even a fairly modest principle of equality of opportunity. However, it is worth noting that the current allocation of responsibilities among nurturing agents has not succeeded in reliably securing even the basic developmental interests of many children. Even a cursory examination of UNICEF's *The State of the World's Children 2006*[2] reveals that the basic needs of millions of children in the world are far from adequately met. Given the general moral priority[3] that typically attaches to meeting the basic needs of children, we have reason to consider changes in the allocation of nurturing responsibilities.

We have reason to doubt that the MPT provides a sufficient account of the entitlements of children that can be derived from an ideal of impartiality. A broad consensus exists among defenders of an impartialist conception of justice that significant resource and opportunity inequalities between persons are illegitimate if they arise because of the way social and political institutions respond to certain irrelevant traits. The MPT fails as an interpretation of impartiality because it is compatible with great inequalities in the life prospects of children that are traceable to morally suspect sources. For example, a society in which every child's basic needs were met but in which white children were provided with substantially better health care and education than black children would be unjust even though the MPT was satisfied. A just society does not permit the opportunities persons have to lead a decent life to be unfairly influenced by factors such as person's race, sex, class, ethnicity, class background, religion, or disabilities. Of course, an impartialist theory of distributive justice need not condemn all inequalities in the life prospects of persons as unjust. A just distribution should display sensitivity to the choices that responsible persons make about how to conduct their lives.[4]

In many responsibility-sensitive theories of distributive justice, the share of resources (for example, income and other goods) to which persons are entitled can vary significantly providing two conditions are satisfied. First, permissible inequalities must be traceable to the choices individuals make (for example, about how hard to work, what occupations to pursue, or what risks to take). Second, the options to which individuals respond in exercising choices about how to conduct their lives must be available to all on the basis of equality of opportunity. On this view, for example, it is not objectionable per se if doctors earn more than manual labourers, providing persons can choose whether or not to pursue a career as a doctor or labourer and that the opportunity to pursue these options is available to all on a fair basis. But if medical schools set a standard of admission for women that is twice as high as the standard set for men, then even though women can choose to pursue a medical career, they are unfairly disadvantaged in the competition for spots in medical school compared to men. The idea that resource distribution should be sensitive to the choices of individuals and to elementary considerations of fairness provides reasons to move toward a more egalitarian response to the entitlement problem than is provided by the MPT.

An egalitarian provision thesis (EPT) according to which children have an equal entitlement to at least certain basic resources can be developed in different ways depending on how we interpret the objective of extinguishing the impact of arbitrary factors on a fair distribution of resources. We can distinguish between moderate and strong versions of an EPT. The moderate EPT corresponds to the ideal equality of opportunity that enjoys widespread popular endorsement. The strong EPT corresponds to the ideal of liberal equality defended in various forms by various influential theorists.[5]

The moderate version of the EPT provides a seemingly attractive way of developing a responsibility-sensitive theory of distributive justice that gives content to the idea that one's opportunity to access the benefits of social co-operation should not be determined by traits over which one has no control and which are irrelevant as grounds of entitlement. A good deal of controversy exists about the background conditions that must be satisfied to ensure equality of opportunity is secured for children. It has been argued, for instance, that permitting parents to confer special benefits (for example, private schooling, better health care, etc.) on their children is inconsistent with equality of opportunity.[6] Taking equality of opportunity seriously in the context of children almost certainly involves ensuring a much more egalitarian distribution of basic educational and health care resources than partisans of this ideal in popular political discourse typically realize. This is in part because we cannot justify inequalities in the basic resources that children have access to and which are likely to have a bearing on their sub-sequent opportunities by appealing to the responsible choices made by children. Children, especially young children, lack the capacities for auton-omous self-direction that are prerequisites for holding persons responsi-ble for their choices. So the responsibility for ensuring that children can access, on an equal basis, the crucial resources that have a bearing on their opportunities for leading successful lives cannot lie with children. Nor would fairness allow some children to have access to crucial resources, simply by virtue of the social and economic position of their family, to which children from less fortunate backgrounds lack.

The impulse to eliminate arbitrary sources of disadvantages that equal-ity of opportunity draws upon can also ground an even more egalitarian solution to the entitlement problem than that presented by the moderate EPT. Equality of opportunity is, in principle, compatible with substantial material inequality among children. Thus, equality of opportunity is not vio-lated if some children are poor and others are rich, even if this means that rich children lead better (that is, more comfortable, enjoyable, and stimu-lating) lives than poor children. Material inequalities and the impact they have on the quality of children's lives are only suspect to the degree that they undermine the achievement of equality in the opportunities children will subsequently have as responsible adults to pursue benefits (for example, employment, post-secondary education, positions of power and authority, and so on). In this respect, equality of opportunity is a forward-looking ideal. It looks forward to the opportunities children will have when they are no longer children, but it is insensitive to arbitrary differences in the oppor-tunities children have to lead good lives as children. If we are genuinely con-cerned about mitigating the influence of morally arbitrary factors on the lives of children, we should be concerned not only with whether material inequality affects the subsequent achievement of equality of opportunity of adults but also with whether substantial differences in the quality of children's lives is just.

From the impartialist perspective, it seems unfair that some children, solely by virtue of the social and economic status of their families, enjoy a childhood that is much more comfortable, satisfying, and fun than the childhood of children from less-advantaged family backgrounds. The qual-ity of one's life as a child matters even if it has little bearing on one's life prospects as an adult. We have reason to ensure, therefore, that the access children have, as children, to good lives is not unduly determined by factors, such as family background, over which they have no control. Arguably, the ideal we should aim for is not mere equality of opportunity but one that seeks to equally indemnify persons against all morally arbitrary sources of disadvantage that impair their overall life prospects. A more fully egalitarian approach to the entitlement problem would require a form of nurturing compatible with providing all children with good and equal life prospects. Therefore, on a strong EPT, all children have an entitlement to an upbringing that ensures that their welfare and development interests are equally well served (relative to their generational cohort) and that they enjoy an equal opportunity among their generational cohort to lead a good life.

The choice between the MPT and some version of the EPT has a bearing on how responsibilities for rearing children are best distributed. For example, ensuring that children have access to equally good educational opportunities requires a different responsibility allocation than the allocation needed to ensure that children merely acquire basic literacy skills. However, as I suggested earlier, the solution to the entitlement problem will not entail a complete solution to the allocation problem. So without resolving the entitlement problem definitively, I now want to turn to some features of responsibility attribution that are relevant to framing the allocation problem more precisely.

Framing the Allocation Problem:
Dimensions of Responsibility of Attribution

Three sets of distinctions may usefully be drawn concerning responsibility attribution in the context of child rearing. First, we can draw a distinction between *undifferentiated* and *differentiated* forms of responsibility. A responsibility to meet an entitlement claim is undifferentiated if all agents have the same responsibility with respect to securing the entitlement. For example, all children are entitled to security of the person of the sort that establishes a prohibition against assault. Respecting this entitlement is obviously important to nurturing children. Since all agents have an identical responsibility not to assault children, this is an undifferentiated responsibility. A responsibility is differentiated if different agents have different degrees of responsibility with respect to securing an entitlement.

As a practical matter, most responsibilities for rearing children are differentiated. As I noted earlier, agents have quite different responsibilities with respect to nurturing particular children and with respect to the kinds of nurturing they have responsibilities to provide. There are obvious practical reasons for my having a greater responsibility to secure the health of my son than you do. But I do not think that differentiated responsibilities for child rearing arise wholly out of practical considerations. There are principled grounds for differentiated responsibilities. So although it is true that we all have responsibilities with respect to raising children, we do not, even at an abstract theoretical level, have equal responsibilities for all children. Just what the principled grounds for differentiated responsibilities are is a matter I take up below.

Within the category of differentiated responsibility, we can draw a second distinction between *primary* and *secondary* responsibility. An agent or a group of agents will have primary responsibility with respect to an entitlement claim when they are directly required to undertake efforts to ensure that the entitlement claim is met. An agent or group of agents will have secondary responsibility with respect to an entitlement claim if they are required to undertake efforts to ensure that the entitlement claim is met when the agent or agents charged with primary responsibility are unable or unwilling to do so. To make matters more complicated, there may also be a category of *supplementary* responsibility. Some agents may have special responsibilities to supplement the efforts of agents with primary responsibilities in ensuring that an entitlement claim is met. For instance, we might say a teacher has a primary responsibility to teach my son how to read. The local school board has a secondary responsibility with respect to teaching my son. If the teacher proves incompetent then the board must find a competent teacher. I have a supplementary responsibility to assist my son's teacher's efforts by reading to him. I hasten to add that these distinctions are not meant to be sharp. Sometimes the boundaries between primary, secondary, and supplementary responsibilities will be hard to draw. Moreover, within a given kind of responsibility we can distinguish different degrees of responsibility. Perhaps both parents and teachers have primary responsibility for teaching literacy skills to children, but teachers have a greater share of that responsibility.

The third and final dimension of responsibility attribution I wish to highlight depends on a special feature of children's entitlements. Because children initially lack and only gradually develop capacities for responsible self-direction, their entitlements to a decent upbringing cannot be met simply by supplying them with resources. Choices of various sorts need to be made on behalf of children in order to promote their welfare and other developmental needs, including the acquisition of meaningful autonomy and moral powers. In light of this fact, nurturing agents will have responsibilities not only to provide children with resources but also to guide various aspects of children's lives in suitable ways. We can therefore distinguish *guidance* responsibilities and *cost-bearing* responsibilities. It is important to note that for many important entitlement claims these two kinds of responsibility can be differentially allocated among nurturing agents. For example, we might allocate guidance responsibilities with respect to schooling primarily to parents but allocate responsibility for paying for the costs of education to the community as a whole.

The foregoing analysis draws out some of the assumptions we implicitly make about the attribution of responsibilities. The analysis suggests that we can view the allocation problem as having a triadic structure that focuses on determining (1) which potential nurturing agents have (2) which kinds of responsibilities for ensuring the satisfaction of (3) what kinds of entitlement claims? I have suggested that a theory of children's entitlements will identify the basic nurturing factors that contribute to a decent upbringing. Assuming that we have at least a provisional idea of what the basic nurturing factors are, we can now consider the problem of identifying criteria for the allocation of responsibility.

Responsibility Allocation Criteria: Strategic and Principled

I suggested above that a mixture of practical and principled considerations seem to play a role in how we assign various child-rearing responsibilities. In this section, I want to explore this idea more fully. Are there valid principled standards for the allocation of responsibilities that are not grounded in contingent practical considerations as to which potential nurturing agents are best placed to ensure that the entitlement claims of children are met? One common strain of thinking about the overriding importance of children's interests gives us reason to suppose that responsibility allocation criteria are grounded exclusively in practical or strategic considerations. In many contexts, the standard for assessing child-rearing arrangements appears to be a "best interest of the child" standard. For example, child custody disputes are often resolved by determining what custody and child support arrangements are best for the children, rather than for the parents, in question. The "best interest of the child" standard has obvious attractions for resolving responsibility allocation problems. If treated as a general responsibility allocation standard, it suggests that responsibility for meeting the entitlement claims of children ought to be allocated solely by determining which agents are best placed to meet the various entitlement claims of different children. Allocation of responsibility would, in effect, be determined by appeal to contingent practical or strategic considerations. For example, we might consider the motivation of different agents, the sort of epistemic access they will have to the needs of children, the expertise certain agents have with respect to the provision of certain goods, capacities to bear costs, or even the general efficiency of different responsibility allocations. I will call these *strategic allocation criteria. Principled allocation criteria*, by contrast, provide reasons for favouring an allocation of responsibilities on grounds such as fairness, respect for individual rights, or other considerations other than the conduciveness of an allocation to meeting entitlement claims.

In many of our existing child-rearing practices, we seem to rely on strategic criteria in making allocation decisions. For example, we entrust parents with many responsibilities, particularly guidance responsibilities, because most parents are highly motivated to promote the interests of their children. Parents also have privileged epistemic access to the needs of their children and hence are usually better able than less closely related agents to determine how their lives are to be guided. Parents, however, typically lack the expertise to educate their children, so schools are assigned special responsibilities for instruction. Cost-bearing responsibilities for the education of children are generally widely shared, and this can be explained, at least in part, as a strategic decision—children's entitlement to an education will be more reliably met if the costs of education are socialized. Strategic allocation criteria also seem to explain the way in which the assignment of responsibility can be contingent. Parents can be stripped of their responsibilities for raising children if they fail to meet the needs of their children adequately. In such cases, the responsibility for care is then plausibly assigned to whomever is best able to meet the needs of the children. A general moral urgency is attached to meeting children's entitlement claims. Strategic allocation criteria speak to this urgency in a compelling fashion by insisting that responsibility for rearing children be allocated in ways that maximize the probability that the entitlement claims of children will be met.

Strategic allocation criteria are clearly important, but in my view they constitute only part of a satisfactory account of responsibility allocation. In other contexts, the question of responsibility allocation is typically not settled by simply determining which allocation will best promote a desired outcome. There seem to be principled constraints that affect both who can be assigned responsibility for securing a morally desirable outcome and how much can be demanded of anyone in bringing about such an outcome. The issue of whether, in the context of meeting the entitlement claims of children, there are principled allocation criteria is important, because the implications of relying solely on strategic allocation criteria are far-reaching and potentially unsettling. The worry is that reliance on strategic allocation criteria alone is likely to generate allocations of responsibility that are perverse and unfair, though nonetheless efficient. Consider, for instance, the question of who should assume the primary cost-bearing responsibilities of raising children. Should allocation of such responsibilities be determined wholly on strategic grounds?

Peter Unger notes that we live in a "perennially rotten world"[7] in which the basic nutritional needs of millions of children go unmet. Faced with the task of meeting the entitlement claims of children in such a world, a radical reassignment of the current allocation of cost-bearing responsibilities for feeding children well makes sense on strategic grounds. Many more children would have their entitlement claims met if, say, North Americans were assigned primary responsibility for the costs of feeding children in poorer parts of the world. Personally, I have some sympathy for the idea that such a reassignment of cost-bearing responsibilities would be a good thing. However, I suspect it would strike most people, even among those deeply distressed by world hunger, as counterintuitive. Insofar as affluent North Americans have cost-bearing responsibilities in this sort of case, they are secondary responsibilities. On this view, the duties of affluent people to bear the cost of feeding children arise because those who are reasonably charged with primary responsibility—for example, parents, local communities, and so on—are unable or unwilling to discharge their responsibilities. This tempting response is difficult to defend by appeal to strategic criteria. In the present state of the world, the resources that North Americans can contribute to the alleviation of child poverty are vastly greater than the resources that are immediately available to local communities and parents in destitute parts of the world. In these circumstances, strategic criteria favour assignment of primary responsibilities to those who are affluent.

Of course, it could be countered that I am invoking an unduly circumscribed understanding of the relevant strategic criteria. Perhaps a more sophisticated reading of the criteria, one that emphasized long-term considerations, could justify assigning primary responsibility more locally. Perhaps, then, this sort of case does not tell against exclusive reliance on strategic allocation criteria. Nonetheless, I think this sort of real-world case gives us some reason to consider the idea that there may be non-strategic allocation criteria that have some role to play in constraining the application of strategic allocation criteria. Even in a rotten world, we have reason to think that those who have created and encouraged the creation of children in particular communities have some special responsibilities to meet the entitlement claims of those children.

I now present a somewhat less realistic case as an ancillary way of motivating the idea that not all responsibility allocation criteria are strategic. One difficulty with the previous case is that the distribution of resources among potential nurturing agents is unjust. Assigning primary responsibility to affluent agents for the costs of raising poor children may seem justifiable in light of the fact that the affluent have an unjust share of resources. So let us consider a world in which there is a just distribution of resources among the existing population of responsible adults. Now add the unrealistic assumption that there are currently no children. Assume also that adults are permitted to use their resources in the pursuit of the projects and activities they value. Some will want to have and raise children. In some respects, having a child is a project like any other. The project of creating a family is typically undertaken by parents with the expectation that it will contribute value to their lives. In this respect, it is not fundamentally different than the pursuit of other life projects, such as gardening, having pets, or even playing golf. But the project of having children imposes demands on the rest of the world that are quite unlike those generated by other projects.

To begin with, children have resource entitlement claims that must be met. Allocating responsibility for bearing the costs of these claims on the basis of strategic criteria alone might result in an unfair subsidization of an expensive taste. Adults who have decided not to pursue the project of having children could be assigned responsibility for bearing the costs of children they do not want. In the case of other projects, this kind of subsidization seems unfair. I cannot reasonably expect you to devote some of your resources to my gardening project. So can I expect you to help pay for the costs of my decision to have children? Viewed from the standpoint from which children appear as projects of their parents, the answer seems to be no. To the degree that children can be viewed as expensive tastes, albeit expensive tastes that have independent moral standing, there is a principled reason of fairness to assign the cost-bearing responsibilities of child rearing to parents. Put more formally, procreative responsibility functions as a principled allocation criterion. Some, like Eric Rawkowski[8] and J.S. Mill, seem to view procreative responsibility as a definitive criterion for the allocation of primary cost-bearing responsibilities. Mill says, "It still remains unrecognized that to bring a child into existence without a fair prospect of being able, not only to provide food for its body, but instruction and training for its mind, is a moral crime, both against the unfortunate offspring and against society; and if the parent does not fulfil this obligation, then the state ought to see it fulfilled, at the charge, so far as possible, of the parent."[9]

It seems to overstate the point to claim, as Mill does, that parents have sole primary responsibility for bearing the costs of children. For one thing, procreative responsibility is often much more widely shared than Mill seems to suppose. Other members of the community often play a role in actively soliciting procreation, partly in anticipation of the benefits it will bring. For instance, if couples are encouraged by the state to procreate because the state anticipates that children will generate or preserve some good—whether it is economic (a new worker) or cultural (maintenance of the language)—then the state can reasonably be taken to have some procreative responsibility. Similarly, a society cannot perpetuate itself unless new generations are created. The goal of societal perpetuation can typically not be met unless there is sufficient procreation. Perhaps parents who contribute to this goal by having an appropriate number of children (but no more) have a claim to have their child-raising costs subsidized by those who do not engage in procreation, so as to ensure that costs of social reproduction are shared fairly. Children created under the auspices of such a social policy are not appropriately considered expensive tastes. Instead, procreative parents are doing their part in contributing to an important social project. Even in the case where procreative responsibility is narrowly focused on parents, I doubt that it can serve as an authoritative criterion for assigning cost-bearing responsibilities to parents. Children can be seen only in part as expensive tastes and, to the degree that it is inappropriate to view them in this way, the procreative responsibility allocation criterion will not uniquely determine how child-rearing costs should be allocated. Fairness requires that those responsible for procreation have some special cost-bearing responsibilities, but I do not think they are as extensive as Mill or Rakowski suppose.

A different principled allocation criterion can also be identified by considering the way children figure as ingredients in the life projects of their parents. To the degree that having children is an ingredient in a parent's life project, there is reason to allocate important guidance responsibilities to parents. Parents have a substantial interest in having control over their life projects. In the case of children seen as ingredients in a life project, this parental interest will typically be served by allocating many guidance responsibilities to parents. So respect for the liberty interests of parents to pursue distinctive conceptions of the good of their own choosing provides another principled allocation criterion. Indeed, it is frequently assumed that parents have special rights to shape both the convictions and religious and cultural identity of their children. There are important constraints on the exercise of parental authority that are grounded in the entitlement claims of children. Parents do not own their children, and they must exercise the special prerogatives they have as parents in ways compatible with respecting relevant interests of children and other members of the community. Parents cannot, for instance, subvert the development of autonomy in their children or raise children in such a fashion that they will impose substantial burdens on other members of the community.[10] Nonetheless, providing they respect these constraints, parents have an entitlement of their own to guide aspects of their children's lives. This parental entitlement is grounded primarily in respect for the distinct interests of parents. In some contexts, it has sufficient weight to constrain or trump the allocation of nurturing responsibilities provided by purely strategic criteria. Even if it is true that some children's entitlement claims would be better met by assigning primary guidance responsibilities to adults other than the parents of the children, we have reason to assign primary guidance responsibilities to parents. A reassignment of primary guidance responsibilities from parents to others is only warranted if parents fail to discharge their responsibilities for meeting their children's entitlement claims adequately. The mere fact that there are others who could satisfy the entitlement claims more effectively than parents is typically not sufficient grounds to deprive parents of their special claim to shape important aspects of their children's lives.

A third kind of principled allocation criterion can be located in the idea of reciprocity. The kind and degree of responsibility agents have with respect to one another seems related to the kinds of mutually beneficial interaction that is likely to obtain among agents. The strength of our commitments to one another often seem to be proportional to the degree to which we are participants in a common co-operative venture. Families, cultures, nations, and local communities are, at least to some degree, co-operative ventures. When they function well, these associations generate significant benefits for the participants involved in them, but their functioning well depends on various kinds of reciprocal commitment. I undertake to make my contribution to the co-operative venture partly in the anticipation that others who are part of the same venture can be relied upon both to contribute and to treat me fairly. The mutual commitment we have to one another in such relationships seems linked to the establishment of mutual responsibilities. The closer the relationship in terms of the degree of interaction and in terms of the magnitude of the benefits generated through interaction, the stronger the responsibilities that obtain between co-operating parties. If this is right, then we can see how considerations of reciprocity can play a role in the allocation of child-rearing responsibilities.

Parents and children who form a family represent a particularly close form of association. Parents and children can anticipate special benefits from this form of association and thereby assume mutual responsibilities for ensuring that the entitlement claims of family members are met. Similarly, but somewhat more diffusely, the members of a common society can expect to benefit from the fact that it contains children. As children mature into adults, they will become participants in the shared economic, social, and political institutions that mark out the society as a distinct co-operative venture. Arguably, part of what is involved in setting the fair terms of such societal interaction is ensuring that the entitlement claims of the children of that society are met. Thus, the members of a society have a special responsibility to meet the entitlement claims of children in that society. As the degree of reciprocity diminishes, the strength of certain kinds of responsibility for meeting the claims of others diminishes. This may help explain the phenomenon of diminished responsibility for distant others I noted earlier. But I do not want to overstate the force of this consideration. For example, the presence of some form of reciprocity is not a necessary condition of having a responsibility to meet an entitlement claim of children. Members of an affluent society can still have responsibilities to contribute to the meeting of the entitlement claims of children in a poor society, even if it is true that the affluent society cannot anticipate any mutually beneficial interaction with the poor society. Nonetheless, I suspect that a principle of reciprocity has some role to play in the allocation of primary responsibilities.

Conclusion

I have identified three principled allocation criteria—a principle of distributive fairness linked to procreative responsibility, a parental liberty interest principle, and a principle of reciprocity. (I do not want to suggest that this is a complete specification of such criteria.) If I am right, such criteria have a role in guiding the allocation of responsibilities for the meeting of children's entitlement claims that is different from the role played by strategic criteria. It seems probable that strategic and principled allocation criteria will often point in the same direction. For example, there are both strategic and principled grounds for assigning special child-rearing responsibilities to parents. But this will not always be the case, so we need some account of the way the criteria interact with each other when they point in different directions. My suspicion is that principled allocation criteria function as partial constraints on strategic allocation criteria in two ways. First, they establish a presumption in favour of differentiated allocations of primary responsibilities in a range of standard cases. We assume, for instance, that adults who voluntarily elect to have children must shoulder at least some of the costs of raising children more than those who elect to be childless. Similarly, we assume that parents have a presumptive entitlement to shape the convictions and commitments of their children in distinctive ways. These principle-grounded presumptive allocations of primary responsibilities initially operate independently of strategic allocation criteria. Second, strategic allocation criteria only determine an assignment of primary responsibilities either when principled criteria are silent on how given nurturing responsibility is to be allocated or when the allocation of responsibilities given by principled criteria is insufficient to ensure that the entitlement claims of children are adequately met. In effect, principled allocation criteria provide a backdrop against which strategic allocation criteria are then applied. Strategic criteria might also assume greater direct importance in determining the allocation of secondary responsibilities. If those charged with primary responsibility for meeting the entitlement claims of children fail to do so, then, given the urgency of meeting these claims, it may be appropriate to have failsafe arrangements that are maximally conducive to ensuring that children are justly treated. These are, however, tentative suggestions about the relation between principled and strategic allocation criteria. At this stage I do not have an account of how we should go about weighing the force of the different criteria. Nonetheless, we have reason to think that both sorts of allocation criteria have a role to play in determining how we should discharge our responsibilities to children.

I have suggested that the entitlement claims of children can be determined, at least to some important degree, independently from the resolution of the question of who is responsible for meeting these claims. The egalitarian provision thesis, whether in the moderate or strong version, that I have defended as providing an appropriate response to the entitlement problem is far from being realized even in contemporary affluent liberal democracies. Even the less demanding minimum provision thesis is not satisfied. In my view, meeting even the modest entitlement claims of children will involve a radical departure from the social, political, and economic arrangements that are currently in place. Principled allocation criteria are, to some degree, in keeping with traditional assumptions about the special responsibilities parents have for ensuring the welfare of children. But accepting such criteria and the responsibility allocations they entail does not provide a justification for limiting efforts to meet the entitlement claims of children. From the point of view of justice, we should favour policies and institutional reforms that meet the entitlement claims of children while still permitting the forms of differentiated responsibility for meeting these claims that flow from principled allocation criteria. However, appeal to principled allocation criteria should not, in my view, be presented as a justification of permitting the basic entitlement claims of children to go unmet. Even if I and other affluent individuals should not be assigned primary responsibility for ensuring that hungry children in distant lands are fed, I cannot thereby deny the validity of their entitlement claim to be fed or my responsibility for contributing to bringing about the conditions under which the entitlement claims of all children are met.

Notes

1 Colin Macleod, "Conceptions of Parental Autonomy," *Politics & Society* 25, no. 1 (1997): 120.

2 UNICEF, *The State of the World's Children 2006*, http://www.unicef.org.sowc06/index.php (accessed September 12, 2006).

3 J. Blustein, *Parents and Children: The Ethics of the Family* (Oxford: Oxford University Press, 1982), 112–13.

4 Ronald Dworkin, *Sovereign Virtue: The Theory and Practice of Equality* (Cambridge, MA: Harvard University Press, 2000), 3.

5 See, for example, John Rawls, *A Theory of Justice* (Cambridge, MA: Harvard University Press, 1971); Dworkin 2000; Thomas Nagel, *Equality and Partiality* (Oxford: Oxford University Press, 1991); Eric Rakowski, *Equal Justice* (New York: Oxford University Press, 1991).

6 Fishkin 1983; Vallentyne and Lipson 1989.

7 P. Unger, *Living High and Letting Die: Our Illusions of Innocence* (Oxford: Oxford University Press, 1996), 80.

8 Rakowski (1991), 154.

9 John Stuart Mill, quoted in P. Casal and A. Williams, "Rights, Equality and Procreation," *Analyse & Critique* 17 (1995): 108 n. 27.

10 Macleod (1997).

TWO

Parental Responsibility

JAN NARVESON

Responsibility: A Distinction

In what way, and why, are parents "responsible for" their children? What makes this an interesting question is that the parental relation is both ubiquitous—we all have parents—and unique in that, unlike any other relations to people, parents actually bring children into existence. In one obvious sense, then, they are responsible for their children by virtue of being responsible for the fact that those children exist. One meaning of "responsible" is causal: "x is responsible for y" entails "x brought it about that y happened." But of course, the causal sense is only one among others. Normatively speaking, the claim that x is responsible for y holds where x is a moral agent of some kind, and what is being said about x in relation to y is that if x does or doesn't do certain things to or about y, then x may be *appropriately blamed*. We do not often ask "Who's responsible for this?" when the "this" in question is something good. I'm not sure why, since the meaning can be just the same: where y is a good, we are asking, in effect, "Whom do we compliment, reward, or praise for y"? In what follows, we shall be mainly concerned with grounds for accusation of dereliction and mainly only by implication with grounds for praise for outstanding performance.

The Distinctiveness of This Problem

What makes our question interesting, then, is that a de facto parent could disown responsibility of the kind we are especially interested in here not only by denying that he is in fact a parent of this particular child but more interestingly by denying that he has any duties to or about, or any responsibility for, the child in question. We want to say that such a parent is a bad parent, and there is an air of self-evidence about that. Not only do we want to say that this is a bad parent, but we sometimes take measures to deprive that person of the child in question, compelling that parent to relinquish the child into someone else's care. But...why?

An important point here is that the production of children needn't be and often is not intentional. Children are a result of an activity that can be pursued and often, perhaps mainly, is pursued for quite other reasons. Children resulting from those activities are often an unforeseen or unwanted result of what was undertaken for pleasure alone or for other reasons. In the case of some things of that sort, the option of disowning the result in question is readily available: we simply throw the flawed item into the wastebasket. That has occasionally happened to newborns as well, but most of us regard that as reprehensible.

Why, though? A familiar answer here is that to discard a newborn is to kill it, and to kill a human is murder; so the discarder is a murderer. Without rehearsing too many familiar arguments about abortion, we certainly do have to rehearse one of them straight off: the newborn child, while a human being, is not obviously a fellow moral being, a fellow "person." Newborns, for a short while, are virtually devoid of the complex of qualities that make us think of people as distinctive and interesting and important—albeit, of course, that for most parents newborns are welcome and prized. However, the would-be discarder of a newborn obviously does not share that assessment of that case: she neither welcomes nor prizes the organism that she disposes of. There is a very interesting question what our attitude ought to be toward such people; but at least it is not obvious, on cool reflection, that they are to be regarded as murderers, or indeed as doing anything seriously wrong *to* the organism they discard. If we take the view that abortion is inherently permissible—a view that certainly would be implausible if human organisms prior to birth were as capable as we of rationality and personality—then it is hard to see why a few hours or days after being born makes the case radically different from the few days or months before.

What must be appreciated, then, is that a view of what we ought to do about our children takes very little from the sheer fact of producing them, and is based much more on the fact that they develop into humans who, from a pretty early age, do have personalities and minds of their own. Soon, in short, we are dealing with people, and we have responsibilities to them as such. But unlike most people, these are ones we care deeply about, and so we devote much more time and energy—especially emotional—to them than we do in dealing with others, even friends and neighbours. Or, rather, most of us do. We do so because we care, which of course implies that we *do* care, and the trouble is that some parents evidently do not. Such parents are happily atypical, but we do need to ask what is the basis for condemnation of their attitudes. The worry here is that maybe it's just the "parents union" against the others; and no doubt we parents are in the numerical majority—but why does that justify *us* in telling the others what to do?

The Value of Children

New people are good things for a community. Indeed, new people grow up and *become* "the community"—without them there would be no such thing. If there are to be new people there must be newborns, and if we value those new people, then we must value newborns—others as well as our own. Even so, that does not of itself supply sufficient reason for condemning the parent who is inclined to discard her newborn. What it does do, however, is to give us reason to supply her, the "wanna-not-be"parent, with a better option, that of letting someone who does want it take on the responsibilities of parenthood in its case. The value of children as members-to-be of the communities we live in is sufficient to insist on the latter and deny parents, in anything like normal circumstances, the option of disposing of unwanted children by inflicting death on them. And their value when grown up also implies concern about their manner of treatment when young: thus abuse that cripples or otherwise damages the growing child, including abuse that cripples the child psychologically, is of legitimate concern to the rest of us.

Still, it is also not obvious, even granted my claim that new people are in general valuable, that each adult in a community has the responsibility to do all that he or she can do for any given newborn, nor, in particular, to add to the community as much as possible. Indeed, the reverse is nearer the truth: it is obvious that they are *not* thus responsible. Normal biology sees to it that new people are continually produced, given normal sociology. Moreover, there have been times and places where the community might do better to rid itself of the child in question, as being a potential severe burden on others: malformed, demented, incompetent, and so on. How much responsibility the *rest* of us have to promote or provide good lives to miscellaneous children other than our own is the question. And the most reasonable answer in general is—not very much. We lack the resources to do much along that line, for one thing; and in any case, we rarely have any right to interfere with other parents' parenting activities.

In this chapter, however, I wish to table many of those difficult and important subjects. I shall speak, instead, to the subject of children who *are* wanted by their parents, and who are or, with reasonable luck, would be welcome additions to the community. The rest of us tend to cheer when our friends and relatives have children and to wish anyone contemplating parenthood well. That is as it should be. But talk of parental duties and responsibilities suggests something rather sterner: when have we *not* lived up to our responsibilities with regard to their upbringing? Thinking about that implies, of course, the need for a plausible view about those responsibilities. Just what are we parents responsible for, and why?

A major problem in considering this question is that we do not have a very good idea of what we are responsible for in my first sense of "responsible": we don't actually know very well which of the myriad traits of our grown-up children are the way they are because of something their parents did—especially, something we did in the sense that we planned to do it and our plans worked out. What parent isn't familiar with the syndrome that attempting to get the child to do *x* is a very good way of getting him or her to do *y* instead? Who of us, when looking at our late-teenaged children, doesn't see traits which they evidently got from us, though we hoped they would not?

A good deal of the philosophical problem here is that it seems clear that much about a child comes from within the child, somehow: there are all sorts of respects in which we can do what we will, but the child is going to grow up *its* way, not ours. The only responsibility we can claim in those respects is genetic, and of course most of us know practically nothing about genetics, so the claim doesn't amount to much. We are responsible for producing the child in the first place, and if it goes bad, that reflects badly on us. Yet at many points, it may have been beyond our control. And how much is within our control is a difficult question, apart from the possibility of disposing of our children altogether—an option discussed (and deplored) above.

Welfare

We can put our question broadly in terms of the child's well-being or welfare: To what level of it are parents to be held responsible?

One popular view is that parents have moral obligations *to* their children, to provide some hard-to-define but high level of benefits to them. There are problems with that view that are, too often, not sufficiently appreciated. Some will be mentioned, or at least implied, below, but we need to make a distinction. The claim that we owe something *to* person A is ambiguous. It may be that I owe it directly to A, because of some relation fundamentally between myself and A. In a frequent and familiar kind of case, this relation will be that I have undertaken a commitment to A, by agreeing with A that I shall do it, in return perhaps for some service A has rendered or will render to me. But that can't be the fundamental reason why I owe my children anything. Obviously I cannot have promised *them* anything before they were born, nor, for that matter, for quite some time thereafter. I can, certainly, do things for my children in the hope or even expectation that they, in later life, will reciprocate, for example by caring for me in my old age. But that can hardly be construed as involving any sort of promise on their part. One's hopes and expectations along this line might be fulfilled, but that can't be the reason they will be. What can be such a reason, however, is a broader intergenerational argument. As the children grow up, we point out to them that we are doing well by them, expect care from them when older, and point out that they too will be in the same position in relation to *their* children, and so they'll do well to fall into place in this ongoing process.

On the other hand, it may be that I owe something to A because I have promised B that I will do something for A (say, promised a friend I will do a favour for his child), or have some other obligation to B that requires doing something for A in order to fulfil it. Typically, we can owe our spouses something of this kind, for instance.

Those who think that we owe something to our children directly, just because they *are* "ours," have some explaining to do. The fact that I could do a nice thing for person A certainly means that, prima facie, it would be *nice* of me to do it, but it certainly does not entail, as it stands, that I have any sort of *obligation* to do it. Why, then, does the fact that it is I who (in co-operation with one other person) cause A to come into existence constitute a reason why I should be morally obligated to perform many more useful services to A? That we normally love the child does not answer this question; rather, it explains why it scarcely needs answering: since we love them, we want what is good for them. But if someone says that we are *obligated* to love them, the reply has to be that we cannot sensibly be obligated to feel a certain way about anything. So it is obligations to do what a loving parent would do for her children even if we do not love them ourselves that need explaining, and it is not very clear how we can do this.

I am aware that it has been popular to plump for "equality" as a requirement of justice; Colin Macleod in this volume, for example, assumes it. I find the assumption unbelievable, if taken literally, and unpromising if taken in any other way, but this is not the time to discuss that large subject at any length. In any case, I find the idea of "equalizing" one's situation with that of a four-year-old fairly mind-boggling.

It would seem, then, that we must switch over, at this point, from concern about rights to something else. The popular view, that we *owe* a whole lot to our children, would indeed account for the tendency to regard the discarding of infants, or the neglect of older children, as terrible. My intent here, however, is to develop a reasonable idea of what a reasonably responsible, good parent will do, without invoking any special assumptions. I do this in the hope, and perhaps the expectation, that my fellow parents will see the idea as the right one, or at least as a plausible one, once we view it from the larger perspective that is appropriate to social philosophy, rather than the narrow though extremely important viewpoint of the normal, concerned parent who wholeheartedly wants the best for his or her child.

Irvine's Argument

William Irvine[1] takes what appears to be a very different view of the matter. He opens the question by making a distinction between two views ("models," as he calls them) of parenting—the "ownership" view and the "stewardship" view. The names indicate the difference: on the first view, children are ours in the sense that we, their parents, *own* them, whereas on the second, children are ours only in the sense that it is we in particular, rather than someone else, who are charged with taking care of them. The first view has it that the parents fundamentally may do whatever they wish with their children. The second, on the contrary, states that the parent is to have the attitude: "Their interests first, his interests second ... he would regard himself as having lots of duties with respect to his child, but few rights."[2] Irvine develops the idea by comparing the situation of parenting to the situation of literal stewardship, in which the agent is appointed to care for something belonging to someone else in the latter's absence. In the case of children, however, it's more a matter of taking care of something on behalf of a *future* owner: the child himself, who upon maturing will be living the life bequeathed, as it were, by its former caretakers.

Irvine notes the possibility of further models, among which a *liberation model* would be of interest. According to it, "children should be treated by their parents as equals—that is, they should be treated more or less the way you would treat your (adult) next-door neighbor."[3] I agree with Irvine in rejecting this model on the ground that children simply are not "equals" and treating them that way could easily get both children and parents into real trouble, were the parents to take it very seriously. But the difference between ownership and stewardship remains.

However, there is an initial problem, for we have to bear in mind that an owner, since he has choice in the matter, *can* and we may well suppose very often *would* treat his children just as he would on the stewardship model. Even if we say we own them, we can nevertheless choose to treat our children that way. After all, as Aristotle says, we are motivated to take care of what is ours. And moreover, most people do just that: they take excellent care of their children, and do so at least in part precisely because they are *theirs.*

The question, then, would have to be this: What differences would stem from taking each view seriously and typically, on the face of it? We can imagine parents whose main interest in their children is to exploit them in some way, for the parents' advantage to the maximal degree. We can also imagine—indeed, we don't need to imagine, for we all know many of these—that parents take the stewardship view very seriously, making major sacrifices for their children and putting them first in all things. Then our question is, Which if either of these gives us the right picture? We soon see that, in fact, the contrast is not so obvious as it may seem.

To see why, let's look at a further problem about this distinction that emerges when we consider Irvine's normative defence of the stewardship view. Why, he asks, would we think that view is correct? After all, wouldn't the first view be more in our own interest? But Irvine, in somewhat Rawlsian spirit, asks us, in effect, to look at it from the point of view of the child. "Which model would you want your future parents to raise you in accordance with—the ownership model or the stewardship model?"[4] Surely, he suggests, it would be the stewardship model. And I shall assume that he's right about that. The trouble is, though, that he's right for the same reason that we would all no doubt prefer a better deal to a worse. Given your choice between worse and better, no doubt you'll take better. By definition, the stewardship view favours the child, and so if she were to call the shots, that's the shot she would call. The question is, though, so what? What would that prove? The trouble is that, as with Rawls's familiar veil-of-igno-rance scenario, there is an air of unreality about this. A fundamental feature of the situation is, quite simply, that children do not have their choice about this. Parents do, and children don't. Arguably, it does not matter how things would look if they were wholly different from the way they are, for we live in a world in which they are this way, and that's that. If we parents choose to insist on looking at the whole situation from our children's point of view, that's our right. But that isn't going to convince anyone who chooses *not* to look at it that way, because he simply doesn't have to. If, as Irvine accepts, the job here is to try to persuade parents to take the stew-ardship view, we will have to do better than merely point out what follows from it if we were the children instead.

Another reason for advocating this position is that we ourselves were once children, and we can appreciate how things were. We might think this is our chance to do better. But that, so far, looks only a matter of hap-penstance psychology. Perhaps others would react to their childhood by treating their own children no better than their parents treated them. It has happened, after all. We philosophers need to do better than that, one would think.

In fact, Irvine is aware of the point, and improves on his argument[5] by suggesting that the parent who practiced "ownership" even though rec-ognizing that if he were a child he'd want stewardship would be in an uncomfortable dialectical situation with himself. Irvine describes a "rein-carnation experiment" in which you are reincarnated as a child of various possible sets of parents. "What the reincarnation experiment might reveal to someone is that she would not want herself as a parent, if she had any say in the matter. Surely it would be wrong for this person to foist herself, as a parent, upon some child."[6] But it is clear that we have now moved a long way from the pure stewardship view to something much less apparently demanding. We are now asking whether our behaviour as parents falls below the threshold of acceptability. The truly bottom-level threshold would be the line below which one would think it better not to exist at all—better dead or not born than to have *this* parent, behaving *this* way as a par-ent. We should agree with Irvine that if it seems reasonable to think this about a given case of parenting, then this person shouldn't be in the par-enting business at all. Still, that leaves lots of room above that line but below the utopian line—a parent who is acceptable by this criterion can be still be much less than an absolutely ideal parent. And, importantly, the new idea leaves room for a more reasonable division between oneself and one's children than All for Them, Nothing for Us.

We should also admit that the terms of this dichotomy are misleading. Parents, after all, identify with their children. They tend not to see what others might view as sacrifices as really being sacrifices at all. We want our children to do well, and we want this because they are ours. They may be viewed as a price, but even so, as a price we are eager to pay. For example, a mother who likes her martinis might nevertheless stop drinking during pregnancy if she believes that this might damage her future child. She might view it as either a sacrifice she's ready to make, or even hardly a sacrifice at all, considering that her interest in her child is much greater than her interest in martinis. Still, she sees it as part of her own interest, even her own self-interest, to do this.

This makes the statement of our question much more complex. On one hand, there may be parents who lack all identification with and interest in their children. This could easily lead to neglect and to subsequent emotional and other deprivations that we would be concerned about. On the other, there will be parents who do identify with and care about their children. But that doesn't assure us of the desired responsibility, for some parents may have values such that, as we see it anyway, if children are brought up with those values, they could emerge with serious problems. But this is a different type of irresponsibility, if that is the right category for it, than the former.

The Default Proposal

What I think has been somewhat pushed into the background in Irvine's treatment is the surrounding community. Who, after all, is essentially concerned about parental responsibility? Parents tend to be so concerned for the reasons just given: these are our children, we love them, we want what is good for them. But the worrisome cases are those parents who, even if they see it that way, also have ideas about what is good for their children that actually lead to harm to those around them. At that point, these others come into the act in a major way. We all have a legitimate concern that parents raise their children in such a way as not to be, as we may put it, *net negative* to the community. We want everyone's children to grow up to be useful, but at any rate certainly not detrimental to the rest of us. I suggest that we have a right to the latter. Parents owe us responsibility to that level.

That their children not grow up to be a net cost to the rest of us in the community is what we might call the "default" notion: parents can impose risks on other people—adults in particular, but probably others too—by their irresponsible behaviour in not preventing, or even encouraging, harmful behaviour on the part of their children. This being so, and the parents being in a position to prevent this, we can insist that they do so.

However, that does not, as it stands, supply a direct duty to promote the welfare of one's children, as such. Thus, suppose that parent P rejects child C, and nobody else picks up the option, so that C dies in the street, or the garbage, or whatever. Why is that terrible? It doesn't obviously impose a cost on us. It may, of course, and in typical cases does, deprive us of a potential source of benefit. But then, as noted, it is not obvious that just because I can do you a benefit, I therefore owe it to you. It is more obvious that I do not. And, too, it is fairly obvious that the thing for the rest of us to do in relation to a parent who would throw her newborn out with the garbage is to make it worthwhile for her to give it, instead, to some among us who would give it the needed care.

I have previously argued[7] that there is something close to a "natural" criterion for minimal regard for the welfare of children: others will take your child if you don't want it, and we the community may reasonably insist, then, that you take good enough care of it so that the child would not obviously be better off with almost anyone else who would have it than it would by remaining with the rejecting actual parent. I am taking it that there is a very strong natural presumption in favour of children remaining with their natural parents. Thus the treatment by its natural parents must be *very* bad before we resort to the drastic alternative of forcibly separating it from them. And I take this to be a very low standard—so low as to be, perhaps, not very interesting. Western middle-class TV viewers are accustomed to looking at naked children in huts or slums in Africa or India and shaking their heads in disdain; but we don't appreciate the fact that children in those communities have been brought up in this condition for millennia and managed to make it, often enough, and their parents and their communities are quite happy with the results. At the least, we have no case for forcibly depriving these parents of their offspring. Very little in the way of major concern for welfare flows from this source, so far as I can see.

Moreover, most of us appreciate that there are things like love and understanding and insight that parents characteristically have for their own children that are worth a great deal more than nice clothing, lots of tasty food, and the other desiderata we are used to thinking of as the natural and expected lot of children. Granted, up to some point the child might do still better if it had both the advantages of its parents' affection and the toys, clothing, food, beds and bedrooms, and the rest of it; but the former come first. They come so far first that to separate a poor but otherwise well-loved child from its parents in order to provide it with more goodies would be, in a word, monstrous. To be sure, this sort of love and understanding could possibly come from someone who is not a biological parent of the child in question. But it is very difficult for them to become fully satisfactory substitutes.

A Higher Standard? A Distinction about Welfare

Obviously a parent's normative situation is not mainly directed toward staving off justified kidnapping by the community. The question of interest here is whether parents may properly be held responsible—by themselves as well as others—for providing something much above that minimal level. An obvious candidate would be a maximizing one—that they are responsible for providing the *highest* level of welfare for their children that is possible for persons of their means and capabilities. That was Irvine's view, in effect. I have rejected his view: parents may reasonably hold that they can't afford to do this or that for the child, that their own interests count significantly, and that their responsibility to their own children is to do as well as possible given those constraints. The parents, say, are successful authors or professionals who are ready to make some sacrifices, but not to put their careers in jeopardy. But in putting the question that way, we of course raise the question, in just what does the "welfare" of children, or for that matter of people in general, consist? Or is welfare even the right category? More generally, perhaps, the question is: In what does the good life of an individual consist, and how do we decide for a given turn in life which way is the better way for that person?

Reflection on that question, I think, especially for present purposes, forces us to distinguish between what we may regard either as two somewhat different meanings of the term "welfare," or two very different types of welfare, either of children, or of anybody. We needn't dwell on the differences, if any, between these two ways of putting the distinction. But perhaps, if the preceding point is right, we should identify the first as "welfare, strictly speaking" and the second as having to do with good lives, more generally. For the moment I'll call them "Welfare I" and "Welfare II."

Welfare I

The first meaning is one in which an obvious and ubiquitous component of welfare is health. That we not be diseased, too weak to make our way about, blind, deaf, and the rest of it, is something we all want, for ourselves and those we love, and for anyone else who isn't an outright enemy of mankind. Insofar as we have a decent grip on it, the same goes for mental health.

It is often supposed that more income means more welfare, but whatever merits that may have for the other sense of "welfare" developed below, we should not regard it as even partially definitive of the first sense. What belongs under the notion of welfare in my first sense would be a function of income only if one spent it on a certain rather narrow category of things: food enough to permit not only continued life but continued decent health (but not such as to qualify one as a gourmand); clothing and shelter sufficient to keep one warm and dry in the ambient conditions (but not more—not, say, stylish); and exercise enough to keep one's body functioning satisfactorily (but not enough to get one into the Olympics). On other fronts, things like jobs, suitable mates, and the having of children of their own are relevant to my first category only insofar as they contribute to bodily and mental health. Beyond that, I want to put them in my second category.

It is roughly correct, I think, to say that this first sort of welfare is common conceptual territory to us all. One person's welfare of this sort is about the same as anybody else's. What is conducive to this first sort of welfare, of course, varies enormously. Some people, for example, require medicines to sustain life that would actually kill others. (My physicians tell me, for example, that I will die promptly if administered penicillin; but penicillin saves many other lives.) But the point is that what these varying remedies and requirements are conducive to is pretty much the same for us all.

No doubt there are value judgments at issue in each component of Welfare I, but I think it safe to say that the rough content of welfare in the first sense, so far as it goes, is not very much in dispute. There isn't much disagreement about which bodily condition is (physically) healthier than which—little doubt that one who can walk and run enjoys more of that sort of welfare, other things equal, than one who cannot, that one who is down with measles is less well off in this respect than one who is not, and so on. There is room for real and important dispute about who is to be held responsible for the welfare of whom, but there is little room for dispute what it consists in, insofar as this first, rather modest sense of the notion of welfare is concerned.

More difficult is the notion of mental health, though here again we do not lack paradigm cases of ill health: insanity, dementia, paranoia, severe depression, and many more, are all recognizably undesirable deviations from the condition we would like to enjoy. And speaking of "enjoying," I am willing to add one more idea to Category I: I suppose that there is a general sense of health and of that sort of well-being that we vaguely have in mind when we ask of a friend, "How are you?" One who is literally feeling fine, I think, does actually *feel* fine; that is, there is a general complex of sensations that goes with having all of one's bodily and mental components in good working condition. This might be called the "phenomenal bloom" of good health. But if that bloom is not brought about by the presence of the actual, concrete conditions making for good health, it is not clear what could be done about it, and so its presence on this list is marginal.

I have no intention of trying to be very precise about health of either kind, however. Rather, my intention is merely to identify a broad idea that, I hope, we are all familiar with, and to distinguish it from another notion, also familiar, which I take up next. For this other notion is quite another matter, and complicates our inquiry enormously.

Meanwhile, we may agree on another thing: there is, I take it, no serious dispute that it is—again, other things being equal—*better* that people should be better off than that they should be worse off—that the welfare of people, in this aspect, is a good thing, something that we should all be in favour of in general, special considerations (such as criminal guilt) aside. But recognition of such goodness, of course, does not straightaway entail obligation, nor even significant moral responsibility. That is the utilitarian mistake—to suppose that all that matters is the welfare or utility or the recipient of an action's effects, while the question of who brings this about is another matter entirely and up, so to speak, for moral grabs. But the utilitarian mistake really is a mistake; we may not run roughshod over agents. On the contrary: agents are the central personages in morals—not mere "patients," possible beneficiaries of actions. The most we are entitled to say is that it is better, other things equal, that a given person should have more welfare than less.

Welfare II: The Good Life

Suppose we are perfectly healthy in all respects; but now, what are we to do with this well-functioning body and soul of ours? The second meaning of "welfare" or perhaps better "well-being" would be, approximately, the *overall value* of the life of the individual in question. To promote clarity for present purposes, let's leave on one side the first meaning of welfare in this overall goodness of life, so that the two types are kept separate for purposes of discussion. Of course I don't want to say that they are sharply separate in our lives themselves—obviously they are not—but only that they are fairly well distinguishable. It is precisely because they are, however, that we have the sort of problems to be discussed next.

We can open this by putting a point about the relation between the two sorts of welfare in economic terms. Health, unfortunately, isn't always cheap. There are people who never see a doctor in their entire lives, and never need to, and whose diets and upkeep are practically costless. But for others, of course, it is not cheap at all. An ailing person can cost someone a great deal of money, time, attention, and more. Much more importantly, there can develop conflicts between that sort of welfare and the other sort roughly distinguished in the preceding. Good lives, whatever they are, are compatible with fairly high levels of sickness; they are sometimes quite short (for example, the composer Schubert, who died at thirty-one); they are often poverty-stricken; the level of cuisine or even sanitation enjoyed by someone with a good life might be quite low. Below some point, of course, one doesn't really "have a life"; but that point is very, very low, and the point is that, above it, trade-offs between welfare of the first sort and well-being of my second become fairly familiar. It is easy to imagine—indeed, we don't have to imagine, since there are plenty of real cases—that someone might prefer more books, or more chemical apparatus for his experiments, or a better violin, to medical treatment for ailments he reckons he can live with, or even ones he knows he can't live with for very long; or she might prefer spiritual contemplation to more nutritious food, and so on indefinitely.

We may put this by saying that very, very few of us give our own health and Category 1 welfare *lexical priority* over other things. Do necessities come before luxuries? Not always, for most of us. Most of us will draw some kind of curve mapping bundles of "luxuries" and "necessities," and as our incomes increase, the budgets available for necessities may increase—but not as fast. Even in higher regions of that curve, we won't devote resources first to health and only second to assorted interests of other kinds. Trade-offs start early on and continue indefinitely. Few will sacrifice career, love, or many other things for the sake of a slightly healthier or slightly longer life.

Indeed, I think it very clear that no reliable generalization can be made about the proportions in question. We must eat enough to live if we are to live even until next week, but we might choose to live on potatoes, water, and cheap vitamin pills and spend the rest of our budgets on recordings of Haydn quartets. The son of an upper-middle-class American family might run off to join an obscure sect, knowing that his level of comforts and, probably, health, and even the duration of his life will be much lower from the trade-off. It happens.

All this makes it extremely difficult to generalize about children's "needs," as is so often done. What children need to live one sort of arguably good life will be almost inconceivably different from what some other one does. So if we suppose that we can talk of "doing the best for our children" with a straight face, the onus is on the supporter to show the other people—his neighbours, people on the other side of the mountain, or of the world—that what he says makes clear sense. It does, of course, make sense that a parent will have a view about what makes for a good life for her child, but in order for this to go into a general formula, usable for all, we need much more than one plausible view by one person. And the next person's view, we may be sure, will be different. Nor, of course, can we ever forget that the child's own view, when it develops enough to be able to have one, is likely to be different again.

In short, this distinction is going to have to be confronted seriously by anyone who insists that parents are responsible for something like "maximizing the welfare" of their children. If what is meant is that we are responsible for maximizing their Category I welfare against our budget constraints, then my reply even to that modest suggestion is: forget it! Many parents have sacrificed not only some of their own Category I welfare, but also that of their children, in order to improve the children's education. No doubt they sometimes reckoned that in the longer run, this education would enable the child to do so much better in life that his long-term Category I welfare would also be higher. But sometimes, I suspect, not. In either case, it could have been quite rational to do this.

The Parental Budget

No matter what your view, how much we can be responsible for about children depends, first, on how much what we do to them affects them and in what ways, and second, how much we know about the first. Most modern parents are familiar with child rebellion, at various levels. There is no ready cure for this, and it would be rash to assume that there is, nor even that the cure for one case, if found, would be equally efficacious for another. Almost all of us are simply unable to be responsible for producing a first-rate mathematician or violinist: either the child is capable of becoming that or he is not, and if he's not there is nothing we can do to make it so. We are able to be, in some degree, responsible for enabling the first-rate mathematician or violinist to emerge in the rare cases where that is in the genetic cards: we can provide the child with the sort of environment in which his mathematical or musical capabilities come to the fore—distinct, say, from his abilities as a dramatist or a used-car salesman. But when we do this we will, at the margin, also provide him with an environment that hobbles or totally defeats many other potentialities. But because this is so, any parent in a position to supply those incentives and conditions must make a value judgment: is it *better* to do just that? Or should we attempt to steer him gently in some other direction?

The "Open Future"

In a famous article, Joel Feinberg held that children have a right to an "open future": We are, he held, responsible for not foreclosing future possibilities that the developing child might want to take advantage of.[8] The child, then, is to have as nearly open a future, as many possibilities to choose among, as possible. Part of the thrust of that article was to deny parents the right to subject their children to, say, an intense religious upbringing accompanied by the closing of their minds in the direction of any other creeds, cutting them off from external sources of religious persuasion or knowledge. But we can easily imagine any number of other ways in which a parent might be thought to be violating this supposed right.

In a recent discussion, however, Claudia Mills has exposed this idea to trenchant and, to my mind, definitive criticism.[9] It is, she holds, "both impossible and undesirable to try to provide children with an 'open' future in any meaningful sense."[10] As to impossibility, her point is simple: any particular future is incompatible with an indefinite number of alternatives. To choose, indeed, is always and necessarily to foreclose. Moreover, if we think that some kind of life is indeed the best one, then to try to hold other options open will appear pointless or even self-defeating. Why distract the child with visions of sugar plums when potatoes are best for him?

The Feinberg-type view has been much too widely accepted by well-meaning philosophers, but its conceptual underpinnings, as Mills details, are hopelessly incapable of providing a solid case for it, and the overall output is to constrain parents, including well-meaning ones, to an extent that surely violates their rights as parents. Academic writers love to play god: we suppose that we see things from an Olympian point of view that entitles us to tell others how to run their lives, including, as in the present case, how to bring up their children. But we are not gods, and we have no entitlement to do violence both to logic and to the persons whose responsibilities we write about. We will have to do the best we can given our partial and limited understandings of the options and the capabilities of our children (or ourselves) for capitalizing on given ones among those options.

The failure of the open-futures requirement is no small thing. Parents are, by their sheer existential relation to their children, in a position to do some shaping of their lives and futures, and must in the process address themselves to questions of whether they might be forcing the child into a mould ill suited to its nature. Some will do this better or worse than others, no doubt. But try they must, and no abstract principle of the open-futures type can both clearly and plausibly constrain them in this. The most we can say is that children will grow up to be people with the full rights and respon-

sibilities of adults and that parents can sometimes do what will clearly dis-
enable them from performing satisfactorily in those respects, but that
beyond that we must do our best as we see it. The rest of us can suggest and
propose and mount arguments, but in the end most of the decisions are the
parents', until their children grow to the point where their own views about
what to do in life have the same kind of decisive weight against their parents as any adult's does against any other adult's views.

The general point is that the parent can do only so much, be at most only
to some degree successful in realizing his or her ambitions for the child:
first, because of the decidedly less than infinite malleability of the child
and, second, because the parents themselves will lack income or the necessary qualities of leadership, communication, and many more to succeed
more fully. The other general point is that we must perforce make choices
and so must perforce make value judgments. And of course that brings up
the question what the basis of those is to be.

The Moral Minimum

A major part of the strength of the case for the default view described previously—that at the least we must bring up our children so that they don't
become threats to others—is that we now have quite a good idea how to
bring up children in such a way that they don't become delinquents, or
more precisely, a few fairly clearly describable things to avoid in the course
of their upbringing, the avoiding of which makes it highly probable that they
won't emerge as delinquents.[11] And so we can give parents-to-be their
choice between bringing up their proposed children so that they don't
become such, or else not having children at all. (There will be cases of
parental incompetence; in such cases, the presence of other adults who
are ready to take over the responsibility allows for as satisfactory a solution
as we can have to it.) It would be very sad indeed if the choice were more
complicated in the following way: bring up the child so that she becomes
a brilliant virtuoso *and* a kleptomaniac, or else leave her in need of external changing of her diapers but no threat to the neighbours. I suppose it is
logically possible that some such choices would have to be made, but it is
almost impossible to suppose that if we could foresee any such thing, we
could do nothing about it. But in general, I don't expect we would be faced
with these particular kinds of difficult choices, and so, once again, I leave
the subject on one side.

One firm thesis assumed in this chapter, then, is that parents may properly be held responsible for minimum standards of moral behaviour on
the part of their children, in the fullest sense of the word "responsible":

I would argue, even, that parents should, up to some point, actually be liable for the wrongful actions of their children. (Here the reader may wish to compare the much heftier program of political interventions sanctioned by Irvine in his newer book, *The Politics of Parenting*.[12])

By contrast, the responsibility that parents typically feel for their children beyond this minimum belongs not to the arenas of obligation and duty, especially, but to virtue theory. To be a good parent is to do well by one's children, and a reason for doing so is that we quite rightly regard it as a virtue to be a good parent. What makes it reasonable to hold good parenting in high esteem is that children, being future people, are indispensable to the community, as I noted at the outset. Having children is necessary for there being any community at all, of course, and, more to the point, having at least moderately good children is necessary for a good community. This interest is enormous. Almost everything any of us has is supplied by other people, and virtually everything that makes those things valuable is due, eventually, to the ingenuity, energy, perseverance, and other attributes of mostly unknown other people. From anybody's point of view, other people are a good thing, and apart from the extremely rare case of imminent starvation (once thought, wrongly, to be common[13]), more people are better.

Beyond all this, however, there are internal values of parenthood, and those, I think, are where most of the action lies, in most cases of parenting that we, in fairly affluent societies, know about. No doubt the fact that there are these values has to do with factors traced by evolutionary biology, but although that is of some interest, it is really beside the point in the one-on-one situation of parent and child. What *we* feel is a surge of emotion upon seeing this face, watching this or that behaviour. What *we* feel is an intense interest in the future of this little human. And what we feel counts, just as such. We can identify at least three components of these parental feelings.

First, of course, there is the emotional payoff of parenthood, experienced by nearly all parents who share in the joys and sorrows of their children.

Second, or perhaps a subclass of the first, there is what we might call a matter of personal aesthetics: children are legendarily cute and charming and immensely more interesting than even the best pets.

A third source has to do with the satisfaction of seeing a child develop into what we can reasonably hope to be a valuable adult, leading a good life.

The Value Judgments: Whose, and Why?

The expression "valuable adult" is, unfortunately, much less than perfectly clear. Valuable, we might ask, to whom, and for what? To the individual himself? Or to those around him? Hume summarizes the criteria of virtue as those qualities of mind or character that are "agreeable or useful to self or others." But there can be tension among these: both between what is either agreeable or useful to oneself and what is so to others and what is so either to some adults as compared with others, or even to some at the expense of others. We must worry particularly about divergences among the following: (a) a life good according to the parent who is trying to get the child to live that life; (b) a life good according to the child himself; (c) a life valued by the community or perhaps by humankind at large. And here we get into interesting moral problems. Suppose that the parent's vision of the child's future differs from (a) that of his community and (b) that of the child himself? The popular deontology implies, I think, that (b) would have absolute precedence over (a). But this, I think, is not reasonable. It can, and is rather likely to, impose unacceptable costs on the parents. It could, for that matter, impose unacceptable costs on the community. There needs to be a reasonable compromise among these three points of view. All, it seems to me, are relevant. I next make some suggestions as to where the proper mean lies in cases where these conflict.

The case for allowing the parent a substantial area of proper influence is basically simple: the parents bring the child into existence, and for some time thereafter they bear the major, and often the entire, costs of its upbringing. They are entitled to try to get a reasonable return on their investment—a return in the way of satisfaction with the sort of person their child turns out to be, insofar as they have been the ones who caused it to become that way. It is in a basic way true of parents that the children they have are "theirs," though the implication that they also fully *own* them in the sense of being able to do anything they want with them is one we can find good reason to back off from. But, the point is, not very far, and not nearly as far as many writers seem to want to.

The case for supposing that the child's own point of view is fundamental is quite different. In a sense, the child doesn't care where it came from or "who" it is. Children emerge from the womb into a world not at all of their own making, a world with which they must somehow make peace as they grow up, a world they will be trying to make the best of, such as it is. But in the earliest stages, these children have virtually no control over their environments—depending on what you count as "control" (and bearing in mind, for example, the many nights when parents are wakened by infants needing attention). Especially, these infants have no articulated program of interests to be pursued by appropriate strategic and tactical reasonings. As they grow up, of course, their repertoire of such interests expands, and, as it does, the child becomes more and more a distinct individual to be dealt with, more like the adult friends and associates we deal with. In short, when the child has ideas of her own, plans and intentions, then the question of respecting them will arise. There is, to be sure, a good chance that those plans and intentions are going to be very different from what they would have been had the genetically same child been brought up by a completely different set of parents, in different circumstances. And there is also an extremely good chance that they will be unpredictably different given everything we know—such as that is.

As with anyone else, our available options for attempting to get children to do what we want them to are (a) by persuasion—reasoning from premises that individual shares; (b) by what we may, with some reservations, call "non-rational persuasion"; or (c) by using force or the threat of same. One could, of course, lump all three under the first heading, but the point here is to attend to the differences among these. Obviously, the threat of force constitutes a reason for the other person to respond, namely by accommodating to the wishes of the forcer; but that isn't what is normally meant by "reasoning." Similarly, displays of emotion may persuade, but again these are not the sort of thing usually meant by "reasoned argument."

Our relation to our children is normally such that our own emotional expressions and responses to what they do, plus our indications to them of likely emotional responses in future should they do this or that, are much more likely to be effective than is the case with strangers or, perhaps, friends. Just which kinds of effects they will have is not so predictable.

The use of physical punishment to affect children's behaviour was extremely frequent in earlier times, but is now, happily, frowned upon by most of us—as well it should be. It was formerly believed that a parent who "spared the rod" would "spoil the child," and if that were true the question would arise whether we ought to prefer child spoilage to child torture; and if this really were the choice, then it would be difficult to avoid the conclusion that it would sometimes be our regrettable responsibility to use force in bringing up our children, insofar as it bore on their learning to respect the rights of other people. But fortunately, we do not generally have to make this choice. Perfectly well-behaved children—such as mine, and probably yours—need never have been spanked or otherwise subjected to corporal punishments.

A further reason to avoid corporal punishment of children is to get them, in turn, used to the idea that that is the wrong way to deal with people. And this is important enough, I think, to be accounted a responsibility of parenting.

Our question is whether there are any serious restrictions on the use of these methods, and the answer, so far, is that the third is to be avoided altogether, at least with most children. But what about the second? It is inevitable in part, of course. But also, it is possible for parents as well as children to use emotion as a sort of threat—to play emotional games with them. And this too, surely, is to be avoided. Displays of emotion should be genuine, so that the child gets the right message—that is, that the parent really cares, rather than that he or she is engaging in manipulation. Taken more broadly, we can accept that a fair part of parenting consists in interacting with our children on a common emotional wavelength—shaping them, no doubt, in the process, but in what we take to be good ways.

Still, this leaves us with the primary emphasis on normal rational persuasion and suggestion. With reasonable luck, children will be disposed to do what parents tell them to do, or strongly suggest that they do, or even what they just advise them to do. But luck does run out, and then what? I do not see that there is an easy answer to this question. And it is, after all, a great part of what parenting is about. Coercion is a last resort, but it cannot be rigidly ruled out. It should, rather, be ruled very far back in the queue, hopefully there to remain. Discussing with the child, pointing out what the consequences are and getting them to size these up in a coherent way, as well as just plain making deals with them to mutual advantage—these should be the main stuff of parental life, once children become sufficiently mature.

Responsibility in General

We must then return to the question of the extent of our responsibilities in training or, more generally, affecting the development of our children. When is it true that a certain parent is or was responsible for the presence of a certain behaviour in that parent's child? When is it true that the parent must or ought to *take responsibility* for such things?

We can be responsible only for our own acts, and what is caused by them. We often enough say that we are responsible for someone else in some way, but to say this is to say that we have access to a repertoire of actions that can be expected to affect the behaviour of this other person or persons, and so our responsibility is to avail ourselves of the appropriate selection from this repertoire. To the extent that a child is "ours" in the sense of acting under our own influence, we can take responsibility; to the extent that it is under its own steam, we can't.

But it is very often true that we could probably have done something to bring it about that the child wouldn't do the sort of thing it has in fact done. The situation with children generally seems to be that a certain general profile of practices will normally result in a child who does not injure people, steal their property, or insult them readily and seriously, and that this general profile is familiar to most of us. Normally intelligent and otherwise capable people will know, generally, about these things and act accordingly. Or so we hope. But if not? We would then have a case for urging some sort of training regime on such parents. But what about imposing it on them, or even taking the children out of their hands? That is a recourse fraught with perils, for one thing. And there is the matter of parental rights as well. We interfere all too readily with these at present, in my view. We may remonstrate, yes. And we may launch lawsuits against their parents for serious violations of our rights by children brought up irresponsibly. But here the default view set forth previously comes strongly into view. Other people's children are not ours. We may not press our own ideas about what is good for them on their unwilling parents without pressing cause. And that pressing cause had better take the form of danger to *us*, rather than danger that the child will not, as we think, do as well as it might.

The interesting further question is: when do we credit the growing child with ideas and values of its own—ideas that the child itself has to take responsibility for, rather than its parents? Surely the answer is: pretty soon. In supposing that children "behave," we automatically credit them with *some* level of independent thought. The level increases as time goes by, and as it does the possible responsibility of parents for what they think in some way diminishes. I suppose my parents must have asked themselves, "What did we do wrong?" in contemplating the career of their errant son, but it seems to me that the answer might very well be, "Nothing—it's all his fault!"

All of which leads to a need to ponder the general idea of parental responsibility. There is a general tendency for children to "take after" their parents—as well as another tendency, only slightly less general, for them to rebel. Parents try to teach their children various things, and the children have a way of learning something rather different from what the parents intended. How is one to generalize in the face of this?

Perhaps we can say this: when parents tried their best to bring it about that their children have characteristic F, and the children in question did in fact end up having that feature, then the parents in question get some credit, if F is a good thing. Or if it's a bad thing, and they failed to prevent it and could, then they get some blame. We can appraise parental intentions irrespective of success, after all. And when they fail, as they so often do, we can ascribe it, sometimes, to incompetence, though probably more often to forgivable ignorance or the General Persnickitiness of Things. At any rate, I think that's a process with fairly severe limits. The more intelligent the child, the more severe the limit, I should think; but in all cases, those limits are there.

This brings us, of course, to the interesting question of attending to the child's own interests, as developed and seen and understood *by it*, as distinct from the parents in question. To attack this question generally, let me first set out briefly a threefold distinction I am accustomed to making in the political field, but which is also, I think, applicable here.

Three Views of Politics

There are, according to this analysis, three sorts of political outlooks:

1. Thrasymachian: the state exists to line the pockets of the rulers. More generally, people in positions of power over others should use that power in their own best interests.
2. Platonic: the state should promote the good of its subjects, but the state decides what that good consists in.
3. Liberal (as represented, somewhat, by Glaucon in Plato's *Republic*, by Epicurus, and later by the classic liberals—Hobbes, Locke, Kant, etc.): on this view, the state exists solely to promote the good of its subjects— but, in *their* view of what's good for them, not someone else's.

I presume all of us who engage in this kind of discussion are liberals when it comes to political philosophy proper. The question is whether we should be liberal when it comes to parenting. When our children become independent persons, with views of their own good and the capacity to pursue it, the answer is, of course, in the affirmative, and for the same reason. But children are born approximately nowhere in this regard; they spend their early lives turning into persons with the capacities in question. And parents have influence—some, at least, and certainly highly variable, but still, *some*—over the course of this development. The question is, are they constrained to be liberals from the word go?

It is not clear that this is possible, and at the very start, surely, it is quite impossible, unless we want to impute innate ideas on such subjects to organisms incapable of formulating them. Soon enough, though, children begin to have ideas of what they want, and conflicts between parents and children on some of those things inevitably begin to take shape. Is the parent constrained, whenever there is a possibility of such a conflict, to give in to the child? Do children have something like absolute priority? The general answer is: certainly not.

There is, of course, the extremely important issue of the long run. Children's ideas of what is good for them are often very limited by inadequate information or an incapacity for formulating ideas of their own more distant futures. We often do correct children's behaviour in light of this. An infant heading out into the busy traffic will be snatched up by its parents, however liberal, on the obvious ground that it is not in the child's interest to be run over, and if the child claims to differ, the time to discuss the question is later. True, but many questions about what the child is to do in later life will not be answerable in so obvious a way. We impute to the child the desire to live a long, healthy life, and some things we can teach it will serve that end; insofar as the child appreciates the basis for such corrections as we may impose in light of such things, we can be fairly confident of cooperation from the child on those matters. But on many matters, that won't really be in question.

Even when it is, there may be real conflict. Suppose the child becomes enamoured of the military life, and wants nothing so much as to join the army as soon as possible. What does a pacifist parent do about that? Or a parent with severe doubts about the foreign policy of the government sponsoring that army? Suppose the child is bent on a university education and professional career for which we are sure he is unsuited: is the parent obliged to allow the child to have its way in the matter? What if she wants to marry some lout of whom we have the gravest doubts? Those who think that our own interests in such matters simply don't count may be accused of not having a life, and probably also of not really having much interest in their children. But people often do have such interests, and such things do matter a lot to them. We academics, I think, have little reason to think of ourselves as being above all that and able to say, grandly, what the interests of the children are and that they are all that matter. We are wrong on both counts. Not only do parents have very differing views about what those interests are—and legitimately so—but, being people, they cannot rationally be required to forget about their own interests when they differ.

Again, the parent may have a great interest that the child learn the agricultural techniques and disciplines on which its parents and their parents and so on for a long time have been dependent. Such parents will likely not raise the question, even, whether to send the child out into the fields to help out and to learn the family's way of making its living. In affluent societies, though, the question is likely to arise. What then? How much may the parents insist on the assistance of their children? The answer is surely not zero, or anywhere near it.

What about religion? Many parents will want to pass on the family religion to their children. Some among these will succeed in this without really trying, and certainly without raising difficult questions. But some of us will insist that it is in the child's true interest to be able to examine the tenets of this creed: they have, we might think, a right to address the difficult questions. In some case, to be sure, this will be a moral imperative: a religion that preaches death to all unbelievers, for example, is one that the rest of us can insist on expunging. But beyond that? Very little indeed. If parents insist on setting out for the wilds of unknown North America on the *Mayflower*, children in hand, others who think they know better are not entitled to stop them.

The model I shall recommend here, broadly to be put in the liberal category, is that on all such matters the parents have a responsibility to make the child who is of an age and mentality to understand the matter aware of problems and doubts about such matters, and to resolve conflicts that may arise regarding them by discussion, as well as to encourage the child in reading relevant literature, and so on. Yet if we say this, we will also encounter parents who will have no truck with such skepticism, as they see it. Are we to say that such parents are not merely wrong but in fact irresponsible? This is not, it seems to me, easy to do. Indeed, that stance may in turn be accused of illiberality. Parents have children voluntarily, and, as pointed out previously, they reasonably expect a return on their parental investment. Part of that return will be seen by some in religious or other ideological terms. It is not clear that we outsiders are on firm ground in requiring them to raise their children to question the family faith, or the like, short of the case where that faith can be shown to be likely to create grave harm to others.

Summary on Parental Responsibility

Where, then, is parental responsibility to be found, and what are its limits?

First, and obviously, it lies in providing those minimal conditions needed for the child to function and develop, which means especially that its physical health should be attended to. Major failure on this front, especially in circumstances of tolerable community affluence, can reasonably be met with offers of help and even with outright intervention by others in the community—though what constitutes the boundaries for such a failing is hard to say, short of likely imminent death or lifelong malformation.

Second, parental responsibility lies in treating the child in a way conducive to its developing into a decent person, one who respects the rights of those around it. Here the boundaries are clearer, and the case for intervention in the case of failings strong. And even for this purpose, the prominence of the factor of parental love and concern becomes evident: the loved child will likely treat others well, the unloved one will only too likely turn antisocial.

Third, it consists in nurturing the child in such a way as to enable it to live a good life. But at this point the question "Yes, but what is that?" and the entailed further question, "In whose view of what a good life for it would be?" confronts us seriously and drains high-level philosophical answers of most of their impact. The best we can do by way of answer, I think, is to say: At first, the parents' view is rightly dominant; later, however, the offspring's own view has primacy; and on the way from the first to the second, we are to proceed without violence, with as much reasoning as reasonably possible, and in every case with affection and respect.

I think those are the best answers we can manage, but I concede that they will not satisfy a good many who think about this and am certainly ready to hear more.[14]

Notes

1 William Irvine, *Doing Right by Children* (St. Paul, MN: Paragon House, 2001).

2 Ibid., 213.

3 Ibid., 228.

4 Ibid., 242.

5 Ibid., 248–50.

6 Ibid., 249.

7 Jan Narveson, "A Contractarian Defense of the Liberal View on Abortion and the Wrongness of Infanticide," *Values and Moral Standing: Bowling Green Studies in Philosophy* (BGSU Phil.) 8 (1986): 76–89. A restatement is found in my more accessible *Moral Matters*, 2nd ed. (1999), chap. 8 (Peterborough, ON: Broadview Press).

8 Joel Feinberg, "The Child's Right to an Open Future," in Feinberg, *Freedom and Fulfillment*, 76–97. (Princeton, NJ: Princeton University Press, 1992).

9 Claudia Mills, "The Child's Right to an Open Future?" *Journal of Social Philosophy* 34, no. 4 (Winter 2003): 499–509.

10 Ibid., 499.

11 The most layman-available scholarly responsible source is probably James Q. Wilson and Richard J. Herrnstein's *Crime and Human Nature* (New York: Simon & Schuster, 1985), chaps. 8–9. This work exhaustively reviews the literature on the particular topic of crime and childhood upbringing.

12 William Irvine, *The Politics of Parenting* (St. Paul, MN: Paragon House, 2003).

13 Ronald Bailey, ed., *The True State of the Planet* (New York: Free Press, 1996).

14 The author's previous paper, "Children and Rights," presented at the conference on Children's Rights, held at the University of Western Ontario in March 2000, now in Jan Narveson, *Respecting Persons in Theory and Practice* (Lanham, MD: Rowman & Littlefield, 2002), chap. 15. The present chapter leans on the previous one, though there is no sentential overlap.

THREE

Children, Caregivers, Friends

AMY MULLIN

This essay will compare friendships between morally competent adults with relations between young children and their caregivers. By "young children," I mean those of preschool age. My arguments are positioned with respect to a debate within feminist theory over the relevance of the mothering relation for thinking about the ethical nature of other human relationships. I distinguish my view both from those who claim that the caregiver–child relation should have a privileged role and from those who argue that this relation serves best as a point of contrast to caring relations between adults, rather than a paradigm for them.

A comparison of the caregiver–child relationship and caring relationships between adults reveals both continuity and difference. An overly sharp distinction between them distracts us from the possibilities for mutuality and reciprocity in relations between caregivers and young children. It makes it difficult for us to understand how children can make the transition from one type of relationship to the other as they mature, and can mask the extent to which degrees of dependence and even occasional paternalism may exist appropriately within some friendships.

In the next section, I discuss feminist debates over whether or not mothering should serve as a model for other caring relations.

Feminist Debates about Mothering

Can relationships between caregivers and young children serve as an ethical model for other caring relationships? Feminist theorists disagree. Jean Elshtain, Virginia Held, Paul Lauritzen, Nel Noddings, Sara Ruddick, Caroline Whitbeck, and Cynthia Willett either state or imply that the mother–child relation can serve as a valuable model for other sorts of ethical relationships.[1]

What do we mean by speaking of the mother–child relation? Mothers continue to care for and think about their children when those children reach adulthood and beyond. Yet maternal care for a baby and that for a middle-aged son going through a divorce would have little in common. Those who speak of the mother–child relation almost always intend the term to describe relations between mothers and their young dependent children. They speak of children being dependent on their mothers for their preservation, growth, and social acceptability, and they do not describe these children as being greatly influenced by others, such as teachers. This suggests that the children they have in mind are young, generally younger than school age. Many of these theorists, including Held and Ruddick, believe that both men and women may "mother" a child, although more women than men currently mother. Despite intending the term "mothering" to be gender-neutral, many feminists use words more typically associated with women in order to reflect the fact that throughout history, and still today, women have performed the bulk of this work.

I turn now to claims made for the paradigmatic status of this relation. Virginia Held writes that if we are to understand human relationships we must replace "the paradigm of economic man with the paradigm of mother and child."[2] Cynthia Willett writes that relationships between mothers and young children are important for developing ethical theories because: "From the standpoint of the mother–child relation, we can address the major concern of contemporary ethics, namely the possibilities of a prosocial desire."[3] Paul Lauritzen claims that the intellectual and emotional skills required for rearing children can serve as a model for a feminist ethic of care and compassion.[4] Nel Noddings uses the relation between a mother and her child as an example of natural caring, and as a model for a feminist ethic of caring.[5] Sometimes the paradigmatic status of this relation is implied rather than explicit. Lorraine Code observes that neither Whitbeck nor Ruddick explicitly claim that the mothering relation is paradigmatic: "But the generalizability claims that they make carry paradigmatic implications."[6]

Those theorists who claim or suggest that the mother–child relationship carries paradigmatic implications tend not to explore issues of the continuities between the mother–child relation and other ethically significant personal relationships in detail. For instance, in Held's contrast between the mother–child relation and contractual relationships, she does not consider where we might place friendships. Friendships clearly line up alongside the mother–child relationship in comparison to contractual relations in that the former are paradigmatically both caring and non-contractual. However, to the extent that friendships involve reciprocity of exchange of goods and services, as many argue that they do, this would align them in some respects with contractual relations. Friendships would be decidedly less formal, and they are relationships in which we typically do not intend to use legal frameworks to enforce the reciprocity. The emphasis on reciprocity of exchange, however, would suggest that friendships have something in common with both types of relationships Held contrasts.

In sharp contrast with those feminists who defend the paradigmatic status of the mother–child relation, Linda Bell, Claudia Card, Lorraine Code, Mary Dietz, Marilyn Friedman, Jean Grimshaw, Sarah Lucia Hoagland, and Barbara Houston argue that mothering should not have a central place in theorizing other sorts of ethical relations. Hoagland writes: "I do not think that mothering can be used as a model for an ethics of caring."[7] Friedman argues that mothering is a poor model for friendships between mature adults.[8] Some theorists of friendship see the contrast between friendship and the parent–child relation as so great that they have generated a debate over whether or not parents can ever become friends with their children.[9] While this debate about the nature of relationships between adult children and their parents is distinct from the question of whether or not friendships have much in common with the relationship between young children and their caregivers, the debate is clearly generated by the assumption of a major contrast between friendships and relations involving caregivers and children.

Focusing on questions about the similarities between the caregiver–child relation and other personal relationships may give the impression that the former are only worthy of philosophical discussion if they can serve as a model for other relationships. This is clearly not the view of philosophers like Ruddick, who have written extensively of their significance, and it does not seem to be the intent of the latter group. For instance, Code recognizes that mothers are an important influence on children's moral development, and the relationships between caregivers and children are ethically significant at least for that reason.[10]

In their relationships with their caregivers, children learn how to trust, receive, give, and care. Even if there are no significant points of contact between relationships shared by children and their caregivers and other types of ethically significant relationships, the former will be ethically important not only because of their role in shaping children's moral development but also because they draw upon moral capacities from both caregivers and children.

This essay seeks to compare relationships between caregivers and children to friendships between morally competent adults. With reference to the debate over the paradigmatic status of the mother–child relation, I will agree in important respects with those who argue significant differences in the two sorts of relationship militate against using the mother–child relationship as a model for ethical relationships more generally. For brevity, I will call these the "naysayers."

Three Disagreements with the Naysayers

I will also disagree with them in three respects:

(1) My first disagreement is not only with the naysayers but also with those who claim that relationships between caregivers and young children can serve as a model for other relationships. The range of relationships between caregivers and the children in their care is reduced to the dyadic, familial relationship between a mother and her child. Despite definitions of mothering, by Ruddick for instance, that equate mothering with gender-neutral provision of childcare,[11] mothering relationships as analyzed by Held, Noddings, Ruddick, and Willett conform in most respects to practices stereotypically expected of middle-class mothers with relatively non-involved but income-providing partners. As Jean Grimshaw observes, this causes Ruddick to "conceive of mothering as a task whose demands arise simply within the mother–child nexus and to adopt an ahistorical view of the ways in which these demands are understood."[12]

These theorists understand mothers to be solely or chiefly responsible for the care of children. Each is expected to do her caring work alone in a private home, to have long-term responsibilities toward her child, a great deal of power to make decisions on behalf of the child, and authority over the child. However, many children in contemporary Canada, the United States, and Europe, as well as most children in developing countries and in other historical periods, have not been cared for in this way. In contemporary Canada and the United States, many children are cared for by a group of caregivers working together, for instance in a childcare centre. Often children's caregivers are paid, the relationships are not expected to last long, and caregivers' responsibilities and power are limited. Patricia Hill Collins, bell hooks, and Alison Bailey have all pointed to ways in which Ruddick's account ignores the role of "othermothers" within African-American communities who voluntarily take on the role of a child's mother. Some of these other mothers simply replace a child's "biomother," others share the work of raising a child.[13] We need to acknowledge and theorize about the range of relationships between young children and their caregivers, not simply the relationships between children and some types of mothers.

This criticism chiefly applies to the work of Elshtain, Held, Noddings, Ruddick, Whitbeck, and Willett. However, for the most part despite their critics' recognition of the limitation of this model of caring for children,[14] the naysayers themselves do not seek to provide a richer understanding of the range of relationships between children and their caregivers, but instead criticize the mother–child relation as if it were a good model for all relations between caregivers and dependent children.[15] Some of the similarities between relationships involving mature adults and relationships of children and their caregivers may be harder to observe when we conceive the work of caring for young children in accordance with the ideology of motherhood.[16]

The ideology of motherhood, like all ideological constructions, makes claims both about what its subject is like and what it should be like, often blurring the line between the two. Patrice DiQuinzio labels it "essential motherhood" and writes: "Essential motherhood represents women's mothering as natural … inevitable, instinctive, and properly contained in its appropriate social realm, the private sphere."[17] Essential motherhood requires "women's exclusive and selfless attention to and care of children" based on women's supposedly natural capacities for empathy and self-sacrifice.[18]

I believe the ideology of motherhood also assumes that mothers should meet all the emotional needs of their young children,[19] care for their bodies, and keep them safe, while fathers provide the material resources required for this mothering work. In broad strokes, according to the ideology of motherhood, with the exception of the necessary provision of material resources, mothers are thought to be necessary and sufficient for the happiness of their children, and children are thought to be necessary and sufficient for the happiness of their mothers.

Like most feminists, I think the ideology of motherhood is false as a description of the wide variety of situations in which children are cared for, and deeply flawed as an ideal. As a result, I rework the question about whether relations between mothers and children can serve as a model for other ethically significant relations. This essay is part of a larger project of studying a range of relationships between caregivers and children in order to contrast and compare them to relationships between morally competent adults. The caregivers can be male or female, paid or unpaid, and have long-term or short-term relationships with a child, but they will not be considered caregivers for the purpose of this essay unless they are on intimate terms with the child and strive to meet his or her needs for preservation, growth, and development.

(2) I have a second point of disagreement with the naysayers. Those who argue that we should not use the relationship between caregivers and children as an ethical paradigm do not adequately distinguish among various features of the relationships between caregivers and the young children in their care. Three facts are conflated: (a) the fact that children are dependent upon their caregivers, (b) the fact that children and their caregivers have different abilities and different social power, and (c) the fact that young children, unlike most of their caregivers, are often legitimately believed not to be the best arbiters of their own interests. Dependency, inequality, and paternalism,[20] are seen as necessarily connected. I do not object to the depiction of relationships between young children and their caregivers as ones in which the caregivers may legitimately make decisions for children in seeking to promote their interests (provided that there are safeguards on what caregivers determine those interests to involve; see Ramsay in this volume). I agree that this is the case. However, I think the naysayers are too quick to suppose that all relationships involving dependency and inequality will promote paternalism. This leads into my third point of disagreement with the naysayers.

(3) Naysayers make an overly sharp contrast of relationships involving caregivers and dependent children with relationships between adults who are equals in every respect. They also suggest that the former relationships necessarily lack mutuality. For instance, Friedman writes: "Relationships vary considerably. We can relate to others in ways which approach equality and mutuality, or we can relate to others in ways which involve forms of dependency or hierarchies of power and authority."[21] The dependency, inequality, and paternalism that characterize relations between children and their caregivers are contrasted with features presented as appropriate to friendship. The latter is described as a relationship between equals, in

which neither is dependent upon the other, and neither makes decisions for the other. As we shall see, it can come to seem as if any failures of reciprocity, such as prolonged dependency of one person upon the other, and any significant inequalities in power and ability between the two parties, inevitably lead to paternalism. Moreover, just as the caregiver–child relationship is presented as dyadic, friendship is also presented primarily as a relationship between two individuals, instead of a social network.

Code makes a similarly sharp contrast between friendship and the caregiver–child relation in *What Can She Know?* She claims that: "Friendship can occupy the space claimed for the best forms of maternal thinking."[22] Yet the best relations between caregivers and young children involve dependency and severe inequality in both power and abilities, and this is not how Code conceives of friendship, which is presented as a relationship between equals.

Friendship and Reciprocity

Of the naysayers, Friedman gives the most extensive account of friendship and it is to her analysis of friendship, and its contrast with the caregiver–child relation, that I turn. In her "What Are Friends For?" Friedman argues that reciprocity in care is a moral requirement in relationships between "morally competent adults." In some sense this is uncontroversial. Adults should not seek to exploit one another and should be willing to give as well as receive. Sandra Bartky[23] and Claudia Card[24] examine failures of this kind of reciprocity. For instance, Bartky argues that in relationships between women and men who are their social superiors, women's caring attention to their male friends—such as attempts to boost their self-esteem and validate the men on the latter's terms—often are unreciprocated and can lead women to compromise their values and minimize their own self-esteem.

These theorists are right to argue that a friendship in which only one party seeks to provide emotionally significant care can be damaging to the psychological health of the giver and moral status of the receiver. Card warns, "lack of reciprocity is probably a major cause of the breakup of friendships among peers."[25] In particular, she worries that in our close relationships, when only one person in a relationship values the other apart from his or her utility, this lack of reciprocity of valuing harms the self-esteem of the person who is not independently valued.[26] However, questions remain about what is required for reciprocity. There are various types of reciprocity, often not clearly distinguished, including reciprocity of valuing, reciprocity of caring, and reciprocity of the exchange of goods and services.

Some types or reciprocity have little to do with others. Moreover, honouring some of them requires us to forgo insistence upon others. Reciprocity of caring should not lead to reciprocity in the exchange of goods and services should the needs and resources of the parties involved differ sharply. If two people care for each other and strive to meet each other's needs when they can, yet one friend has more resources than the other, perhaps financial resources, perhaps availability of leisure time, reciprocity of caring would discourage demands that the friend with lesser resources seek always to provide gifts of equal value to his more well-off friend, or refuse to accept gifts whose overall value he could not reciprocate. While we might insist that he could or should give his friend other kinds of goods and services (thoughtful phone calls, emotional boosting during difficult times) of "equal value," it seems perverse either to insist upon the equality of value, or to attempt to provide some common measure, whether in terms of money or utility, which would make it possible for us to assess whether or not he has reciprocated equally. Moreover, it seems equally perverse, should one friend have more serious needs than the other, for him to refuse to accept help at the point where he predicts that he is unlikely to be able to reciprocate, and perverse as well for his friend to stop giving so as to preserve the reciprocity of the exchange of goods and services.

One reason that demands for reciprocity of exchange of goods and services seem perverse is that those demands conflict with another type of reciprocity, one that is more essential to an intimate friendship, and that is reciprocity of valuing. Since reciprocity of valuing is contravened whenever a person is not valued apart from his or her utility within the relationship, it cannot be said to exist in relationships that cannot tolerate failures in the reciprocity of exchange. If friendships decrease in moral value[27] when friends are not equally useful to one another, giving and taking in approximately equal amounts, then those friendships do not actually involve reciprocity of valuing.

Theorists of friendship generally insist upon both equality overall and the equality of giving and taking in particular within a friendship. For instance, Joseph Kupfer argues that the reason to think parents and their grown children might be friends is because "young children become adults able to contribute to their parents' lives in ways comparable to what their parents have done for them."[28] By contrast, the reason he decides parents cannot really be friends with their adult children is because the history of the inequality between them prevents them from interacting as equals forever afterwards.[29] Nicholas Dixon, who argues that friendships might be possible between people who are not equal, such as an able-bodied person who physically assists her disabled friend, suggests that this is because "the alleged inequality in such relationships may be only superficial, since the able-bodied person may gain just as much in terms of emotional satisfaction and intellectual stimulation as she gives in physical assistance.[30] While I certainly would not dispute the possibility, it troubles me that friendships are presented either as no longer possible or as morally flawed whenever the "give and take" involved are not roughly equal. Are inequalities of resources and needs always a threat to the moral value of a relationship between adults? To suppose so conflates willingness to give and ability to give.

I find it implausible to think that the kinds of support we provide for our friends, whether in the provision of meals for someone temporarily bedridden, assistance in caring for the children of a recently bereaved friend, or support for a friend who challenges social mores, would or should always be reciprocated equally. I find it more plausible to demand that the various parties to a friendship be prepared to meet the needs of their friends, depending upon their resources and abilities, but not that they should seek to provide goods and services of equal value to what has been received (it also is difficult to conceive of what we might count as the common measurement that would reveal whether or not equality of value had been achieved). To the extent that a friend refuses to accept help because she does not expect to be able to repay it, I hope that most of us would see this as a weakness in the friendship. Similarly, we do not expect caregivers to refuse to provide, or children to refuse to receive, that which they do not expect to be reciprocated.

Audrey Thompson points out that "the distinctive character of responsibility in friendship, which we might call co-responsibility, calls for shared rather than distributive attention to the conditions of the friendship."[31] She argues that if one friend has significant obligations to spouse and daughter as well as to work and an aged parent, and the other friend has obligations to work and a spouse but not to dependents, it would be inappropriate for the friends to impose equivalent demands upon one another. Her suggested solution is for one friend to assume some of the burdens of caring for the other's dependents, not in order to receive quid pro quo extra attention from the more burdened friend, but instead as "the boundaries of the friendship are widened to include caring for what the friend cares for."[32] However, Thompson then goes on to make an absolute contrast of friendship to relationships between parents and children. She states that the latter relationships preclude mutuality since "caretaking imposes necessarily differential responsibilities, whereas caring between equals allows for co-responsibility."[33] Here I think it is troubling that her solution to the situation where friends do not have equal time and resources to devote to a relationship is that one friend care for the other's dependent daughter. For her, caregiving that meets dependency needs is something that an adult may provide a child, but not something that one adult friend may provide for the other. Despite her call for co-responsibility that does not require reciprocity in the sense of equivalence in the exchange of goods and services, whenever differential care is provided, it is directed to one's friend's dependents, and not to one's friend, for this would be caregiving of the sort appropriate for parents to provide to children, not for equal friends to provide at times one for the other. Caring for equals is contrasted with the caring an adult may provide to a child, and dependency is considered appropriate only for the child.

Marilyn Friedman, in a move similar to Audrey Thompson's, appears to allow for a broader notion of reciprocity than that of equivalent exchange, but holds back from making sense of dependency in friendship. Friedman argues that she does not require a "*quid pro quo* accounting of services in personal relationships." However, while she may not require an *accounting* of services, she does seem to require that the goods and services exchanged be equivalent in value. She writes: "Something is amiss...if a close personal relationship between morally competent adults lacks an overall approximate reciprocity in the diverse ways of caring. This mutuality seems, on the face of it, to be a moral requirement for those morally competent persons who genuinely care for each other."[34]

In a footnote to this paragraph, Friedman observes that "My generalization is intended to allow for exceptional cases; sometimes one partner is infirm or otherwise deeply needful of care and unable to reciprocate this care for a prolonged period of time."[35] However, she does not tell us what justifies the exceptional cases, or whether she believes the relationship is sustainable (either practically or as a moral relationship) if the inability of one partner to reciprocate on an equal basis is sustained, or can be expected to continue indefinitely.

In the same footnote, Friedman goes on to distinguish between mutuality and reciprocity, but makes it clear that reciprocity is a necessary though not sufficient component of mutuality: "'Reciprocity' suggests that specific actions are met with corresponding actions as repayments; 'mutuality' suggests, in addition, the sharing of interests or concerns. 'Mutuality' identifies a richer relationship than that of mere repayment for good turns rendered. Nevertheless, reciprocity is not irrelevant to personal relationships; it would seem to be a part, even though only a part, of what mutuality involves."[36]

I believe that Friedman is mistaken to claim that mutuality always requires reciprocity in the broad sense of repayment for care received. As I will argue later, we can see mutuality in relations between children and their caregivers even before reciprocity is aimed at, and certainly before it is achieved. However, I believe that this is true not only of relations between children and caregivers. Close personal relationships between morally competent adults do not require this kind of reciprocity to involve mutuality and to be morally valuable relationships.

Friedman's concern, echoing Bartky and Card, is that women, particularly in their relationships with men, will care for more than they will be cared for, either because they are actively abused or because they are exploited by having their caring activities taken for granted and not reciprocated. There are real grounds for this concern. We often encounter relationships where one member has sufficient emotional and financial resources, as well as time and talent, to provide for the other member's needs, but chooses not to do so, or to do so in a very limited way, while continuing to draw upon the other person's resources.

However, there are also relationships where failures of reciprocity are not due to one person's unwillingness to do her or his fair share, or lack of commitment to the relationship, but to the person's lesser resources or greater needs. Sometimes, as Friedman indicates, this period of greater need may be prolonged—in fact, it may be permanent. For example, one friend, due to aging manifested during the relationship, may come to have physical limitations, which make it more difficult for her to provide goods and services to her friend, even while she continues to care for and about the friend, to value the relationship, and to have mutual interests with her friend. The physical limitations, such as difficulty walking, chronic fatigue, or problems with fine motor control, may also limit her opportunities for employment, reduce her income, and lower her social status as compared to her friend. Reciprocity, independence, and equality of status may therefore all be threatened.[37]

Except for one footnote, Friedman ignores friendships that face these kinds of issues. This failure on her part is linked to her sharp distinction between "caring by mature persons for those dependent on them and the caring that can and should go on among morally competent adults."[38] Because she considers only these two alternatives, she risks making all persons who are dependent upon others for care, whether or not they are mature, appear morally incompetent (surely not her aim). While this stark contrast is particularly clear in Friedman, it operates as well in other theorists of friendship. For instance, Laurence Thomas privileges reciprocity of self-disclosure as the criterion of friendship. He considers the objection that this obscures other features of friendship, such as providing material help to one's friend, and notes that he has "assumed that by and large companion friends are self-sufficient or, in any case, that the material help each provides the other is quite ancillary to the friendship."[39] This ignores the many times in which friends are not self-sufficient and have real dependency needs and makes an overly sharp distinction between the affective component of a friendship (which involves the exchange of confidences) and material help. Those who care for young children are well aware of the emotional intimacy involved in acts of bodily care, and the provision of material help to adults, including such actions as helping one's friend recover from surgery or illness, can be similarly deeply emotional.

Caring for Young Children

Friedman rejects the possibility that work focusing on the philosophical significance of care for dependent children may be relevant for thinking about relationships between adults. Ruddick argues that maternal thinking is characterized by concern for a child's preservation, growth, and social acceptability. This involves seeking to ensure that a child thrives physically and grows and develops emotionally, intellectually, and morally. As a result, the characteristic virtues aimed at in maternal thinking involve being responsive to growth, accepting of change, and attentive to particularity, context, and individual differences. If we view friendship between two people as static, these aims and virtues do not apply, but if we see friendship as characteristically long term, and capable of accommodating and encouraging change, then they do seem relevant. Friedman argues that: "Morally competent adults, in relationships with each other, do not usually have mother like responsibilities for each other's preservation, growth, or social acceptability."[40] If we think of mother-like responsibilities according to the ideology of motherhood, in which one person is assigned moral and legal responsibility for achieving these outcomes for her child, then friendship is indeed dissimilar. However, if we reject this ideology, and refuse to limit responsibility for children's development to one or two persons who may have insufficient resources and talents to achieve their aims, then the contrast is not as great.

Nonetheless, in some respects, Friedman is surely right; there are significant differences between caring for children and caring for adults. One involves the extent to which young children often lack insight into their long-term interests and needs and may lack the ability to delay gratification in order to meet those long-term needs. While children at different ages have different levels of insight into their needs and interests, and caregivers should never ignore children's expressions of those interests, caregivers also have responsibilities to look out for children's long-term interests, as well as the capacity to help shape what those long-term interests may turn out to be. This makes the work of the caregiver morally difficult, but we must be careful not to make moral judgments about this relationship that would be appropriate only if the relationship were one of morally competent adults.

Linda Bell, following Sartre, makes this mistake, and considers all relationships between caregivers and children to involve violence: "To keep the child from consequences she or he does not intend, the adult limits the child's freedom. Though done with the best of intentions for the child's welfare and though perhaps truly necessary to keep the child from harm or to provide for her or his future freedom, the limitation is nonetheless violence."[41] She therefore argues: "Vulnerability of the child and the power imbalance between the child and adult(s) render this relationship inherently violent and thus a poor model for caring and moral adult relationships."[42] While Bell is right to argue that the paternalism of the child–caregiver relation "simply cannot be taken as a model for relationships between individuals who are both responsible adults,"[43] she is wrong to consider vulnerability of one person in a relationship, and a power imbalance between the parties, always to threaten the moral status of that relationship. Relationships between mature adults should not characteristically involve profound paternalism, but they may well involve unequal vulnerability and dependency. Of course vulnerability may be abused, and one person may illegitimately take another's dependency as a sign that she lacks the capacity to make decisions for herself. However, since friends are paradigmatically vulnerable to one another in many ways, it is odd to think that we need to worry about only the kinds of vulnerability produced by dependency.

Although Friedman is right that caring for adults differs significantly from caring for children, she is like Bell in making too close an equation between inequality, dependence, and paternalism. Friedman rejects the caregiver–child relation as a model for ethics and replaces it with friendship,

characterized in opposition to the former. Instead we should look to paradigmatic features of various types of caring relationships to investigate
whether or not one type, such as friendship, may sometimes have features
associated more often with relationships of another type, such as the relation between caregivers and children. While there are important differences between these types of relationships, there can also be interesting
points of similarity, particularly when one adult is dependent, temporarily
or permanently, partially or totally, on another or others for her preservation or her spiritual, intellectual, or emotional growth. This dependence
may be much easier for both the dependent person and her supporter to
bear when a network of persons shares the task of providing support, as
Aronson argues.[44] However, this response to dependence is obscured by
most theorists' emphasis on friendship as dyadic.

One of the reasons Friedman downplays areas of overlap between relations between caregivers and the children in their care and relations
between friends has to do with her uneasiness about relations of dependence between mature persons. Another reason may be that Friedman
reduces the former to familial relationships. This is because she ignores the
relationships between children and those of their caregivers who are not
bound to them by familial ties, and because she also downplays the extent
to which men and women who care for children may challenge the roles
socially ascribed to family members, particularly challenging the ideology
of motherhood.

What are some of Friedman's worries about family ties? She considers
them to involve "great differences in status and power between family
members" often due to age differences or gender inequality.[45] This is often
true, however she also claims that kinship relations are marked by a "crusty
rigidity."[46] She describes family ties as nonvoluntary; they are socially
ascribed relations.[47] When we recognize that caregivers are not always family members, some of these worries about the caregiver–child relationship
may be diminished, and certainly the contrast Friedman draws between
friendships and the caregiver–child relationship need not be so sharp. Differences in status and power due to age and ability remain, but there is no
reason to think that all relationships between children and their caregivers
will be characterized by crusty rigidity or governed by expectations about
relations between kin. Moreover, even when caregivers have some abilities
that the children in their care lack, the children may have some abilities that
the caregivers lack. For instance, some quite young children serve as trans-
lators for their immigrant parents, others care for an ill parent or assist a
parent by providing information he or she lacks, for instance due to blind-

ness. However, while some caregivers may voluntarily choose to work with children, the children in their care generally cannot opt out of the relationship. This may seem like a sharp distinction between friendships and the role children play in their relationships with their caregivers, but just because a friendship may be voluntarily started does not mean that a friend can easily opt out of her ties to those upon whom she depends.

Just as some of Friedman's concerns about the caregiver–child relation are better represented as criticisms of traditional mother–child relations, so too are some of Hoagland's. For instance, in her "Some Thoughts about 'Caring,'" Hoagland worries about the inequalities involved in relations between mothers and children—both in that mothers are expected to care for their children (perhaps unconditionally) without being cared for in return, and in that mothers have authority to make decisions for their dependent children. Here it is unclear whether Hoagland finds the inequality itself troubling, as she objects to Noddings's focus on "the unequal relationship between mother and child"[48] or whether she worries only that the authority of the parent may lead to domination of the child.

She suggests that "group mothering may be the key" to avoiding one mother's singular authority over her children.[49] In group mothering, inequalities of power and ability between adults and children would remain, as would children's dependence upon the adults. Presumably paternalism would also be involved, at least in relations with very young children, but there would not be as many opportunities for abuse of power, and the entire burden of a child's needs would not be placed on any one person. This suggests that inequality and dependence, and potentially also paternalism, are not in themselves problematic features of relations between adults and children, although they may become so when one person has sole responsibility for and authority over a child.

Paternalism is rarely appropriate in relations between morally competent adults, but I am reluctant to say that it is never appropriate in friendship. If limited to specific periods of time and specific areas of decision-making, in times when moral competence and autonomy in general may be compromised due to significant stress, such as bereavement, temporary drug or alcohol abuse, an area where our friend is massively self-deceived, and similar threats to the friend's insight into his or her interests and situation, then paternalism between friends may be a legitimately caring act. Friends may act to prevent their friend from making irretrievable decisions in times of grief, or when judgment is clouded by alcohol, rage, or massive vanity. One friend may try to keep another friend, who has just had a sexual relationship end badly, from engaging in a sexual encounter he suspects his friend would deeply regret. Another may temporarily remove a large supply of sleeping pills from the medicine cabinet of a just-widowed friend. These decisions may be mistaken, and the mistakes could have very bad consequences, but I do not feel that we would always take occasionally paternalistic acts of this sort to nullify a friendship. In fact, we may feel that failures to intervene in these ways, when no one else is as well acquainted with the shaky or vulnerable nature of our friend's ability to think about his or her long-term interests, would be a failure of friendship. We can sometimes make too sharp of a distinction between moral competence and incompetence. We need to recognize that we may make poor decisions about alcohol or suffer stressful events that temporarily render us incompetent, and that friends are sometimes aware of their friends' areas of weakness and vulnerability and can sometimes legitimately seek to shield one another from the effects of bad decision-making.

Nonetheless, I would agree that there is a significant difference of degree in the amount of paternalism appropriate in caring for young children and caring for our friends, albeit one that shifts slowly as the child ages and develops his or her abilities. What about those other prominent features of caring for young children, inequality and dependence? Hoagland suggests: "The very purpose of parenting, teaching, and providing therapy is to wean the cared-for of dependency."[50] I agree that in most cases, although not all, these practices do and should aim to end dependency in the one cared for. In other relationships, however, enabling the cared-for person to mature or develop her skills may not end dependency. Sometimes all that can realistically be aimed at, even in relations between morally competent adults, is diminished dependency. For instance, a frail senior may depend upon his partner for some kinds of care; a woman may depend upon her network of friends for support in her terminal illness.

Do these kinds of relationships necessarily lack mutuality and reciprocity? For those who think that mutuality must incorporate reciprocity of exchange of services, it appears that they do. By contrast, Noddings, thinking about relations between infants and adults, offers a minimalist notion of reciprocity in which mere acknowledgement of care received is a kind of reciprocity. Hoagland worries that in this model, "there is no need for the child to turn and exhibit concern for the mother's projects."[51] She writes that "Nonreciprocity-beyond-acknowledgment" does not show respect for the other, and undermines the ability of the cared-for to learn to become caring. However, is this a problem with the caregiver–child relationship per se, or is it a problem with Noddings's characterization of that relationship, particularly when the child is still an infant?

Mutuality and Reciprocity between
Children and Their Caregivers

On my view, mutuality and reciprocity, of varying types, are not only possible but should be aimed at by both children and their caregivers. First, relationships between children and their caregivers can involve mutuality in the absence of various sorts of reciprocity. Second, we should tolerate the lack of reciprocity only when the child lacks the abilities required for that kind of reciprocity. Third, children at various ages are capable of various sorts of reciprocity, and even young children are capable of the kinds of reciprocity that involve intent rather than equivalence in exchange, for instance reciprocity of valuing and reciprocity in seeking to give one another joy.

Children are capable of much more than mere acknowledgement of care received, and the mutuality of relationships between caregivers and children can come in the form of shared activities and shared joys, rather than in children's contribution to those of the caregivers' projects that existed before the relationship.[52] Children and their caregivers, including those caregivers who are only with a child for a few months or a few years, share stories and share experiences. Both sides may engage in self-revelation (with the adult keeping to age-appropriate topics). Young children and their caregivers may mutually maintain the living space they use to eat, sleep, and play. This is not to say that the contributions of the children and the adult caregivers will be equal as they tidy, fix meals, or play together, but it is to insist that children are capable of contributing to the tasks involved in their care. In good relationships, children and their caregivers have mutual trust, are physically affectionate with one another, and share some aspects of a sense of humour. Such good relationships are rewarding for the caregivers as well as the children and are one explanation for the interest some women and men have in paid caregiving as a career, despite the poor financial compensation.

Many caregivers seek to teach children physical, emotional, and moral skills by means of play. Some of this play, particularly when a caregiver is not expected to be the sole adult participant and available for the entirety of a child's waking hours, can be fun for the caregiver as well. While many of these forms of mutuality require a child to seek to reciprocate the care she receives, they certainly do not require her to be equal in her contributions to what he or she shares with the caregiver. Moreover, some of what children give to their caregivers does not involve any specific intention to give. For instance, some of it comes in the form of a transformation of the caregiver's world. Christine Gudorf talks about some of what her physically disabled children have given her: "new communities, new loyalties, new insight—new identities."[53]

Reciprocity requires both parties to seek, explicitly or implicitly, to provide something to the other. The reciprocity may be in the exchange of goods and services, and it may aim at equivalency, or it may be reciprocity in valuing, or reciprocity in seeking to bring one another joy. Mutuality is broader. Mutuality is a matter of what the relationship to which each contributes achieves for the other, such as moments of fun, opportunities for growth and learning, and the making of new connections to others outside of the immediate relationship. This should not be taken to excuse those who have the ability to contribute more directly to the other person and choose not to because the other is seen as unworthy of care, but it does provide us with models of reciprocity and mutuality that permit the participants, whether children or adults, to be unequal in status, abilities, and resources, while still having an ethical relationship.

If friendships between mature adults may involve varieties of inequality and dependency, and absence of reciprocity of some kinds, does this mean that relations between caregivers and young children can or should be friendships? We often hear of parents mistakenly trying to be friends with their young children. The mistake here is not the pursuit of mutuality. Possibilities for mutuality and reciprocity should not make us forget that relations between caregivers and young children continue to involve not only more inequality and dependency than is typical in friendship, but also some significant paternalism on the part of the caregivers. Caregivers have responsibilities to strive to preserve children's lives, health, and opportunities. (See Macleod and also Narveson, in this volume, for related discussions of responsibility toward children.) These responsibilities may require them to override children's wants and decisions, albeit reluctantly, when those children do not manifest the capacity to make reasonable and informed judgment about what is required to meet their needs, or what are likely to be the consequences of their choices. While friendships between mature adults can also accommodate some paternalism, relationships between young children and their caregivers will involve far more frequent occasions of appropriate paternalism.

Abandoning reciprocity as a goal to be worked toward within the child–caregiver relationship would have many negative consequences. Failure to work toward reciprocity within that relationship threatens the moral development of the children, who learn to subordinate others' needs to their own. It threatens the happiness and mental health of the caregivers. It weakens the relationship between the child and his or her caregivers, and it deprives both caregivers and children of real joys, including but not limited to the opportunity to learn about those who differ from one's self.

When we make an overly sharp contrast between friendship, seen as a relationship involving mutuality and reciprocity, and relations between caregivers and children in their care, we make it difficult to see how children could make the move from one type of relationship to the other. We impede working toward mutuality and reciprocity as goals in caregiving, and we also discourage people from engaging in caregiving, leaving the work instead to those who are most culturally devalued, because of their sex, class, race or ethnicity. However, my encouragement of the pursuit of mutuality and reciprocity in relations between children and their caregivers is not meant to burden caregivers and children with the expectation that they will share all of one another's interests, anymore than I would endorse the ideology of motherhood's expectation that one person can and should meet all of the needs of a child.

Networks of Caregivers

Instead, this should give us reason to strive towards caregivers working in groups or networks. The networks should be small enough to coordinate the work of caregiving and to let the children and caregivers form intimate bonds, yet large enough to minimize the potential for abuse of authority and the stress of people seeking to meet needs they are not suited to, or lack the resources to, meet. One reason the networks must be reasonably small is that caregiving requires intimacy of at least some types. Caregivers require intimate knowledge of the bodies, moods, and character traits of those they care for, if they are to meet their needs. This intimate knowledge, however, makes those who are cared for particularly vulnerable to abuse by their caregivers. While groups of caregivers are as capable of abusing the vulnerability as individuals are, and so the potential for abuse can never be reduced to zero, it does seem plausible that members of a caregiving network would be more nervous about abusing those they are supposed to care for, when they know that evidence of this abuse would be available to others in the network. They might also be less likely to abuse the children in their care if they were not overwhelmed by the demands of those children and the social expectations about their ability to meet those demands.

Another potential advantage for providing care for young children in networks concerns the paternalism involved in this work. As Grimshaw observes, Ruddick can make it seem as if discovering what a child really needs is solely a matter of attentive love.[54] Yet what someone is taken to need depends also on ideologies imposed on this caregiving work, social expectations of the child, and possibly unconscious expectations and needs of the caregiver him or herself. If caregiving for young children were provided by groups working together, the caregivers would need to become aware of their conception of the long-term interests and short-term needs of the child and then possibly defend or alter that conception when faced with the alternative conceptions of the other caregivers. Even if the power dynamics of the caregiving network were such that one or two persons' conceptions of the best interests of the child were more likely to dominate, the process involved in articulating that conception (if only so the other caregivers can be expected to share it, or act on it), could at least help to expose that conception to the scrutiny of other adults, and would require articulation and therefore conscious reflection. This could be a safeguard against some of the abuses potentially involved in paternalism. (See Brennan and White, in this volume, for a related point about the role for third parties, other than a child's parents, in protecting children's rights.) Whenever the caregiving network is relatively homogeneous, however, this would not prevent the conception of the best interests of the child from being parochial, and possibly sexist, racist, or classist. (The arguments of Narveson in this volume point to another reason for sharing responsibility for children in this way, in that parents would be less likely to raise children to be sexist or racist, and hence the children, once raised, would be less dangerous to others.)

Speaking of caregiving networks in the context of childcare may seem like a radical proposal, given our common understanding of this work as being done by lone individuals (typically mothers) or pairs (typically parents). However, this common view fails to acknowledge the many ways in which the ideology of motherhood is already undermined. It ignores practices like other-mothering and the involvement of an extended community in rearing a child that Bailey, Collins, and hooks see occurring in many North American black communities. It ignores the roles played by many people in caring for a child, including medical professionals, neighbours, and extended families. It also ignores the fact that childcare is often shared by parents and paid caregivers. In part, what I am proposing is that we begin to think of this work as shared by a network, rather than of one caregiver as a surrogate for another. Sociologist Lynet Uttal argues that parents sometimes think of paid caregivers who care for their children as temporary surrogates or replacements for the parents. She notes that a few parents instead think of themselves as working in coordination with their caregivers. I find the latter approach preferable for a variety of reasons, and I believe it is not only parents who need to think of paid caregivers in this way, but also the paid caregivers and the wider society.[55] This approach would facilitate recognition that all of those who provide significant care for a child have insight into the needs and abilities of that child, and all have a legitimate interest in securing the child's well-being. It is also important to remember that, just as children may grow to accept unjust relations between the sexes when they observe significant disparities in the role of men and women in their care, so, too, they may grow to accept unjust relations between social classes or races when they observe how hierarchically their caregivers interact with one another. Thinking of the caregiving that is already shared as part of a network of providing care makes some of these caregivers more visible to those with more power and may provide an opportunity to reflect more self-consciously about the power dynamics involved in the network. Finally, when thinking about who is part of the network of caregivers, we should also remember the role, historically and internationally, that children have played as caregivers of younger children. The role of children as companions for and teachers of younger and similarly aged children should be encouraged and celebrated, so long as we see them as sharing in the work of caregiving with others, including adults, who have skills and capacities that they themselves lack.

The dependency of a child makes some forms of caregiving more ideal than others, especially those that limit opportunities for abuse of authority, and encourage the sharing of the work and decision-making involved in caregiving. (The argumentative framework presented by Macleod, in this volume, suggests that reasons of this sort, for sharing responsibility for children, could be both strategic and principled.) This may have things to teach us about relationships between mature adults, particularly when one or some of those adults have needs that make them obviously dependent on others. We might be prompted to move toward a model of friendship in which people participate in social networks, rather than solely dyadic relationships.

Conclusion

Appreciating both the differences and the commonalities between the caregiver–child relation and friendship between mature adults can help shape our ideals about both sorts of relationship. By contrast, when we are given only two models of relationship, friends who are equal in status and who contribute equally to the relationship, and caregivers providing care to dependents, particularly parents to children, all failures of reciprocity threaten to reduce a dependent person to the status of a child. However, there are important differences between dependency in relationships between morally competent adults, and relationships between a child and her caregivers. Although I have argued that paternalism may occasionally be appropriate in friendships, in most friendships between morally competent adults, including those involving substantial dependency, we should not take the person who is dependent to have less insight into her interests than the other person. While morally competent adults can sometimes misconstrue their own interests, and friends may occasionally have more insight into one another's needs than into their own, there is no reason to think that dependency alone makes one incapable of understanding and seeking to realize one's goals. In fact, experiences of dependency can help clarify what matters to one most.

We need not interpret all relationships in which one party has more ability or more resources than the other as morally compromised, because we need not see all such relations as equivalent to the caregiver–child relation, which involves inequality, dependency and extensive paternalism. Hoagland argues that differences in ability need not compromise our seeing our intimates as equal.[56] She is right to try to make space for relations between peers that do not involve equivalence in abilities, but there also needs to be space to recognize that sometimes these differences in abilities—and differences in needs—will make one person dependent on another or others, and this should not make us see the dependent person as incompetent. When friendship is presented in sharp contrast to the caregiver–child relation, we may well be tempted to see the person with lesser abilities or more needs as like a child and incompetent to make decisions for herself. As long as we recognize that dependency need not entail paternalism, and that inequality need not preclude reciprocity of some sort, we should avoid this temptation and may operate with richer and more complex conceptions of reciprocity and mutuality in both the caregiver–child relationship and friendship between mature adults.

NOTES

1 Some of these theorists, such as Elshtain and Ruddick, also make claims about the significance of the mothering relationship to political thought. Their claim is engaged by Patricia Boling ("The Democratic Potential of Mothering" in *Political Theory* 19 (1991): 606–25) and critiqued by Mary Dietz ("Citizenship with a Feminist Face: The Problems with Maternal Thinking" in *Political Theory* 13 (1985): 19–37). I will not discuss the relevance of the caregiver–child re-

lationship to political thought, but I do find some interesting parallels between the debate over its significance for ethical thought and the debate over its significance for political thought. In particular, those who dispute the significance tend to conceive of politics as a place where equals meet, and deny the significance of meeting dependency needs for politics. See, for instance, Dietz, page 34.

2 Virginia Held, *Feminist Morality* (Chicago: University of Chicago Press, 1993), 195.

3 Cynthia Willett, *Maternal Ethics and Other Slave Moralities* (New York: Routledge, 1995), 53.

4 Paul Lauritzen, "A Feminist Ethic and the New Romanticism: Mothering as a Model of Moral Relations," *Hypatia* 4 (1989): 40–42.

5 Nel Noddings, *Caring: A Feminine Approach to Ethics and Moral Education* (Berkeley: University of California Press, 1984).

6 Lorraine Code, *What Can She Know? Feminist Theory and the Construction of Knowledge* (Ithaca: Cornell University Press, 1991), 90.

7 Sarah Lucia Hoagland, "Some Thoughts about 'Caring,'" in *Feminist Ethics*, ed. Claudia Card, 249 (Lawrence: University Press of Kansas, 1991). See also Barbara Houston, "Rescuing Womanly Virtues: Some Dangers of Moral Reclamation," in *Science, Morality and Feminist Theory*, ed. Marsha Hanen and Kai Nielsen, *Canadian Journal of Philosophy* Suppl. Vol. 13 (1987): 237–62: 253.

8 Marilyn Friedman, *What Are Friends For? Feminist Perspectives on Personal Relationships and Moral Theory* (Ithaca, NY: Cornell University Press, 1993), 151.

9 See Laurence Thomas, "Friendship," *Synthese* 72 (1987): 217–36, and Joseph Kupfer, "Can Parents and Children Be Friends?" *American Philosophical Quarterly* 27 (1990): 15–26.

10 Code, 90.

11 "To be a 'mother' is to take upon oneself the responsibility of child care, making its work a regular and substantial part of one's working life." Sara Ruddick, *Maternal Thinking: Toward a Politics of Peace* (Boston: Beacon, 1989), 17.

12 Jean Grimshaw, *Philosophy and Feminist Thinking* (Minneapolis: University of Minnesota Press, 1986), 248.

13 See Patricia Hill Collins, "Shifting the Center: Race, Class, and Feminist Theorizing about Motherhood," in *Representations of Motherhood*, ed. Donna Bassin, Margaret Honey, and Meryle Mahrer Kaplan (New Haven, CT: Yale University Press, 1994); bell hooks, *Feminist Theory: From Margin to Center* (Boston: South End Press, 1984); and Alison Bailey, "Mothering, Diversity, and Peace Politics," *Hypatia* 9 (1994): 188–98.

14 See, for instance, Code, 94.

15 Hoagland and Card both briefly explore possibilities of group mothering.

16 The mother–child or parent–child relationship is typically contrasted with friendship with the former described as formal and highly structured and the latter as minimally structured. See, for instance, Thomas, 218–19. I believe the contrast would not be as sharp if we considered a range of caregiver–child relationships.

17 Patrice DiQuinzio, *The Impossibility of Motherhood: Feminism, Individualism, and the Problem of Mothering* (New York: Routledge, 1999), 10.

18 Ibid., xiii.

19 The ideology of motherhood is targeted at mothers with fairly young children.

20 I use "paternalism" in a gender-neutral way to describe any relation in which one person makes decisions for the other on the basis of what the decision maker believes to be the best interests of the one decided for.

21 Marilyn Friedman, "Friendship and Moral Growth," *Journal of Value Inquiry* 23 (1989): 3–13: 3.

22 Code, 96.

23 Sandra Bartky, "Feeding Egos and Tending Wounds: Deference and Disaffection in Women's Emotional Labor," in *Femininity and Domination: Studies in the Phenomenology of Oppression*, 99–119 (New York: Routledge, 1990).

24 Claudia Card, "Gender and Moral Luck," in *Identity, Character and Morality: Essays in Moral Psychology*, ed. Owen Flanagan and Amelie O. Rorty, 197–216 (Cambridge, MA: MIT Press, 1990).

25 Ibid., 205.

26 Ibid., 205.

27 For instance Friedman argues that ethically ideal friendships require reciprocity of exchange.

28 Kupfer, 15.

29 Kupfer, 16.

30 Nicholas Dixon, "The Friendship Model of Filial Obligations," *Journal of Applied Philosophy* 12 (1995): 77–87: 81.

31 Audrey Thompson, "Friendship and Moral Character," *Philosophy of Education* 45: 72.

32 Ibid., 72.

33 Ibid., 73.

34 Friedman, *What Are Friends For?* 159–60.

35 Ibid., 160.

36 Ibid., 160.

37 Friedman argues that mutuality is reinforced by "an approximate overall equivalence of status and authority of the friends, and by an approximate equivalence in their mutual confidences and disclosure of vulnerabilities" (210). The latter seems uncontroversial. The former is what I contest in this essay.

38 Ibid., 155. See also pages 188–89.

39 Thomas, 227.

40 Friedman, *What Are Friends For?* 151. Despite this, Friedman argues that friends can be an invaluable resource for enabling moral growth, including the growth possible when we "learn to grasp our experiences in a new light or in radically different terms" (196). She also argues that we depend upon others for our social acceptability, even when we are adults, even when we are morally competent adults (207). This suggests there are similarities between friendship and maternal thinking as Ruddick describes it.

41 Linda A. Bell, *Rethinking Ethics in the Midst of Violence: A Feminist Approach to Freedom* (Lanham, MD: Rowman and Littlefield, 1993), 201.

42 Ibid., 200.

43 Ibid., 201.

44 Jane Aronson, "Lesbians Giving and Receiving Care: Stretching Conceptualizations of Caring and Community," *Women's Studies International Forum* 21 (1998): 505–19.

45 Friedman, *What Are Friends For?* 214.

46 Ibid., 219.

47 Ibid., 209.

48 Hoagland, 250.

49 Hoagland, 253. See also Claudia Card, "Against Marriage and Motherhood," *Hypatia* 11 (1996): 1–23: 16–17.

50 Hoagland, 251.

51 Ibid., 254.

52 Another way to think about reciprocity between parents and children is to think that children, as they mature, will have opportunities to repay their parents, perhaps when the parents become dependent. This type of reciprocity would be available only when the caregiving relationship is itself long-term.

53 Christine Gudorf, "Parenting, Mutual Love and Sacrifice," in *Women's Conscience: A Reader in Feminist Ethics*, ed. C. Gudorf and M. Pellauer, 179 (Minneapolis, MN: Winston Press, 1985).

54 Grimshaw, 248.

55 Lynet Uttal, "Custodial Care, Surrogate Care, and Coordinated Care: Employed Mothers and the Meaning of Child Care," *Gender and Society* 10 (1996): 291–311.

56 Hoagland, 251.

FOUR

Parent Licensing and
the Protection of Children

MARK C. VOPAT

In 2005, the United States Department of Health and Human Services' Administration for Children and Families published its 2003 report on child maltreatment. According to that report there were 2.9 million referrals concerning the suspected abuse or maltreatment of approximately 5.5 million children. Of these suspected abuse reports, 1.9 million were referred for investigation. Of these remaining cases, 906,000 resulted in a determination of abuse or neglect.[1] Given that some instances of abuse cannot be proven due to a lack of evidence, and that others are never reported in the first place, it can be safely assumed that these numbers underestimate the amount of actual abuse.

One of the disturbing facts made vivid by the aforementioned report is that in a given year nearly a million children in the United States are maltreated—and to date our responses have been reactive rather than proactive. The call for licensing parents stems from the desire to prevent—not just treat—the abuses children suffer each day at the hands of abusive and incompetent parents. It is this desire for a proactive solution to the problem of child abuse and neglect that motivates those who advocate licensing parents. Unfortunately, current parent-licensing proposals have faults that make them an undesirable solution to the problem of child abuse and neglect. On one hand, parent-licensing proposals such as Hugh LaFollette's[2] are far too optimistic regarding the predictive accuracy of psychological tests used to predict abusive behaviour. On the other hand, Jack

Westman's[3] approach suffers less from its particular content, and more from its reluctance to call for universal licensing. In this chapter, I argue for a minimalist conception of parent licensing that corrects the problems found in the aforementioned accounts. The proposal to be presented here is minimalist in the sense that the intention is not to ensure that children are raised only by the best parents, but the more modest goal of ensuring that children are reared by minimally competent parents.

Because nearly all parent-licensing proposals are modelled on the procedures found in adoptions, I begin by briefly examining adoption practices in Canada, as well as adoption and foster parenting practices in the United States. An additional reason for examining adoption is that it constitutes what I consider implicit parent licensing. For those who would argue that licensing parents is a radical departure from our current normative views on the nature of the relation between children, parents, and the state, adoption criteria indicate that the step from the implicit parenting licensing of adoption to explicit licensing for all parents is a small one. Next, I examine the parent-licensing arguments of Hugh LaFollette and Jack Westman and present a few objections that can be levelled against their proposals. Following this, I present what I take to be reasonable criteria for a minimalist parent-licensing scheme. Finally, I discuss some of the objections to parent-licensing proposals generally and argue that a minimalist conception is not susceptible to such criticisms.

Precedents for Parent Licensing

Parent licensing is often perceived as a radical departure from our normative conceptions of the role of societal institutions and their relationship to the family. But parent licensing is not in actuality a radical departure from adoption and foster parenting practices. In the next section, I outline some of the requirements prospective parents in both Canada and the United States must go through in order to adopt, as a prelude to discussing explicit parent-licensing proposals.

Whether or not we refer to it as licensing, society has been implicitly licensing parents for decades. The adoption criteria that parents must meet in order to be deemed suitable parents are tantamount to a licence to parent. All proposals for explicit parent licensing borrow from or make reference to adoption criteria. What follows is a brief summary of the types of conditions parents must meet in order to adopt a child.

Adoption Criteria in Canada

Although the rights of children fall under the purview of the Canadian Child and Family Services Act, the actual procedures for adoption are determined by each province. There are some differences in adoption criteria, but most of these differences tend to revolve around the sexual orientation of the couple attempting to adopt. Once these differences are factored out, the requirements that must be fulfilled before an adoption can take place are similar across the provinces. In all cases, before a child can be placed in a home, a "home study" is required to assess the suitability of the prospective parents.

The home study is a report that indicates whether or not the prospective parents, or parent, are able to provide for the physical and emotional needs of a child. Some of the factors that must be taken into account when a social worker is preparing a home study are:

1. how the prospective adoptive parents' reason for adopting a child might affect their ability to meet the needs of the child;

2. whether there is or was drug or alcohol use on the part of the prospective adoptive parents, or any member of the household of the prospective adoptive parents, that might limit their ability to protect, nurture, and care for the child;

3. whether the prospective adoptive parents, or any member of the household of the prospective adoptive parents, have had a child in their care that was found to be in need of protection;

4. how the physical and mental health of the prospective adoptive parents impacts on their ability to meet the needs of the child;

5. the prospective adoptive parents' ability to provide stable and continuous care of the child;

6. a description of the prospective adoptive parents' personalities, interests, and values, in order to identify the personal factors that may be helpful or limiting in meeting the needs of the child to be adopted;

7. the results of a criminal record check that are relevant to the ability of the prospective adoptive parents to protect, nurture, and care for the child;

8. the results of a prior contact check that are relevant to the ability of the prospective adoptive parents to protect, nurture, and care for the child;

9. the results of a medical report from a health care provider attesting to the prospective adoptive parents' mental and physical health; and

10. any other factors that are relevant to the best interests of the child.[4]

In addition to the home study, there is a required educational component. This educational component may be required if a prospective adoptive parent is attempting to adopt a special needs child. Furthermore, a yearly home study is required until such time as a child is placed permanently with a family.

Adoption Criteria in the United States

Just as in Canada, the criteria that determine who is eligible to adopt are not federally determined, and vary from state to state. Although differences exist between states with regard to adoption criteria, they all have requirements similar to those found in Canada. For example, in New York State the home study is referred to as an "adoption study" and contains a list of things which may and may not be considered when evaluating the suitability of the prospective parent(s). Below are some of the characteristics that may be considered in an adoption study:

1. capacity to give and receive affection;
2. ability to provide for a child's physical and emotional needs;
3. flexibility and ability to change;
4. ability to cope with problems, stress, and frustration;
5. feelings about parenting an adopted child and the ability to make a commitment to a child placed in the home; and
6. ability to use community resources to strengthen and enrich family functioning.[5]

In addition to these, applicants must be able to show that they are in good health, that they can reasonably be expected to live until the child's "age of majority," that their family size does not affect the quality of life of the child, and that their income, with or without public assistance, can insure that the child's proper nutritional, health, housing, and clothing needs are met. Furthermore, the prospective parents must be able to demonstrate their ability to take advantage of "human and organizational resources to strengthen their own capacity as parents"—though this is not an educational requirement such as those found in the Canadian adoption criteria. Finally, an applicant cannot be a current drug or alcohol abuser, subject of an investigation for child abuse or maltreatment, or have a felony conviction for physically injuring a child.[6]

All of the aforementioned criteria apply to things that may be considered when determining whether an individual or couple is fit to adopt. By statute, however, marital status, length of marriage (unless under one year), fertility, sex preference, religion, race, ethnic group, employment, and education of the prospective parents may not be considered to determine parental fitness.

There are additional criteria that may or may not be considered, depending on the particular circumstances surrounding the adoption. For instance, the geographic stability of one's employment, child care experience, sexual practices, and sexual preference may be taken into account if it can be shown to relate to the best interests of the child. If an evaluation enters into this extremely personal realm, a clear explanation of the relevance of the inquiry must be provided to the applicant.

Foster Parenting Criteria

There is another area in which society imposes de facto licensing requirements, and this is in the area of foster parenting. Foster parenting requirements are in many respects similar to those found in adoption criteria already mentioned.[7] As with adoption, the requirements an individual (or couple) must meet to become foster parents vary from state to state. Generally, all prospective foster parents must:

1. be eighteen years old or over;
2. be in good health;
3. meet the state's home safety standards;
4. have sufficient income for family needs;
5. be emotionally stable and have character references;
6. have no criminal record;
7. have sufficient bedrooms;
8. be willing to work with social workers;
9. agree to discipline without physical punishment; and
10. agree to attend foster parenting workshops.[8]

The licensing of foster parenting is essentially the same as that of adoptive parents, and it is this similarity that is relevant to both recent statistics on child abuse and neglect and a minimalist parent-licensing proposal.

Effectiveness of Implicit Parent Licensing

What is striking about both Canadian and United States adoption criteria is their effectiveness at preventing child abuse. At this point I am going to make an assumption that appears warranted by abuse statistics. According to findings by the United States Department of Health and Human Services, 75% of all child-abuse perpetrators were parents, but only .5% of these parents were foster parents.[9] Given that foster parents must meet nearly the same criteria that adoptive parents must meet, it is reasonable to conclude that the statistics that apply to foster parents apply to adoptive parents. The assumed correlation of the rates of abuse between foster and adoptive parents is further bolstered by independent studies of the incidences of abuse in adoptive families. For example, Richard Barth and Marianne Berry cite several studies that looked at the reasons for "disruptions" of adopted children, and found that abuse was the least likely reason for removing children from their adoptive parents. As they note:

> Most studies of adoptive families find extremely low rates of abuse. Sack and Dale found that not one of twelve children (with an average age of five and one-half years) with histories of physical abuse prior to adoption were re-abused despite the difficulties of an adoption breakdown (Sack and Dale 1982). Of the eighty-two disruptions studied by Boneh, 20% resulted from the agency's request for the child's removal, but fewer than 10% involved abuse by the adoptive parents (Boneh 1979). Barth and Berry (1988) found reabuse an even rarer reason for disruption. Since adoption disruptions occur in about 11% of all adoptions of older children (Barth et al. 1988), abuse of adoptive children would be about 1%. National studies of child abuse and neglect confirm this estimate indicating that adoptive parents are alleged perpetrators in 1% of all reports despite their representation of approximately 3% in the population at large, indicating that adoptive placements are unusually safe. (Russell & Trainor 1984)[10]

That the rate of abuse of adopted children is extremely low—regardless of whether the child had suffered abuse at the hands of their biological parents—is very telling. In either situation, the percentage of abuse cases in adoptive homes is commensurate with the numbers of reported instances of abuse of children in foster care. This data seems to support the conclusion that the standards parents are held to in foster and adoptive situations make it less likely that a child will be abused or neglected. It is this connection between adoption and foster parenting criteria and the prevention of abuse that suggests to many the need to license parents.

There is additional reason to believe that licensing parents would lessen the instances of child abuse and neglect. A survey of abusive and/or neglectful parents cites the following reasons for their abusive behaviour: 88% cite substance abuse, 51% poverty or economic strains, 39% lack parental skills/abilities, and 27% cite a cycle of domestic violence. Each of these conditions is addressed in one or more of the aforementioned adoption criteria, suggesting that were these problems in parents identified early enough, the abuse suffered by children could be avoided.[11]

Explicit Parent-Licensing Proposals

Explicit parent-licensing proposals are essentially the application of adoption criteria to all parents. There are three prominent parent-licensing proposals that have garnered some attention over the last two decades, namely those proposed by Hugh LaFollette, Jack Westman, and Katherine Covell and R. Brian Howe. Since Covell and Howe's proposal is based on the model proposed by Jack Westman, the specifics of their system of parent licensing will not be presented here.

Hugh LaFollette

LaFollette's parent-licensing proposal is based on the argument that society is justified in regulating activities it deems to be harmful or potentially harmful to others. Just as incompetent drivers, doctors, or lawyers, etc., can cause harm to others, so too can incompetent parenting cause harm to both children and society. What follows from this general theoretical position is society's right to be sure individuals have a minimal level of competence before being allowed to perform certain functions. As LaFolette states:

> Any activity that is potentially harmful to others and requires certain demonstrated competence for its safe performance is subject to regulation—that is, it is theoretically desirable that we regulate it. If we also have a reliable procedure for determining whether someone has the requisite competence, then the action is not only subject to regulation but ought, all things considered, to be regulated. It is particularly significant that we license these hazardous activities, even though denying a license to someone severely inconveniences and even harms that person.[12]

LaFollette's argument can be summarized as follows:

1. Parenting is an activity potentially harmful to children.
2. A parent must be competent if he or she is to avoid harming his or her child.
3. Society has a right to regulate potentially harmful activities.
4. Society ought to regulate potentially harmful activities.
5. Incompetent parenting is a harmful activity.
6. Therefore, society ought to regulate parenting by licensing parents.[13]

According to LaFollette, there are no real theoretical objections which can be levelled against his position. So long as we accept that parenting is a potentially harmful activity, we cannot argue against parent licensing without concurrently arguing that *no* harmful activity ought to be regulated.

Although LaFollette makes a compelling case for parent licensing, his theory is not without its detractors. In "Licentious Licensing: A Reply to LaFollette," Lawrence Frisch questioned whether the psychological testing called for in LaFollette's proposal is an adequate measure of future parental performance. He writes: "There are many matters in which such divine foreknowledge would be useful, but lacking divinity, we must rely on other methods. LaFollette falls back on statistics. He envisions tests capable of predicting future abusive behavior, while asking us to forgo our own serious doubts about sociologists' ability to prognosticate, because 'even if such tests are not available we could undoubtedly develop them.'"[14] Not only is the predictive ability of testing troubling, but the determination of what is actually being tested for is also cause for concern. Is negligent and/or abusive behaviour a moral or psychological defect of the individual? Given the subjective and value-laden nature of mental-illness classification, we should be wary of tests whose results may lead to the denial of parental rights.[15]

Another apparent criticism of LaFollette's parent-licensing proposal, as well as of licensing schemes in general, is that a system of parental monitoring would better accomplish the goals of a parental licence. David Archard has argued that while a parental licence may initially exclude some obviously bad parents, it is no guarantee against the indeterminate number of parents that may end up abusing a child later. What is required is a system of parental monitoring, rather than one of licensing. As Archard notes:

> Such monitoring is required by the logic of LaFollette's own argument. Any license may be revoked upon evidence of subsequent and seriously harmful incompetence in the activity for which the license was originally granted. Thus, LaFollette would have to be assured that even licensed parents were still fit to care for their children. My point is that, having already excluded those who can be confidently picked out as very bad prospective parents, monitoring alone does all the work that LaFollette's more cumbersome and impractical licensing scheme is designed to do.[16]

Though LaFollette's licensing proposal has some shortcomings, this is not one of them. While it is true that monitoring is an essential part of ensuring licensed parents continue to be good parents, monitoring alone is not enough. Monitoring is essentially a reinforcement of the status quo, as mechanisms for monitoring are already in place. School teachers, doctors, and social workers are already required to report suspected child abuse. Licensing would limit the need for intervention on the part of the monitors already in place by preventing the initial abuse. Archard's claim that monitoring, along with removing children from obviously unfit parents, is sufficient ignores the fact that we do not currently have the means of recognizing *obviously* unfit parents. Licensing is an appropriate first step in the protection of children.[17]

Jack Westman

According to Westman, parent licensing is a way to uphold four principles:

1. Human rights principle: The child has a right to be free from abuse and oppression.
2. Civil rights principle: All individuals, including children, should have equal access to opportunities to develop their potential in life.
3. Common good principle: Society has a right to regulate activities that are potentially harmful to others and society generally.
4. Humanistic principle: The future success of children depends upon forming affectionate attachment bonds with their parents and indirectly with others.[18]

According to Westman, parent licensing would not entail the creation of another public bureaucratic nightmare. Parental licensing could be handled by agencies that are currently responsible for licensing in related areas, for example, marriage and birth authorities. The practical aspects of instituting a policy of parental licensing fall into five categories: (1) timing, (2) criteria, (3) administration, (4) denial, and (5) competency:

1. Timing refers to when a licence would be granted to an individual or individual. According to Westman, a licence could be obtained prior to, or along with, a marriage licence. It could also be obtained during pregnancy, or immediately after birth when registering the birth of the child.
2. Criteria for licensing would include (a) adulthood, (b) the parents agreeing to care and nurture the child and not to abuse it, and (c) completion of a parenting course or its equivalent.
3. Administration of licensing would be handled at the state and local level. The licences would be administered by marriage and birth authorities, and appeals would be handled by existing social services. Those parents deemed to be vulnerable could be offered support services early to help avoid their abusing their children later. In borderline cases, provisional licensing could be an option. Licences would have to be renewed with every new child.

4. Denial of licences would occur when it is determined that competence as defined by current legal definitions is lacking in the parent or parents. It should be noted that competence is not couched in terms of "good" and "less good" parents, only competent and incompetent. The standard of denial is *not* the "best interest of the child" standard.

5. Although adoption practices have something like parent competency testing, Westman does not believe it would be practical to institute such a test for each parent at this time, although he does not rule out such tests in the future.[19]

Parent licensing in practice would operate in a manner similar to current social worker interventions in abuse cases. As Westman writes: "If a mother could not meet the licensing standards, child protection laws would be invoked at the time of a child's birth. The custody of the child would be with an agency, and the child's placement would be determined by the circumstances of the situation, as it is now."[20]

The overarching ideal is to change the way we have dealt with children and child abuse and neglect. Rather than use the perpetrator–victim model, we should adopt a prevention/treatment model. The latter approach allows us to simultaneously prevent harm to children and support, encourage, and aid individuals in becoming responsible parents.

The main fault with Westman's proposal is his reluctance to call for mandatory licensing. Westman contends that licensing could be encouraged by tying licensing to tax breaks or credits, and the receipt of social services. Although doing so may seem like a way to gradually introduce a social policy such as licensing, it ignores serious considerations of social justice. Voluntary licensing would result in discrimination against those of lower economic classes. Individuals who could forgo the tax breaks or who do not need social assistance could simply refuse to be licensed. Conversely, those who require social assistance for basic survival would be forced to agree to licensing.

Furthermore, merely encouraging parents to obtain licences ignores the fundamental rationale behind licensing, namely that licensing parents is a means by which the state fulfills its fundamental duty to protect the interests of children. To hold that only impoverished parents need to be licensed not only reinforces the stereotypes of the poor being more inclined to criminal behaviour, but it obscures fundamental considerations of justice. We owe a duty to all children whether they are rich or poor. Licensed parents are not a gift we bestow on the poor unfortunates of the inner city or the rural countryside but are a dispensation of a duty owed to all children.

Licensing, if it is to accomplish the presumed goal of preventing child abuse and neglect, must be mandatory for all prospective parents.

Conclusions

Although there are some problems with each of the proposals, the central arguments presented by both LaFollette and Westman seem relatively unobjectionable. Both make compelling cases for the implementation of licensing of parents. LaFollette's argument that society is justified in regulating potentially dangerous activities is bolstered by the numerous statistical studies on the relationship between poor parenting and social cost.[21] Similarly, when we add Westman's human-, civil-, and humanistic-rights-based arguments to the mix, the arguments for licensing parents become even more compelling. Although the courts have not been consistent on these matters, there are ample precedents that hold that children are entitled to the same rights and protections as adults.[22]

The compelling nature of the central arguments of each of the proposals indicates that the objections to parent licensing are not moral objections but practical ones. Further evidence for this conclusion is derived from the general lack of criticism of parent-licensing proposals. As was noted in the previous section, Frisch does not object to licensing on the grounds that society does not have the right to regulate parents in this manner; rather, he argues that society would most likely do it badly. In the section that follows I offer a licensing proposal that avoids the shortcomings of both LaFollette's and Westman's proposals.

Minimalist Parent-Licensing Proposal

In addition to problems specific to each of the aforementioned parent-licensing proposals, there is the ever-present objection that parent licensing would be susceptible to the abuses of power that inevitably occur when the state regulates any activity. Enforcement of a policy of parental licensing could potentially cause more social harm than the good intended. Although the concerns surrounding the abuse of power are legitimate, I believe they can be mitigated by *constructing a policy of parent licensing that is intended to weed out only the very worst parents.* Furthermore, such a policy would limit, as much as possible, the subjective elements found in licensing proposals such as LaFollette's.

A minimalist licensing proposal is one that does not try to address all instances of poor parenting. Nor does it attempt to predict which parents might neglect or abuse their children as indicated by some type of psychological evaluation. Rather, a minimalist account attempts to remove children from obviously dangerous parental environments. Such a policy would address the four main reasons given by abusive parents for their behaviour. As previously stated[23] these are (1) substance abuse, (2) poverty or economic strains, (3) lack of parenting skills, and (4) cycle of domestic violence. Each of these reasons for abuse can be turned into more or less objective criteria for determining parental fitness. The following criteria correspond to the aforementioned reasons. A parent would not be granted a licence unless:

1. they pass a drug test;
2. they are able to provide proof of residence and employment (or, alternatively, receipt of welfare benefits);
3. they are at least eighteen years of age and have attained a high school diploma; and
4. they pass a background check that shows they have not been convicted of domestic violence or violence against a minor, or had another child in their care need protection.

To these four criteria, I believe a fifth should be added:

5. they sign an agreement that they will not neglect or abuse their child.

Each of these criteria (aside from the fifth) addresses one of the reasons given by parents for their abusive behaviour. By applying these criteria to all parents, it should be possible to reduce the number of children abused each year. Parents who fail to meet these criteria would be denied the right to raise a child.

Drug Testing

One contributing factor to child abuse is substance abuse by parents. In order to remove the children from the neglect or abuse that often accompanies parents addicted to drugs and alcohol, a mandatory drug test is a reasonable requirement.

Requiring parents to pass a drug test is fairly intrusive, and there are those who might argue that it would unfairly penalize the recreational user, but that objection fails to take into account the context in which licensing occurs. If the drug test is being administered to the mother, then the recreational use argument is unpersuasive, as drug and alcohol abuse are known to have adverse effects on developing fetuses.

On the other hand, drug testing of the father may, prima facie, appear more problematic. Here too the context in which licensing is taking place must be considered. Licensing would in all likelihood take place at or around the time of the child's birth. Individuals that could not set aside their drug use at this time (a time when clarity of thought and readiness should be at premium, given the impending birth) are demonstrating, at best, questionable judgment. Setting aside the morality or immorality of recreational drug use, drugs and alcohol affect perception and judgment. It is not unreasonable to require that a parent remain clear-headed immediately before, during, and after the birth of his child. A lack of such willpower may be indicative of just the sort of abusive or addictive personality that the drug test is meant to detect.

Residency and Employment

The residency and employment requirement is meant to insure that parents have the resources necessary to provide for the essential needs of the child. As was the case with substance abuse, the intent here is to avoid the economic hardships that contribute to parents becoming abusive. By insuring that parents have prepared themselves for the costs and housing needs that parenthood necessarily entails, we can remove some of the strain that may contribute to parents abusing their children.

Those who could not provide proof of employment or receipt of welfare benefits could also be licensed provisionally, with a full licence being granted once they had found employment or had contacted the appropriate social services department. In such cases, the children could be monitored by social services until such time as a full licence was granted.

Education

A further clarification should be made with regard to the high school education requirement. Such a requirement needs to be conjoined with a mandatory child development or parenting class requirement before an individual is granted a high school diploma. This could be accomplished on either the state/provincial or federal level. Thus, it is not in virtue of possessing a high school diploma that one is assumed to make a better parent; the high school diploma would simply allow us to assume a certain minimal level of parental knowledge.

There are instances in which the education requirement would prove problematic. One such case is that of Old Order Amish communities. Although I believe the decision for reduced educational requirements supported by the United State Supreme Court in *Wisconsin v. Yoder* is fundamentally flawed, this exception entails that some individuals may not be able to comply with the education requirement.[24] In such exceptional cases, separate parenting classes could be required for those that did not complete high school (or the high school parenting class).

Background Check

The most straightforward of conditions that must be met before parents could be licensed is a background check for previous abusive behaviour. Abusive individuals, particularly those that have not sought counselling, present an immediate threat to the well-being of a child. If it is irresponsible for a society to allow an abusive parent to maintain custody of a child, then it follows that it is equally irresponsible to place a child into a situation in which it is likely to suffer abuse and neglect. Such situations pose a clear and present danger to the well-being of the child, and as such society is justified in removing the child from the parents.

Agreement Not to Abuse

The final requirement (appropriated from Westman's proposal) would have parents sign a formal agreement not to neglect or abuse their child. Admittedly, I do not believe that having parents agree not to maltreat their child will in anyway stop abusive parents from doing so. The agreement is in fact symbolic—it makes a statement to the effect that we as a society believe parenting to be more than a lifestyle choice, that it is a serious endeavour not to be undertaken lightly by those who engage in it. Furthermore, this symbolic aspect of licensing parents points to an additional goal of licensing, namely, the desire of society to reproduce some of the attitudes toward children that are exemplified by adoptive and foster parents—attitudes that are beneficial to a child's well-being.

Administration and Enforcement

Failure to pass all the requirements does not necessarily entail that one would not be licensed. Licensing need not be an all-or-nothing affair, and provisional licences could be granted in certain circumstances. For instance, those under the age of eighteen could receive a provisional licence so long as there was a parent or guardian who agreed to supervise them. Also, as in the case of the Old Order Amish, accommodation could be made for those that maintain ways of life that are outside mainstream society.

There are, of course, instances that would warrant immediate denial. Failure of the drug test or a history of violent or abusive behaviour would constitute such grounds. In such cases, children would be taken into protective custody until a social worker had the opportunity to evaluate the situation.

Objections to Parent Licensing

There has been very little discussion in the philosophical literature with regard to the issue of parent licensing. The vast majority of the debate has dealt with the nature and extent of parental rights—whether parents can be said to have rights, whether children have rights, or how we are to properly balance parents' rights or interests against those of the child. Consequently, the objections presented in this section are, by and large, those implied by any number of views on the nature of the parent–child relationship.[25]

The licensing of parents has as its goal the prevention of child abuse and neglect. Although the intention may be laudable, there are six obvious objections that can be levelled against any licensing proposal. First, it may be argued that licensing amounts to an unjust prior restraint of the individual, since parents could be denied the right to parent prior to any substantiated abuse. Second, licensing is seen as objectionable because it would result in the imposition of majority standards in parenting. Third, a policy of parent licensing would be susceptible to abuse, and thus the social benefits would not outweigh the social costs of licensing. Fourth, there is the argument that the state does not have the authority to license parents—that the family is essentially a pre-social institution that is outside the purview of the state. Fifth, there are concerns surrounding the ways in which the state would have to intervene and essentially redistribute children in cases where parents are deemed unfit. Finally, there is the argument that says the state licensing parents will justify the imposition of requirements that are more draconian than the minimalists ones proposed here.

Unjust Prior Restraint

The first objection to licensing is that it amounts to an unjust prior restraint, since the parent has not been found guilty of abusive behaviour. This objection would carry some weight if the minimalist licensing proposal being advocated here relied upon some form of questionable psychological or sociological test purporting to predict the likelihood of a parent being abusive.[26] The minimalist account I have presented here does not rely on such questionable psychological evaluations; rather, it relies on factors that contribute to abusive behaviour.

Even though the parents who would be denied a licence had yet to abuse or neglect their child, we can still legitimately keep them from raising their child. The United States Supreme court has long recognized that demonstration of a "clear and present danger" can warrant prior restraint. It is socially irresponsible, for example, to place a child in the care of a parent who is a substance abuser, has a history of abusing children, or who cannot provide for the basic needs of a child. Such cases do present an immediate danger to the child, and, as such, the prior restraint is justified.[27]

Imposition of Majority Standards

A second objection to licensing parents is that licensing would result in the coercion of minorities to accept majority ways of parenting. Such an objection would be telling if a licensing proposal required uniformity in parenting. A minimalist account does not attempt to create good parents or the best parents, nor does it attempt to standardize parenting. The goal of parent licensing is to weed out the worst parents. The minimal education requirement, which may be construed as imposing majority standards, is meant only to inform parents or prospective parents about the objective needs of children. Such a class would provide knowledge only about the basic nutritional, educational, and emotional needs of children.

Utility Considerations

A third objection to parent licensing stems from the claim that the benefits of licensing are outweighed by the potential harms. This objection holds that activities regulated by the state are subject to abuse. Once given the power, the state will insinuate itself in other aspects of our personal life. While it is true that whenever authority over an activity is granted to the state there is the possibility of abuse, these concerns can be mitigated by making the criteria for licensing as objective as possible. A minimalist approach relies on criteria that do not permit large degrees of interpretation. By minimizing the subjective elements in licensing (the elements most susceptible to abuse), it is possible to implement a policy of parent licensing that is fairly administered.

Limits of State Authority

As was previously mentioned, the issue of parent licensing has taken a back seat to the issues surrounding the nature of the relationships among children, parents, and the state. The central issues surrounding these relationships have to do with the nature and extent of state power in relation to the rights of parents and children. From the debate surrounding these complex relationships, comes the objection that the state does not have the authority to regulate parenting as it does other activities. There are several ways in which this objection can be interpreted. To say that the state lacks the authority to regulate parents may mean that there must be a compelling state interest. On the other hand, the prohibition of state interference may be seen as an unjust violation of the assumed private sphere of the family. Finally, it may be argued that state intervention in the form of parental licensing constitutes a violation of some strong conception of parental rights.

It is generally acknowledged that the state is justified in regulating activities that impose a substantial social cost on others, especially when such costs are unjustly imposed. The demonstration that poor parenting amounts to a compelling state interest has been convincingly made by Hugh LaFollette when defending his own parent-licensing policy, and statistics on the financial losses incurred by society due to poor parenting are staggering: $56 billion due to abuse, and $15 billion due to neglect.[28] LaFollette also notes that over 80 percent of individuals incarcerated were abused as children, and first-degree murderers from middle-class homes with no history of drugs, alcohol, mental illness, or epilepsy were frequently victims of parental abuse.[29]

While there may be compelling pragmatic grounds for licensing parents, some may argue that there are more compelling moral grounds for not doing so that stem from the conception of the family as a pre-social, private sphere into which the state should not intervene unless it has good reason to do so. Such a view of the family would entail that state licensing of parents constitutes an unjustifiable violation of this private sphere.

Furthermore, this objection to parent licensing is compatible with support for foster and adoptive parents complying with the criteria mentioned in section one. In foster and adoptive cases, the state is creating a family unit where one did not exist previously, and as such it has a duty to act carefully. Conversely, biological families are pre-existing entities into which the state should not generally insinuate itself. According to opponents of parent licensing, the two cases are not analogous, and thus licensing is unjustified.[30]

The problem with this objection is that it misconstrues the nature of the family. Families have no ontological standing independent of the interests of the members that compose them. Rather, families are composed of individuals with legitimate rights and interests—rights and interests deserving of respect and protection. Also, the idea that the family is a pre-social institution consisting of affective relationships that the state has little authority to regulate ignores the fact that historically the family has been the locus of abuse of women and children. To view the biological family as a pre-social unified whole is to make the specious assumption that the interests of all members of the family are the same. As David Archard has pointed out, this assumption has allowed the perpetuation of abusive relationships under the guise of the sacredness of the family. As he states:

And again it is for harms done *within* the private familial space by *some* members of the family to *other* members of the same family that the family as a whole loses its right to privacy. This important difference between the cases of the individual and of the family is obscured by writers who speak of the family as a single unit. Thus, for example, in their influential text *Before the Best Interests of the Child*, Goldstein et al. speak of the value of "family integrity" which encompasses both parental autonomy and privacy. Their conflation of quite distinct rights can only spring from a tendency to view the separate interests of child and parents as unified into that of a single familial interest. This is a not uncommon tendency in liberal writing on the family.[31] (emphasis in original)

It is this last point, namely the idea that children have legitimate interests that demand state protection, that justifies state intervention in the family—biological or otherwise.

Underlying the call for parental licensing is the fundamental assumption that the state has an obligation to protect the rights of children. To assume that parents have *rights* to their children is to take an objectionable proprietary view of the parent–child relationship. As I have argued elsewhere, this property view of the parent–child relationship runs counter to the intuitions underlying a number of theories of the relationship between children and their parents.[32] The vast majority of moral theorists share the view that children have an intrinsic value and legitimate interests deserving of respect. Combining this intuition with the fairly common liberal assumption that the state is the sole entity permitted to use coercive force means that one of the duties of the state is to ensure the protection of the person and interests of all individuals under its authority. Not only are adult members of the state entitled to protection, but so too are children. The state cannot violate the presuppositions that ground it, and so would be responsible for ensuring that social mechanisms are in place to protect all of its intrinsically valuable members. As Jean Hampton writes: "A society that fails to define or develop institutional or social responses to those who are in serious need is failing to respond to the worth of its own citizens."[33] In the case of the parent–child relationship, given the power differential between the two, and the lack of capacities on the part of the children, the state has a fundamental obligation to see to it that the children's legitimate interests are protected. The existence of this obligation is given further credence by the intuitions regarding children that make them fundamentally equal to adult members of society, thus deserving of the respect and protection of the state. Consequently, the state is justified in acting in the best interests of the child to ensure that his or her intrinsic value and interests are respected. In this capacity as protector, the state is justified in dispensing with its duties to children by licensing parents.

Enforcement

Related to the issues surrounding the nature and extent of state power in relation to the rights of parents and children are those that apply to the means by which a parent licence would be enforced. There are three issues that the enforcement of a parent-licensing scheme will have to deal with. First there is the issue of what to do with those that become pregnant without being able to meet the licensing provision. Would the state be able to coerce the unlicensed parent to abort the child? Could the state impose mandatory contraception? A second and related issue is what would happen to the children born to unlicensed parents. Would the state simply remove a child after birth from his or her parents? Finally, there is the issue of equality under the law. Some may argue that a parent-licensing scheme would unfairly impact women; that is, the negative consequences of enforcement would fall disproportionately, if not exclusively, on women. These enforcement issues do generate legitimate concerns about the implementation of a parent-licensing scheme. I attempt here to allay these concerns.

The issue of what to do with those who become pregnant without being able to meet the licensing provisions is handled by a taxonomy of parental rights. There are three types of rights that apply to parents. The first is the right parents have to conceive a child. The second is the right to bear a child, that is, a right to bring a child to term. Finally, there is the right to raise a child.[34] It is only the last of these rights that is regulated by the minimalist proposal offered here.

The right to conceive is the right that individuals have to engage in sexual relationships, the result of which may be the conception of a child. The right to bear is the right women have to choose whether or not bring a child to term. Since my minimalist parent-licensing proposal applies directly to a parent's fitness to raise a child, it would not involve intrusions into bodily integrity. For instance, the state could not impose forced contraception on individuals, nor could it force a woman to terminate her pregnancy. Such intrusions into an individual's life would not be agreed to by those in the initial situation. Regulation of the right to conceive and the right to bear a child would seriously interfere with the ability of an individual to realize his or her conception of the good life. Decisions regarding our sexual practices are some of the most personal and self-defining, including those that involve whether one is going to become a parent. Of course, once the decision has been made to bring a child into the world, the child's fundamental rights (as has been argued) would require protection.

Given that a parent licence applies to the right to raise a child, then the answer to the second question—Would children simply be removed from the parents deemed unfit according to the licensing criteria?—is yes. While this may appear to be a draconian remedy, its severity is somewhat ameliorated by what has already been said about the minimalist proposal. First, parents may receive a provisional licence if they fail to meet some of the licensing criteria. So while being a current substance abuser may disqualify a parent completely, the lack of proper parenting skills may require that they complete a parenting-skills course. Such a provisional licence allows the state to more closely monitor a parent's progress and a child's well-being without resorting to removing the child. Second, though taking a child away from a biological parent is not like taking away a person's property, it is in virtue of this dissimilarity between children and property that such actions are justified. Children are not like property; they are persons with rights that society has an obligation to protect. To leave a child with parents that cannot pass the minimal requirements of a parent licence is morally irresponsible. Additionally, it should be noted that this type of state intervention in the parent–child relationship is not a radical departure from our current practice. As was noted earlier, medical personnel are required to call social services if they believe a parent is under the influence of drugs or alcohol—an action that often results in the child being removed from his or her parents.

A final concern associated with the enforcement of a parent licence is the likelihood that it would disproportionately affect women. While the affects may be disproportionate, they are not arbitrary. It is a fact of nature that women are those capable of bearing children. As was mentioned previously, the choice whether to bear a child resides wholly with the mother. This decision is a complex one involving moral, religious, and social considerations. Though the decision is difficult, its difficulty does not change the fact that once born a child deserves a minimally competent parent.

The extent to which this objection is troubling for the implementation of a minimalist parent-licensing proposal has to do with the background conditions of justice against which it would operate. The minimalist proposal assumes the existence of an adequate system of social services—including *access to adequate health, education, and welfare services*. The inability to meet portions of the licensing criteria should not be the result of inadequate resources, but should reflect an individual's lack of commitment to fulfilling his or her parental responsibilities. The implementation of a minimalist parent-licensing scheme would necessarily require addressing larger questions of social justice.

Slippery Slope Argument

A final objection that may be levelled against parent licensing asks why the justification offered for implementing a parent-licensing scheme doesn't justify more draconian sorts of licensing requirements. If it could be shown that a more intrusive sort of licensing was better able to protect children, then it would seem to follow that the state would be justified in becoming even more involved in parent–child relationships. This is essentially a slippery slope argument: minimally intrusive licensing leads to moderately intrusive licensing, which in turn leads extremely intrusive licensing arrangements.

The problem with this argument is that it mistakenly views the licensing scheme as providing the justification for the amount of intervention the state has in the parent–child relationship. Parent licensing is ultimately justified by how well it contributes to the individual realizing his or her conception of the good life. In a liberal society, we should be concerned with minimizing those things that contribute to an individual's life going badly. Poor parenting in early childhood often results in individuals being unjustly handicapped in terms of their life prospects. Licensing is simply one way society opens up options for the individual, but it is not intended to interfere with the later projects and goals of the individual. Consequently, a parent-licensing scheme would be deemed unreasonable if it undermined other moral commitments necessary for individuals to realize their conception of the good life. For instance, a system of parent-licensing mandating forced sterilization for those who could not meet the licensing criteria would not be socially acceptable. Individuals have an interest in their bodily integrity and in not being harmed. Also, such a policy would also violate a number of other moral commitments (for example, commitments to autonomy, equality, etc.) that we as a society are not willing to exchange for a more intrusive parent-licensing scheme.

Conclusion

I have argued for a minimalist conception of parent licensing intended to take a proactive approach to the problems of child abuse and neglect. I have shown that licensing is not a radical departure from our current foster care and adoption practices and that there is evidence to suggest that the implicit licensing done in the case of the former is effective in preventing child abuse and neglect. Further, I have argued that there are compelling utilitarian and rights-based arguments for endorsing parent licensing. Finally, I have addressed some of the objections that can be levelled against parent-licensing proposals generally. While each of these objections has some merit, I do not believe they are compelling enough to rule out the implementation of a minimalist parent-licensing policy. As Westman writes: "All of the objections to licensing parents can be regarded as insurmountable obstacles, or they can be seen as hurdles to be taken into account in designing and implementing licensing procedures. If undertaken, a process for licensing parents should carefully consider all of the potential problems. It should not be ruled out simply because it has not been done before or because it would be too much trouble."[35]

Notes

1 National Clearinghouse on Child Abuse and Neglect Information, "Child Maltreatment 2003," U.S. Department of Health and Human Services Administration for Children and Families (2005), http://www.acf.hhs.gov/programs/cb/pubs/cm03.

2 Hugh LaFollette, "Licensing Parents," *Philosophy and Public Affairs* 9 (1980): 183.

3 Jack Westman, *Licensing Parents: Can We Prevent Child Abuse?* (New York: Insight Books, 1994).

4 British Columbia Adoption Act, B.C. Reg. 291/96.

5 NYS DSS Standards of Practice for Adoption Services (State of NY, Title 18-DSS, Part 421), Section 421.16, Adoption Study Criteria.

6 An individual may adopt if under investigation, but a review and determination of fitness must be made in writing to explain why the state should allow this person to adopt. NYS DSS Standards of Practice for Adoption Services.

7 The relevance of including foster parenting criteria is the connection that will be made between child abuse rates, foster parents, and adoptive parents.

8 National Foster Parent Association Information and Services Office, 226 Kilts Drive, Houston, TX 77024, http://www.nfpainc.org.

9 United States Department of Health and Human Services, Child Abuse and Neglect Data, http://www.childwelfare.gov/can/index.cfm.

10 National Foster Parent Association Information and Services Office, pp. 333–34.

11 Volunteer Court Appointed Special Advocates (CASA), NCASAA Staff, Statistics on Child Abuse and Neglect, Foster Care, Adoption and CASA Programs, February 2000, http://www.moyu8.cn/live/adoption-statistics.html.

12 LaFollette, 183.

13 Ibid., 184–86.

14 Lawrence Frisch, "On Licentious Licensing: A Reply to Hugh LaFollette" *Philosophy and Public Affairs* 11, no. 2: 177.

15 See Karen Ritchie, "The Little Woman Meets Son of DSM-III," in *Health Care Ethics in Canada*, ed. Françoise Baylis et al., 237–47 (Toronto: Harcourt Brace Canada, 1995).

16 David Archard, "Child Abuse: Parental Rights and the Interest of the Child," in *Children's Rights Re-Visioned: Philosophical Readings*, 116 (Albany, NY: Wadsworth, 1996). Originally published in the *Journal of Applied Philosophy* 7, no. 1 (1990): 183–94.

17 Of course we do make some requirements of parents. For example, child safety seats are legally required for all children under a certain age and or weight.

18 Westman, 245.

19 Ibid., 241.

20 Ibid., 242.

21 The direct and indirect financial losses due to child neglect and abuse incurred in the United States are estimated to be a staggering $94 billion a year. This estimate includes things like hospitalization, chronic health problems, mental health care, child welfare, law enforcement, judicial system costs, and special education. See Suzette Fromm's "Total Estimated Cost of Child Abuse and Neglect in the United States," at http://www.perspectivesonyouth.org/Pages-Articles/Summer-Fall-2004/2-Suzette_Fromm-Total_Estimated_Cost_of_Child_Abuse-Neglect_in_US.html.

22 *Tinker v. Des Moines Independent Community School District*: children are entitled to free speech protection under the First Amendment; *Planned Parenthood of Central Missouri v. Danforth*: constitutional rights do not magically come into being when one reaches the age of maturity. Minors, as well as adults, are protected by the Constitution and thus possess the right to privacy inferred by the Constitution; *Carey v. Population Services International*: state cannot prohibit the distribution of non-prescription contraceptives to minors, as doing so is violation to their right to privacy; *In re Gault*: adjudicatory hearings in the juvenile courts must measure up to the essentials of due process and fair treatment. The assumption by the Court is that the 14th Amendment and the Bill of Rights are not for adults alone.

23 See page 78.

24 *Wisconsin v. Yoder*, 406 U.S. 205 (1972).

25 A number of anthologies address the issues surrounding the relationship among the parent, child, and state: Rosalind Ekman Ladd, ed., *Children's Rights Re-Visioned: Philosophical Readings* (Albany, NY: Wadsworth, 1996); Hugh LaFollette and William Aiken, eds., *Whose Child? Children's Rights, Parental Authority, and State Power* (Totawa, NS: Rowman and Littlefield, 1980); Uma Narayan and Julia Bartkowiak, eds., *Having and Raising Children: Unconventional Families, Hard Choices, and the Social Good* (University Park: Penn State University Press, 1999).

26 Hugh LaFollette advocates such testing in his licensing proposal. Jack Westman does not believe testing would be practical at this time but would be open to it in the future.

27 This type of intervention in the child–parent relationship is currently required
    by nurses who suspect that a parent or guardian has been drinking.

28 CASA Report, February 2000.

29 LaFollette, n. 185.

30 I would like to thank Robert Noggle for pointing out the possible objection to
    parent licensing based on the dissimilarity between biological and adoptive
    families.

31 Archard, *Child Abuse*, 110.

32 Mark Vopat, "Contractarianism and Children," *Public Affairs Quarterly* 17, no. 1
    (2003): 49–65.

33 Jean Hampton, "Feminist Contractarianism," in *A Mind of One's Own: Feminist
    Essays on Reason and Objectivity*, 2nd ed., ed. Louise M. Antony and Charlotte
    Witt, 360 (Boulder, CO: Westview Press, 2002).

34 Westman, 215–16.

35 Westman, 248.

FIVE

Responsibility and Children's Rights:
The Case for Restricting Parental Smoking

SAMANTHA BRENNAN and ANGELA WHITE

This chapter has two parts, the first conceptual and the second applied. The conceptual focus of the chapter outlines the nature and content of the responsibilities that adult members of a society have toward children. The subsequent applied part of the chapter looks at the issues of responsibility for children in the context of parental smoking. We are interested in two questions. First, what responsibilities do we have toward children given their status as bearers of rights? Second, does a commitment to children's rights entail a responsibility to ensure that children enjoy a smoke-free home environment? This chapter argues that given certain reasonable and compelling assumptions, there are prima facie grounds for undertaking to protect children from second-hand smoke, including limiting parental smoking. We expect that most people will find this conclusion surprising and that many people will disagree with it. However, given how compelling we find the initial assumptions to be, we find ourselves driven to this controversial conclusion. We invite readers who strongly disagree with the conclusion to consider which of our initial assumptions might be given up, or on what grounds our prima facie case for restricting parental smoking might be defeated.

Children's Rights and Adult Responsibilities

We are interested both in parental responsibilities for particular children and in state responsibilities for children in general. In addition, we are interested in the responsibilities that apply to adults as members of communities—whether or not they are parents—that are separate from the responsibilities of the state (although we see that the responsibilities held by individual adults are connected to the responsibilities of the state). This chapter will assume that children have rights and will explore the question of responsibilities for children that follow once we think of children as the bearers of rights. For example, one of the implications of thinking about children as rights bearers is the transformation of parental rights from property rights to stewardship rights—rights that are constrained by the good of the interests of the child.[1]

This chapter will restrict itself to the plausible assumption that children have rights. The views in it do not rely on any further moral or political views. We will not assume that there are moral obligations to promote the overall good, to provide a minimum level of income or welfare for all citizens, or to redistribute the overall wealth to promote a more egalitarian society. Instead, we are interested in seeing what responsibilities we have for children when we begin with a fairly minimal set of moral commitments such as those specified by rights against harm.

The Direct Duty Not to Infringe Rights

One kind of obligation we all have toward children is not to infringe their rights. This is a simple matter of what follows from having a right. If a child has a right not to be harmed, then you have a corresponding obligation not to harm the child. It is hard to see how this right differs, in any interesting way, from that of the adult right not to be harmed, morally speaking.

When we think about the standard counter-examples to consequentialist moral reasoning, our intuitions do not change with children occupying the spot of the potential victim. Thus, if we had a version of Judith Thomson's famous transplant case (in which we are asked to consider the moral permissibility of killing one person to save four others) that featured a five-year-old boy as the potential involuntary organ donor, it is not as if we would all agree that, in this case, it would be okay to proceed to chop up one very young person to save four others.[2] In fact, many people would think it is worse to kill one person to save four others if the one were a child. There are a variety of explanations for the intuition that it is worse. We might worry that the child has parents who will suffer, or we might think the child has more at stake in terms of the amount of life he has left to live—but we will not explore that issue in any detail here. What is relevant for our purposes is the idea that it is not a different *kind* of case because a child is involved. Further, the explanation of what would make the act wrong does not seem that different. It is part of common-sense morality that there are constraints that protect persons from acts of harm, even when the acts could bring about more good overall. Rights are the basis of these constraints. Thus, if children have rights not to be harmed, then the simplest and easiest way to demonstrate the responsibility we have toward children is the duty not to infringe these rights. I have this responsibility to my own children, but it is also owed to children generally. But do my rights-based responsibilities to children end here? We do not see quite how this can be so. In subsequent sections of this chapter we look at some more interesting and controversial implications of children's rights, including a look at children's exposure to second-hand smoke as an instance of a violation of the right against harm.

The Responsibility to Educate Children about Their Rights

The rights of children generate at least two distinct sorts of moral obligations. The first is the most obvious. It is the obligation we all have to refrain from violating those rights. The second are the duties that at least some people have to protect and promote those rights. Where the first sort of duties apply equally to all persons, the second sort of duties may be less evenly distributed, generating stronger obligations, for example, for those in a direct custodial or stewardship role. Here we are thinking not just of parents but also teachers, grandparents, community leaders, and so on. This second sort of obligation follows from the ways in which children as right bearers differ from fully competent adult right bearers. One difficulty with children as rights bearers is that they may not know that they have rights. What a right amounts to is the justification of a moral claim or demand upon others. But if a right bearer is unaware that she has a right, she is not in a very good position to make a claim (even if she would be justified in doing so). Thus, we would argue that if children have rights, then it follows that we have an obligation to educate children about rights. This aspect of moral education falls primarily on parents. But since parents can fail to educate children, the task cannot be left to parents alone. Teachers and community leaders (or, when a child is not in the custody of his parents, the representative of the state—likely the child's social worker and/or foster parents) must educate the child regarding her rights to bodily integrity and autonomy. For example, the Ontario Association of Children's Aid Societies (OACAS) undertakes to see that children it its care are aware of their rights. There is a list of the rights children in care have and the list is available in a few different formats and levels, so that the description of the rights matches the ability of the child to understand.[3]

But educating children will not be enough. Sometimes these efforts will fail. We may tell children about their rights, but they might forget or fail to understand. Other times a child may know his rights are being violated but not know what to do. Finally some children may be too young to understand or to stand up for their own rights. What follows, then, is a third-party moral responsibility to pay attention to when children's rights may be being violated.

The Third-Party Moral Responsibility to Pay Attention to Infringements

We also have duties to see that the child's rights are not infringed. This falls again primarily on parents as part of the stewardship task, but as parents are, sadly, most likely to infringe children's rights, it cannot be left to them alone. We argue that we have a shared responsibility to interfere when we see a child's right being violated.

The OACAS lays out the grounds on which citizens ought to report suspected abuse or neglect of children.

> A person who has reasonable grounds to suspect that a child is or may be in need of protection must make the report directly to a children's aid society and that people who work with children who suspect that a child is a victim of child abuse or neglect must report these suspicions to the CAS; failure to do so could subject the person to a fine. The Act defines the term "child in need of protection" and sets out what must be reported to a children's aid society. This definition (CFSA s. 72(1)) is set out in detail on the following pages. It includes physical, sexual and emotional abuse, neglect and risk of harm.[4]

This legal obligation bears most directly on those who work closely with children, but as a moral obligation its reach extends much further. Whatever the legal upshot, surely it seems morally right to think we have an obligation to report suspected infringements of children's rights. Most often we discharge this shared responsibility by means of the state through agencies such as the Children's Aid Society and empower that group to act when they have compelling evidence of neglect and/or abuse. But this cannot discharge our responsibility entirely. Now, it could if we employed a vast army of social workers to visit families and check up on children—and some people seem to think we ought to move in just that direction. However, it would make for a fairly unpleasant society and it is hard to imagine how this would be consistent with even a small degree of family autonomy. Insofar as we favour less government in some areas, it is because we think we have very strong moral responsibilities. In political philosophy there is a tendency to think that we must choose between justifying a society that adopts a large state apparatus as a means of seeing that our collective or shared responsibilities are met or settling for a society in which each person decides for him- or herself whether and how to help others. There exists a space between government and autonomous family units, and it is at the level of community. One answer to the question of how we discharge our shared responsibilities is that we contract out some of this work to an agency that will be more efficient at seeing that accusations of child abuse are properly investigated and that alternative housing arrangements can be made for children who must be removed from their family homes. But we do not get rid of all of our responsibility in this way. Some remains attached to individuals. Thus, those who see children suffering at the hands of their parents but who wait for the authorities to step in are making a serious moral mistake.

In conclusion, we have argued that from the claim that children have rights three further duties follow. First, we have a direct duty not to infringe the rights of children. Second, we have a duty to educate children about their rights. Third, we have a further duty to protect children from having their rights infringed. In the following section we explore the practical implications of these duties in the case of children's rights and the harm that follows exposure to second-hand smoke.

The Case of Children's Rights and Second-Hand Smoke

We will now move to consider what follows from adult responsibilities for children's rights in the case of childhood exposure to tobacco smoke. This is a useful example because our views as a society have changed as we have become increasingly aware of the dangers of second-hand smoke. If I have a right not be harmed, or subjected to a significant risk of harm, and inhaling second-hand smoke poses such a risk, then that harm makes permissible rules restricting the smoking behaviour of others. Thus, you may not smoke in restaurants in many, or most, North American cities unless the retaurants provide a separately ventilated enclosed smoking area. However, there is nothing to prevent you from inviting a large group of smokers into your home and keeping all the windows closed while children are present. Likewise, you may subject children to long car trips (all the while securely buckled in) while smoking for the duration of the trip. It is difficult to see what would justify imposing such a risk of harm on children if children are protected by the right not be harmed and if legislation to protect adults from environmental tobacco is justified. If harm is the basis for the justification of restrictions in the case of adults, then it seems such grounds ought to extend to children. There are three ways in which the case for legislating to protect children is stronger than the case to protect non-smoking adults. These are as follows:

1. Children typically have less autonomy than adults in terms of controlling their own movements. Where tobacco use is allowed, children often have no way of protecting themselves from exposure to second-hand smoke. Young children cannot leave the house alone while the parent smokes.

2. Children, especially very young children, are usually less aware than adults of the dangers of second-hand smoke. Further, even those children who are aware of the dangers may not be able to successfully argue against their parents' wish to smoke in the home.

3. The risk of harm from exposure to smoke is greater in the case of children. We will address this third point in some detail.

The Harmful Effects of Exposure to ETS on Children

Since the mid-1970s, the negative effects of second-hand smoke, or environmental tobacco smoke (ETS), have been documented and reported to the general public.[5] Second-hand smoke may be defined as "the smoke that individuals breathe when they are located in the same air space as smokers."[6] It includes the smoke the smoker exhales, the smoke emitted by the cigarette when it is not being actively smoked by the smoker, and the smoke that emits from the cigarette while the smoker draws on it.[7] More than forty components of second-hand smoke are known to cause cancer.[8]

Although there is little doubt about the negative effects of ETS, the exact causal relationship between ETS and the harms associated with it are sometimes unclear. However, there is sufficient evidence to establish ETS exposure as a causal factor for some serious health problems, such as increased asthma-related morbidity in children, infections of the lower respiratory tract, increased fluid in the middle ear, reduced lung function, and reduced oxygen flow to tissues.[9] For other risks, the causal links between ETS exposure and the health problems associated with it are less certain.

Children are vulnerable to ETS exposure through the air, but ETS also holds risks for them when they are exposed in utero, either because the mother smokes or because she is in an environment in which others are smoking. The effects on a fetus when the mother is exposed to ETS are somewhat less well understood than effects of the mother herself smoking, but both are known to carry notable hazards for the fetus. When the mother smokes during her pregnancy, she is at greater risk for miscarriage or still-birth, or for other complications during her pregnancy.[10] In infants of both mothers who smoke and mothers who are exposed to second-hand smoke, the same pathological arterial change that causes arteriosclerosis (hardening of the arteries) has been seen in their umbilical arteries.[11]

Also, babies whose parents smoked (either their mothers or their fathers) while they were in utero are at greater risk for being born underdeveloped and/or with low birth weight (LBW).[12] Neonates exposed to ETS are at a greater risk for succumbing to sudden infant death syndrome (SIDS) before the age of one.[13] There is also increased risk for infants exposed to smoke in utero to be born with underdeveloped lungs.[14] Because of their diminished oxygen and nutrient supplies, which have been compromised by ETS exposure, intellectual deficits and behavioural problems may become apparent over time in these infants.[15]

Toddlers who are exposed to ETS are at greater risk for increased fluid in the middle ear, ear infections and hearing problems, tonsillitis, meningococcal infections, upper respiratory tract irritations and infections, which result in cold symptoms and sore throats, hoarseness, wheezing, headaches, fussiness, and greater difficulty recovering from colds.[16] Exposure also increases children's risk for lower respiratory tract infections such as bronchitis and pneumonia, and reduces lung function.[17] Children's risk for asthma is also greatly increased, and in children who do have asthma, the incidence and severity of attacks increase with ETS exposure, requiring more visits to the hospital for treatment.[18] The risks for health problems such as lung cancer and other childhood cancers and leukemia, for heart disease due to unfavourable cholesterol levels and initiation of arteriosclerosis, and cataracts also increase for children who are exposed to ETS.[19] The reduced lung function observed in some children who have been exposed to ETS results in reduced oxygen flow to tissues, the effects of which are comparable to observed effects of anemia, cyanotic heart disease, or chronic lung disease.[20] Overall, the Ontario Medical Association reports that "exposure to second-hand smoke represents a serious pediatric problem which has been estimated to double the risk of infection and death in children."[21] For adolescents, exposure to ETS carries not only the risks of the above health problems but also the greatly increased risk that they will start smoking themselves.

Exposure to ETS holds many health risks for anyone who is exposed to it, but the risks are greater for children because of their smaller body mass.

Because of their smaller size, it takes less exposure to absorb more toxins than a fully grown adult,[22] although there is no evidence of any level of second-hand smoke being safe.[23] In addition, young children may be at increased risk for harm from ETS because their immune systems are less protective.[24]

How widespread is the problem? According to Physicians for a Smoke Free Canada, in 1996–97 nearly 1.6 million Canadian children under the age of twelve were regularly exposed to tobacco smoke at home. This amounts to one-third of all children in this age group. What do these organizations recommend? According to the Ontario Medical Association, given the known and serious health impacts of second-hand smoke on children and adolescents, and also to the child in utero, steps must be taken to eliminate smoking in all places frequented by pregnant women, young children, and adolescents. The Ontario Medical Association concludes:

> Elimination of exposure to second-hand smoke in infancy is especially important as early lung development appears to be a critical determinant of respiratory health. Children of parents who use tobacco may be exposed to second-hand smoke levels in the home which may approach the levels found in bars, creating exacerbated respiratory hazards for them. The only suitable control measure is tobacco use outside the home. Parents must not ignore their responsibility to protect their children from involuntary exposure to second-hand smoke, especially exposure which will increase the children's risk of second-hand-smoke-related death in the future. Based on current information on ventilation systems, second-hand smoke can persist indoors for many hours after tobacco use. Parental tobacco use in another room in the house is therefore similar to having urination allowed only in the deep end of a pool.[25]

The Ontario Association of Children's Aid Societies requires all fostering and adoptive parents to sign a pledge promising that the home will be smoke free. The rationale is based on the known health dangers of second-hand smoke exposure, especially for children under two years of age, as well as the known risk for SIDS, which is increased twofold when the caring adult smokes. Corresponding to the responsibilities discussed in the first section of our chapter, we can see there are three categories of responsibility adults have toward children regarding exposure to second-hand smoke: the direct obligation not to smoke in front of children, an obligation to prevent others from doing do, and an obligation to educate children both about the dangers of second-hand smoke and their rights.

In the following section we examine legislation and polices regarding smoking in the home.

Legislation and Policies Prohibiting Parental Smoking in the Home

Legislation limiting smoking in public places has become widely accepted and endorsed over the past two to three decades. The effort to make anti-smoking measures acceptable to the public began with educating the public first about the harms of second-hand smoke (as well as the harms to those actually smoking), and then implementing legislation incrementally, gradually including more and more public places where smoking often occurred. People seem largely to agree that legislation against smoking is justified on the basis that those who choose not to smoke ought not to have to suffer the harmful effects of smoking because of those who do. Couched in terms of rights, the rights of non-smokers are thought to take precedence over the rights of others to smoke, on grounds that the former group has a right to health that the freedom to smoke does not override. But although the decision to implement legislation against smoking in public places for others' protection is widely accepted, it seems that people generally do not agree with moving legislation into the home. Here we examine the arguments for and against legislating against smoking in the home.

A primary reason for suggesting that we ought to legislate against smoking in the home is to protect children who will be exposed to second-hand smoke. Proponents argue that given how harmful we know ETS is for children, and since they rarely are given the choice of whether or not they remain in an environment that exposes them to these risks, someone else should step in to protect their interests when their parents will not. The parents are viewed as failing to live up to an obligation they have to their children. Presumably, people hold that the courts ought to be the one to do this because there are few others with the authority to dictate to parents how they raise their children.

Generally, both in Canada and the United States, courts do not address the issue of parental smoking around their children unless the issue is explicitly brought before them by one of the parents. Most often, the situation is brought before the courts by a parent who is filing for custody and who argues that the child ought to be placed in a home where she will not be exposed to ETS. This argument has been received in various ways by judges to whom it has been presented. Some have allowed the fact that a parent smokes to weigh heavily on their decision; others have warned that it could have an effect on subsequent decisions about custody, if the parent continues; and still others have ruled that they will not base their decision on the fact that a parent smokes at all. Taking a position that is viewed as more radical, one judge in Cleveland independently raised the issue of parental smoking without its having been raised by either of the parents.[26]

Opponents of this position rarely deny the risks that smoking poses to children's health but argue that these risks do not give the state the right to invade the privacy of people's homes and interfere with the way that people choose to raise their children. Especially in North America, people are reluctant to get involved in the upbringing of other people's children, perhaps because there is a wide variety of opinions about how children should be raised. For example, some prefer to school their children at home, rather than send them to public schools; some refuse certain kinds of health care for their children, on religious grounds. But we do limit other sorts of harms that parents can impose on children.

An argument that is advanced for greater court intervention is that parents' choice to expose their children to ETS is similar to child abuse.[27] Garfield Mahood notes that an important distinction between child abuse and smoking is that child abuse is a criminal offence, whereas smoking in the presence of children is not.[28] However, the argument may be strengthened if proponents are taken to mean that choosing to expose one's children to ETS is a form of child abuse in that it is making a conscious decision to do something that one knows is harmful to one's children.

Mahood points out the difference, in the eyes of the courts, between child abuse and smoking in that the former is categorized as a case for criminal law, while the latter would be an act against civil law and would thus be couched in terms of negligence. The child or someone on the child's behalf would have to demonstrate that the parent failed to fulfill a duty of care owed to the child, that this failure resulted in some harm to the child, and that, furthermore, there was no good reason to excuse the parent's failure to meet the duty owed to the child.[29]

This points to a problem for those who wish to see judges become more proactive about preventing children's exposure to ETS in the home. That is, someone has to bring the case to the courts, since it is unlikely the children themselves would. Typically, family members are reluctant to litigate against each other except in extraneous circumstances, such as custody battles, and people outside the family generally do not involve themselves in other families' private affairs. Currently, although people seem to feel strongly enough to endorse legislation against smoking in public places, studies have shown that they do not support legislating for change inside the home.

When the matter is brought before the courts, judges who refuse to give the matter of ETS exposure any weight at all hold a distinction between the *risks* of ETS exposure and the actual harm that results from ETS exposure. On the basis of this distinction, the judge requires not only that there be a risk from ETS exposure but that there be good evidence that ETS exposure *will* in fact result in some demonstrable harm to the particular child in the particular case at hand.[30] There is a great deal of evidence to support the risks that ETS exposure holds for children, in general. But some argue that given the impact of the judge's decision, and the many other important factors that must be considered when determining whether a child should be permitted to be with her/his parents, such as the effect on the family's emotional well-being, judges ought not to base their decision on a mere *risk* of harm. The judge should take into account ETS exposure only if it can clearly be shown that it does in fact negatively impact on the health of the child in the case in question, for instance, if the child has asthma, which is known to be aggravated or exacerbated by ETS exposure.

Another factor that seems to affect the weight judges are willing to give to ETS exposure is whether it is visitation or custody that is at stake. Judges generally seem much more willing to deny visitation rights to a parent because of his inability to refrain from smoking in the child's presence than to refuse him custody rights on that basis. Two possible reasons have been suggested for this difference.[31] One is that there are more factors to be considered in custody cases, and so the weight of the parent's smoking is lessened. Another is that given the relatively small period of time parents applying for visitation would have to refrain from smoking, refusal may be given a much more negative weight by the courts than if the parent who has primary custody cannot refrain from smoking, since it is a larger undertaking for her not to expose the child to it.

Although judges do not take a firm and consistent stance on the issue of parental smoking in the home, legislators and policy-makers have begun to take measures to prohibit it in places such as adoptive parents' homes and foster homes. Britain has recently passed legislation making smokers ineligible to adopt or provide foster care to children.[32] In Canada, regulations are much less stringent. For example, according to the Children's Aid Society of Eastern Ontario, smoking would not rule a person out as a potential foster parent, although the person may be required to restrict her/his smoking to certain areas of the house, maintaining others as smoke-free.[33]

Opponents often raise issues related to individual adult rights and freedom. In the case of children the relevant rights are the autonomy rights enjoyed by parents. However, once we think of children as also protected by rights against harm, then the parental smoker's right does not include the right to smoke in the home or car or to take the child into other smoke-filled environments. Some may worry about state intervention in the home, yet the concept is not a new one. The homes that we live in and the cars that we drive are strictly regulated. There are building and electrical codes, regulations banning the use of certain products such as cribs painted with lead-based paint, regulations that determine who can and cannot drive an automobile, and laws against domestic violence and child abuse. In addition, the often-invoked spectre of "smoke police" knocking on the doors of family homes need be no more real in this case than it is in the case of legislation requiring child safety seats, smoke detectors, or fences around backyard swimming pools.

Is this position on a child's right to be free from second-hand smoke fundamentally anti-liberal? We do not think so. It is no different from the justification for the many restrictions we impose on adults smoking because of our belief that second-hand smoke is dangerous to other adults. No public health rational exists for providing less legal protection from environmental tobacco smoke (ETS) exposure in the home than in public places.

The more we are convinced that we ought to treat adult persons with as much autonomy as is consistent with maintaining a minimum level of good across the board, the more we are convinced that we need to pay significantly more attention to children. One might argue in the opposite direction. For example, one could conclude that heavy income redistribution is required in a just society given that it would be too intrusive in family to guarantee equal starting points. But if the requirements regarding the treatment of children are rights-based, then paying them back after the fact through redistribution of wealth misses the mark in two different directions. First, it is not clear what amount of money would make up for a miserable childhood—the goods may be not very commensurable. Second, if one has a choice between violating a right and paying restitution versus not infringing it in the first place, the far better choice is not to infringe.

So far we have argued that a child's rights to not be harmed can ground restrictions on parental smoking, though we leave open what form those restrictions might take. From a child's right not to be harmed follows obligations on adults not to smoke around children and obligations to see that other adults also fulfill their obligations. In what follows we discuss obligations that fall on the general public regarding children's rights to a smoke-free environment.

Obligations on the General Public to Provide Children with a Smoke-Free Environment

While policy-makers and legislators have been somewhat reluctant to invade the privacy of people's homes to protect children from ETS exposure, much progress has been made to protect their interests outside their homes.

Legislation has been passed in many Ontario municipalities prohibiting smoking in many places children are likely to occupy.

Regulations against smoking in public places began with restricting smoking in the workplace, as that was identified as the place non-smokers were most exposed to second-hand smoke.[34] In many cases, restricting smoking in the workplace also served to reduce the amount of smoking by employees and resulted in some people's choice to stop using tobacco products altogether. Indirectly, then, workplace smoking restrictions are credited with reducing children's exposure to ETS because of their effects on smokers' use of tobacco products, overall.[35] Measures that have had a more direct effect on children's exposure to ETS are policies and legislation that regulate smoking in public places where children are likely to be. The Tobacco Control Act (1994) prohibits smoking in such places as hospitals and health care facilities, pharmacies, nurseries, schools/colleges/universities, bus shelters, enclosed shopping malls and retail establishments, and video amusement arcades.[36] Eating establishments of any kind were omitted from the Tobacco Control Act, and the decision to allow smoking or not in them has been left to municipalities. Perhaps most notably in Ontario, Toronto has amended its bylaws to make all restaurants and entertainment facilities non-smoking unless they can provide separately ventilated enclosed areas, which are not to exceed 25 percent of the restaurant or bar seating area,[37] a choice many municipalities have followed. Other places—among them Waterloo, Ontario—have chosen to make their eating establishments 100 percent smoke-free. The disadvantage to allowing a ventilated area to remain is that there may be no restrictions on who may enter the smoking area. So if a parent, for example, brings his or her child into a restaurant to eat and chooses to sit in the smoking area, there is nothing to prevent him or her from taking the child in too. Thus, although the separate area protects the other patrons, it does not help children who are there with a smoker. Even in smoking areas that restrict access to adults, there may be little enforcement, because we are often reluctant to interfere with parental choices. Another way the problem has been addressed is to make the establishment smoke-free until a certain hour of the day, after which time children are unlikely to be there.

The approach to limiting the amount of ETS children are exposed to has largely been through public policy, which has become increasingly restrictive about where people can smoke. Besides taking a prohibitive approach to address the problem of second-hand smoke, public policy measures have also heavily relied on public education, although there seem to be few studies to test the accuracy of people's beliefs, and more specifically those of smokers, about the severity of the effects of second-hand smoke on people's health.

Conclusion

We have argued that there are grounds for limiting parental smoking around children and these grounds are connected to the responsibilities adults have toward children that derive from a child's right not to be harmed. These grounds form a prima facie case against parental smoking and in favour of legislation, but we do not suggest here how these grounds might be balanced against competing considerations. We have not considered all relevant objections nor have we examined or endorsed specific forms of legislation in this area. Even so, our conclusions may strike some readers as clearly incorrect. If so, we invite those skeptical of legislating against the exposure of children to second-hand smoke to reconsider some of our starting assumptions. One may decide in the end that children do not have a right not be harmed after all. Or one could argue that an adult's right not to be harmed does not extend to exposure to environmental tobacco smoke and that laws prohibiting smoking in bars, restaurants, workplaces, etc., are similarly unjustified. All we have shown is that given a commitment to children's rights and the belief that legislation against environmental tobacco smoke to protect adults is justified, it follows that legislation to protect children can be similarly justified.

Notes

1 See Samantha Brennan and Robert Noggle, "The Moral Status of Children: Children's Rights, Parents' Rights, and Family Justice," *Social Theory and Practice* 23, no. 1 (1997): 1–26, for some discussion of this idea.

2 Judith Thomson, *The Realm of Rights* (Cambridge, MA: Harvard University Press, 1990), 135.

3 See the Winning Kids website, sponsored by the Children's Aid Foundation, at www.fosteradoptwinningkids.com/website/eng/index.php.

4 Ontario Association of Children's Aid Societies (2006) website pages "What Is a CAS?" and "How and When to Report Abuse or Neglect," at http://www.oacas.org/resources, accessed 25 August 2007.

5 "Ontario Medical Association position paper on second-hand smoke," OMA Committee on Population Health (November 1996), http://www.oma.org.phealth/2ndsmoke.htm; "Cigarette smoke and kids' health," Physicians for a Smoke-Free Canada (n.d.), http://www.smoke-free.ca/Second-Hand-Smoke/health_kids.htm.

6 "OMA position paper on second-hand smoke."

7 Ibid.

8 Ibid.

9 Ibid.

10 Ibid.

11 Ibid.

12 Ibid.

13 Canadian Health Network, "Second-Hand Smoke Kills: Let's Clear the Air" (2001), at http://www.canadian-health-network.ca, accessed 8 September 2007.

14 Ibid.

15 "Cigarette smoke and kids' health," Physicians for a Smoke-Free Canada.

16 American Academy of Pediatrics, "What Is Environmental Tobacco Smoke (ETS)?" at http:/www.medem.com, accessed 8 September 2007.

17 Ibid.

18 Ibid.

19 Ibid.

20 Physicians for a Smoke-Free Canada.

21 "OMA position paper on second-hand smoke."

22 Physicians for a Smoke-Free Canada.

23 Canadian Health Network.

24 Physicians for a Smoke-Free Canada.

25 "OMA position paper on second-hand smoke."

26 Associated Press, "Not around kids, you don't," *The Globe and Mail*, September 13, 2002.

27 Roberta Ferrence and Mary Jane Ashley, "Protecting Children from Passive Smoking: The Risks Are Clear and a Comprehensive Strategy Is Now Needed," *British Medical Journal* 311, no. 7257 (5 August 2000): 310–11.

28 Garfield Mahood, "Smoking in the Home: Social and Legal Implications," Non-smokers' Rights Association (2003), at http://www.nsra-adnf.ca/cms, accessed 8 September 2007.

29 Ibid.

30 Ibid.

31 Ibid.

32 Addiction Research Foundation of Ontario, "Smokers Rejected as Adoptive Parents," *The Journal* 3 (22 May, 1993): 7.

33 "Foster Care Frequently Asked Questions," *Winning Kids*, Children's Aid Society of Eastern Ontario. http://www.fosteradoptwinningkids.com/website/eng/foster/questionsd.php.

34 "OMA position paper on second-hand smoke."

35 Ibid.

36 Tobacco Control Act (1994), Province of Ontario, 9(1).

37 "OMA position paper on second-hand smoke."

SIX

Political Liberalism and Moral Education:
Reflections on *Mozert v. Hawkins*

MARC RAMSAY

The issue of moral education has important implications for our understanding of the parent–child relationship and the child–state relationship. Our conception of moral education should help to elucidate the appropriate division of authority over children between parents and the state. Of course, few authors argue that either party should be granted complete and exclusive authority over children's education. Rather, most authors recognize that both parents and the state have some authority with respect to the content and delivery of children's moral education. But the question of how to establish the appropriate balance between parental and state authority remains controversial. At what point do mandatory state educational programs or requirements intrude upon legitimate parental authority concerning children's moral education?

The most famous case regarding this issue is, of course, *Wisconsin v. Yoder*.[1] In *Yoder*, Amish families sought to exempt their children from state laws requiring school attendance up to the age of sixteen. The Amish objected to mandatory attendance of two years of high school, alleging that high school attendance subjected their children to a variety of worldly attitudes and beliefs that run contrary to Amish traditions and beliefs. Moreover, they claimed that formal schooling outside their community during early adolescence would interfere with their children's development as members of the Amish community.

As Stephen Macedo suggests, *Mozert v. Hawkins*, although not quite as famous as *Yoder*, provides a more useful practical example regarding disputes concerning authority over moral education.[2] In *Mozert*, various Protestant fundamentalist parents objected to their public school board's imposition of a mandatory reading program—the Holt program—that was designed to promote critical reflection but which involved materials and ideas that offended their religious beliefs. The program exposed to children to stories, including science fiction and accounts of persons from various cultures and religions. The parents maintained that several readings from the program encouraged an unacceptable level of toleration of— perhaps even outright endorsement of—beliefs and practices repugnant to their religion. As a remedy the parents proposed that they be allowed to exempt their children from the particular readings that they deemed religiously repugnant. Some local schools did adopt pragmatic compromises along these lines. However, the Hawkins County, Tennessee, board of education voted to eliminate all such alternatives, firmly establishing the mandatory character of the Holt curriculum. The board's policy led to a constitutional challenge by parents. Ultimately, the United States Court of Appeals 6th Circuit rejected the parents' constitutional challenge, thereby upholding the board's authority to make the Holt Series a mandatory element of the public curriculum.

The *Mozert* parents' stance was more restrained than that of the Amish community in *Yoder*, since the former group did not seek to exempt their children from attendance at public schools. But the *Mozert* parents' concerns pose a more serious and troubling question for a liberal democratic society. The Amish are a small isolationist group; they lack both the ability and the desire to exert an influence over the political affairs of the society that surrounds them. Protestant fundamentalists, on the other hand, are a much larger group, one that has been increasingly active in politics over the last three decades. Thus, the moral education of their children is a matter of public interest in a way that the moral education of Amish children is not.[3] For this reason, I frame my discussion of the division of authority concerning moral education around *Mozert* rather than *Yoder*.[4]

Liberals cannot deal with the issues posed by *Mozert* without confronting the divide between political liberalism and autonomy (or comprehensive) liberalism. We need to know how the choice between these rival models of liberalism affects our conception of the parent–child and child–state relationships. Autonomy liberalism would seem to provide the most straightforward justification of the Holt program. Autonomy liberals might see the development of children's capacity for critical reflection on their received conceptions of the good as a value of the highest priority, a value that could trump the religious objections of dissenting parents. Political liberals, on the other hand, eschew appeals to controversial ideas of the good life, preferring to justify liberal political principles on less controversial grounds. For the political liberal, the main goal of moral education is to prepare children for the duties of citizenship and to instill in them a sense of civic respect and tolerance for those with different conceptions of the good.

Macedo argues, however, that *Mozert* provides a legitimate example of a case in which political liberalism's goals of civic education should override parents' religious beliefs.[5] More precisely, Macedo argues that mandatory reading programs are justified because, in addition to serving the goals of civic education, they can be shown to impose no serious costs on either parents' religious beliefs or their related conception of their children's interests. In other words, these programs are unproblematic because they are not disruptive of the legitimate parent–child relationship. For Macedo, this approach stands in sharp contrast to the autonomy liberalism approach, which would confront and refute parents' religious conception of their children's interests. The political liberal holds that such confrontations should, to the extent possible, be avoided.

This chapter has two main goals. First, I argue that political liberalism cannot provide us with an uncontroversial justification of the result in *Mozert*. Instead, we must face up to the conceptual cost that this result imposes on some parents' religious conception of their children's interests. A liberal state should not pretend to deny the reality of the conflict between the state's conception of children's interests and the rival conception held by dissenting parents.

Second, I argue that the *only* plausible moral defence of the outcome in *Mozert* is one that is based on autonomy liberalism, the idea that children have an essential interest in developing their capacity for critical reflection. However, it is far from clear that autonomy liberals should, all things considered, endorse the result in *Mozert*. Once we see that political liberalism's uncontroversial defence of the Holt reading program fails, we are forced to confront the stresses that this program places on the parent–child relationship. Costs to parental autonomy and legitimate questions about the efficacy of the Holt program should give autonomy liberals pause if they are otherwise inclined to impose such programs in the face of serious parental opposition.

In the first part of the chapter, I set out the details of the dispute in *Mozert* and the court's reasons for rejecting the parents' claims. In the second, I set out the dispute between political liberalism and autonomy liberalism. I then provide an explanation of why Will Kymlicka's brand of autonomy liberalism requires us to be sensitive to concerns about indoctrination and anti-religious bias in public education. I conclude this section by explaining why autonomy liberals should be at least somewhat skeptical of mandatory reading programs such as the Holt curriculum. In the final section, I explain why Macedo's efforts to provide a politically liberal or uncontroversial defence of the result in *Mozert* are bound to fail. A liberal state cannot justify the result in *Mozert* unless it is willing both to affirm children's deeper interest in autonomy and to dispute the parental beliefs that oppose this interest.[6]

The Case

The dispute in *Mozert* began in early 1983, when the local school board adopted the Holt series "critical reading" program for students in grades one through eight.[7] The purpose of critical reading programs such as the Holt series is to develop "higher order cognitive skills that enable students to evaluate the material they read, to contrast the ideas presented, and to understand complex characters that appear in the reading material."[8] The plaintiffs (parents' groups and their children) argued that the design of the Holt Series, and its particular implementation in Hawkins County, conflicted with their religious commitments and those of their children.

The plaintiffs listed several examples of the alleged defects in the Holt Series readings. The story "A Visit to Mars" portrays thought transfer and telepathy in such a way that "it could be considered a scientific concept." A story about a boy making toast while a girl reads to him was thought to denigrate the difference between the sexes. Another story about the lives of Catholic settlers in New Mexico was said to endorse Catholicism.[9]

Nomi Maya Stolzenberg provides a thorough catalogue of the parents' objections, some of which are:

- the content of the readings in the Holt reading series is contradictory to the plaintiff's beliefs...
- the readings induce children to stray from the way of God...
- parents face eternal damnation for letting children read the books. Such disobedience to biblical commands results in spiritual or physical punishment...
- the children will be punished with eternal damnation if they read the books...
- the content of the readings is offensive; accordingly, the plaintiffs feel offended by the readings...
- the readings have the potential to make Christian children wish to be other than who they are; to create in them a desire to change from their

heritage to the one positively portrayed in the text; and to lead them to a world view such as feminism, humanism, or pacifism.[10]

An initial decision in favour of the plaintiff's was overturned by the U.S. Court of Appeals 6th district, which ruled in favour of the Hawkins County School Board.

Judge Lively

Writing for the majority, Judge Pierce Lively rejected the plaintiff's free exercise claim on the grounds that the Holt curriculum, as implemented in Hawkins County, did not compel acts contrary to the plaintiff's religion.[11] According to Lively, there was no evidence that children were compelled to make critical judgments about their religious commitments, although he concedes that the reading program encouraged such judgments. However, he also notes that students were free to comment on or interpret the reading assignments in light of their own religious commitments or "value base."

In Lively's opinion, the only conduct compelled by the school board was the activity of reading and discussing the Holt materials. In his view, this counts as mere exposure to different ideas; there is no plausible sense in which reading and discussion (with the freedom of interpretation and commentary noted above) can constitute compulsion to "affirm or deny a religious belief or to engage or refrain from engaging in any act either required or forbidden by the student's religious convictions."[12]

Judge Kennedy

Judge Cornelia G. Kennedy concurs with Lively in holding that the defendant's actions did not compel the plaintiffs to act in a manner contrary to their religious beliefs. However, she also says that even if the plaintiffs had been able to establish such compulsion, she would decide in the school board's favour because of the state's overriding interests in public education.[13]

Kennedy claims that the "opt out remedy" would be too disruptive of teachers' efforts to develop an integrated education program. She also finds a compelling state interest in avoiding religious divisiveness, an interest that she believes the United States Supreme Court has recognized in the specific context of public education. According to Kennedy, excusing students from core subjects because they object to the material in question on religious grounds threatens to exacerbate existing levels of religious tension and divisiveness.

Judge Boggs

Judge Danny J. Boggs's concurrence with Lively and Kennedy is largely a matter of regretful acquiescence. Boggs notes that reading "objectionable" materials does, historically constitute a prohibited act within some Western religions. For instance, "we may recall the Roman Catholic Church's 'Index Librorum Prohibitorum.' This was a list of those books the reading of which was a mortal sin, at least until the second Vatican Council in 1962. I would hardly think it can be contended that a school requirement that a student engage in an act (the reading of the book) which would specifically be a mortal sin under the teaching of a major organized religion would be other than 'conduct prohibited by religion,' even by the court's fairly restrictive standard."[14] So, on Boggs's terms, reading does constitute more than mere exposure to objectionable ideas. In fact, he contends that his colleagues unfairly ignored parents' claims that, according to their beliefs, the reading of certain materials could constitute a mortal sin. Likewise, Boggs maintains that Kennedy's appeals to compelling state interests are based more on the speculative benefits of the Holt program than any clear evidence of a threat to paramount state interests.

Unlike his colleagues, Boggs sees exemptions (the opt-out remedy) as a reasonable method of dealing with the dispute between parents and school boards.[15] However, with some regret, Boggs concludes that the United States Supreme Court is unlikely to recognize First Amendment protections concerning the content of civic education.

Political Liberalism vs. Autonomy Liberalism

Political Liberalism

The dispute between autonomy (or comprehensive) liberalism and political liberalism concerns the proper grounding or justification of core liberal political commitments such as the priority of liberty, fair opportunity, and distributive justice. So-called comprehensive liberals hold that these commitments are justified because each person has a deep and essential interest in being able to develop, reflect upon, and revise her conception of the good. Liberal politics is based on our desire to afford equal consideration to each person's basic interest in personal autonomy. Liberal politics reflects respect for liberty and opportunity because personal autonomy is a crucial, perhaps the crucial, human interest.

Political liberals, however, maintain that the public justification of liberal political principles should not depend upon controversial ideas about the nature of good lives. Some people may value liberal political institutions because those institutions protect and foster personal autonomy and individuality. But other reasonable persons may find such a justification to be incompatible with their deeper moral and religious convictions. The political liberal wants the public justification of liberal political commitments to be one that can enjoy the support of people who don't regard personal autonomy as a deep or essential human interest. For the political liberal, support for liberal political commitments does not stand or fall with public's commitment to the deeper moral importance of personal autonomy. Rather, the political priority of liberty and opportunity is based on an overlapping consensus among various reasonable conceptions of the good.

Political liberals do not deny that some persons support liberal principles for Millian or Kantian reasons. But they maintain that the desire to promote personal autonomy and critical reflection is just one of the many legitimate motives for supporting liberal political commitments. Other persons will explain their political commitments in terms of religious doctrines such as "free faith." Political liberals do not wish to dictate the particular path by which people come to liberal political principles. All parties who can find a way of reconciling themselves with the political features of liberalism are welcome in the political liberal's camp. All reasonable conceptions of the good that are capable of supporting liberal political principles are regarded with equal and impartial respect. Political liberalism does not justify policies by judging or ranking these reasonable conceptions of the good.

Thus, one can see how the rival versions of liberalism might yield different and conflicting accounts of both moral education and the state's legitimate role in securing that education. According to Rawls,

> The liberalisms of Kant and Mill may lead to requirements designed to foster the values of autonomy and individuality as ideals to govern much if not all of life. But political liberalism has a different aim and requires far less. It will ask that children's education include such things as knowledge of their constitutional and civic rights so that, for example, they know that liberty of conscience exists in their society and that apostasy is not a legal crime, all this to insure that their continued membership when they come of age is not based simply on ignorance of their basic rights or fear of punishment for offenses that do not exist. Moreover, their education should also prepare them to be fully cooperating members of society and enable them to be self-supporting; it should also encourage the political virtues so that they want to honor the fair terms of social cooperation in their relations with the rest of society.[16]

Political liberalism's conception of education is supposed to provide citizens with an understanding of their rights and claims. But it does not encourage them to exercise these claims in any particular way. In particular, it does not require them to understand their moral and religious commitments as products of autonomous choice or objects of critical reflection. The other goal of political liberal education is to prepare citizens to be full participants in social co-operation. It seeks to foster the skills necessary for participation in democratic decision making as well the disposition to respect the rights and claims of other citizens whose conceptions of the good may be very different from our own.

Comprehensive liberals might argue that public education should not be confined to the civic goals of political liberalism. After all, if our shared justification of liberal political principles is based on the value of personal autonomy, then personal autonomy is an indisputable good that all persons should recognize. So it would seem that public schools should promote what Amy Gutmann refers to as "rational deliberation among ways of life."[17] Of course, fundamentalist families, such as the plaintiffs in *Mozert*, object to this ideal. But, according to Macedo, comprehensive liberals are prepared to say that these families are wrong and that fundamentalists' false beliefs should not impede the promotion of children's capacity for critical reflection. If parents' religious beliefs stand in the way of protecting and promoting children's interest in personal autonomy, then so much the worse for parents' religious beliefs.[18]

But the political liberal refuses to justify liberal political principles with reference to controversial ideas about the nature of good lives. Because his liberal state does not even recognize a public conception of people's deeper interests, the political liberal's liberal state isn't in the business of promoting such a conception. Thus, he is more likely to endorse a conception of moral education that respects parental authority concerning children's deeper interests. The political liberal will challenge parental discretion and authority concerning moral education only in those cases where parental authority threatens to undermine the civic goals of public education.

But *Mozert* presents a scenario in which the civic educational goals of political liberals such as Macedo *appear* to conflict with parental authority. In particular, the aims of civic education appear to conflict with parents' religiously based conception of their children's interests.

Here, according to Macedo, political liberalism attempts to smooth over the apparent conflict by avoiding questions concerning the truth or falsity of parents' religious beliefs. It asks persons with strong religious commitments to "bracket" their beliefs, to limit their applicability to the political realm. In Macedo's words, "What political liberalism asks of us is not to renounce what we believe to be true but to acknowledge the difficulty of publicly establishing any single account of the whole truth. It invites us to put some of our (true) beliefs aside when it comes to laying the groundwork for common political institutions."[19] Our commitment to political freedom, along with our recognition of the difficulties in "publicly establishing" true claims, is what enables us to limit the applicability of our beliefs. We recognize two distinct spheres of morality: the political morality that allows us to live together in civil society and the private morality of the good and religion. Political liberalism, according to Rawls, does not claim that political values are more important than other principles. Political values apply only within the political sphere itself.

According to Macedo,

> We focus on shared public principles and leave the religious dimensions of the question aside. The public school curriculum would in this way avoid directly confronting or denying the *Mozert* families' contention that the Bible's authority should be accepted uncritically.... By simply leaving aside the religious question as such (at least in the sense of not taking an official position on it), Lively and political liberals leave the school door open to reasonable fundamentalists, that is, to those willing to acknowledge for political purposes the authority of public reasonableness.[20]

Here, Macedo follows Lively in noting that students were not forced to express any particular religious or moral views and that they were free to comment on readings from their own religious perspective.

For Macedo, the court's decision is not based on comprehensive moral or religious ideals. The purpose of the reading program was to instill political virtues of understanding and tolerance. It did not aim to teach children a deeper form of religious tolerance, which would require them to question the truth of their beliefs or regard rival religions as equally valid paths to God. Macedo concedes, as Lively does, that reading programs such as the Holt series make it more likely that children will adopt critical reflection or a deeper religious pluralism. But, following Rawls, Macedo notes that political liberalism endorses neutrality of aim, not neutrality of consequences. There is no avoiding the fact that liberal policies have non-neutral consequences concerning rival conceptions of the good. But if the policies that carry non-neutral effects are vital to the maintenance of shared political values, reasonable citizens will accept these policies.[21]

Autonomy Liberalism

There are several rival conceptions of comprehensive (or autonomy) liberalism. Political liberals usually point to the key historical examples of Kant and Mill. But they also note a number of contemporary examples, including Gutmann, Kymlicka, Ronald Dworkin, and Joseph Raz. What unites comprehensive liberals is their admission that they rely upon deeper moral ideals to justify liberal political principles. Furthermore, they hold that political liberalism's attempt to ground political principles without appeal to any comprehensive ideals is a failure.

In this chapter, I cannot rehearse all the various responses to political liberalism. But the core of my own response is that political liberalism's conception of reasonableness replicates the commitments of Kymlicka's modest brand of autonomy liberalism. In attempting to explain why disputes over moral and religious issues are difficult, political liberals commit themselves to the fallibilist empiricist moral epistemology that makes up the core of Kymlicka's conception. If they refuse to endorse this conception, political liberals cannot provide a satisfactory account of their commitment to basic liberal freedoms.

The strategy of "bracketing" truth provides no help here. The division that political liberalism draws between the political and private spheres is a division that satisfies only persons with comprehensive commitments sympathetic to autonomy liberalism. Fundamentalists whose commitments rub up against or conflict with liberal political principles are supposed to be content with the "official" agnosticism of political liberalism. But from their perspective, the idea that their moral and religious beliefs lack political relevance is tantamount to the claim that their beliefs are false. "Bracketing" beliefs comes at a cost in terms of content of those beliefs.

I do not expect this brief presentation of the problems with political liberalism to be compelling. My purpose here is not to refute political liberalism generally, but to show how autonomy liberals can respond to charges about their view of the scope of state authority concerning education. However, the complaints against political liberalism will come up again in the final part of this chapter, where I argue that political liberals cannot account for the result in *Mozert*.

Kymlicka's Autonomy Liberalism

Perhaps some versions of autonomy liberalism do lend themselves to over-expansive conceptions of public education, ones that encourage aggressive challenges to parental authority. However, it is important to note the respects in which political liberals overstate the controversial character of autonomy liberalism.

Macedo in particular describes autonomy liberalism as a political theory that bases the priority of liberty on a comprehensive view of morality, one that speaks to deeper questions about the good. It is better, however, to describe autonomy liberalism as appealing to what Rawls calls a partially comprehensive view of morality.[22] Autonomy liberals do not believe that liberal ideals dictate every element of good lives; rather, liberal ideals of autonomy and individuality dictate certain crucial conditions of good lives. These ideals dictate the way in which persons should develop and reflect upon their conceptions of the good, but they say relatively little about what sort of projects or commitments people should endorse. As Raz says, the autonomous life is defined more by its history than by its content.

Conceptions of autonomy liberalism can be compared in terms of the models of moral choice and critical reflection they endorse. Political liberals commonly express two sorts of complaints about autonomy liberalism, ones that track different conceptions of choice and reflection. First, Macedo speaks of Gutmann's commitment to a pervasive form of critical reason. Supposedly, the problem with this conception is that it attempts to assimilate all moral questions of the model of scientific discourse. It rules out or disparages moral commitments based on intuition or religious faith.[23]

Raz's conception of autonomy liberalism, however, is intended to avoid the over-intellectualization of deliberation about the good. For Raz, choices about the good are matters of partial self-authorship. In a well-maintained liberal society, citizens are able to choose from a variety of valuable ways of living that are frequently both incompatible and incommensurable with each other. According to Raz, there is no objective intellectual standard that can be used to determine how we ought to choose between these sorts of options. In choosing from such options we, to some degree, define ourselves and set the standards by which our future well-being is to be measured.[24]

However, Raz's explicit commitment to value pluralism also runs afoul of religious faith in another way. Value pluralism cannot be reconciled with the commitments of persons who endorse a monist conception of religious or moral truth. Many believe not only in faith as a tool of moral inquiry but also in the idea, that faith can track a unitary moral ideal, such as the will of God.

Political liberals wish to make room for those with strong commitments to faith-based moral inquiry and monist conceptions of moral and religious truth. On the other hand, the conceptions of autonomy liberalism outlined above appear hostile to these ways of thinking. Kymlicka's conception of autonomy liberalism, however, goes a long way toward avoiding these disputes.

Kymlicka's conception of autonomy begins with the idea that we all have an interest in leading a good life. This seemingly "banal" claim, he argues, has important consequences: "For leading a good life is different from leading the life we *currently believe* to be good—that is, we recognize that we may be mistaken about the worth or value of what we are currently doing. We may come to see that we've been wasting our lives, pursuing trivial or shallow goals and projects that we had mistakenly considered of great importance" (emphasis in original).[25] For Kymlicka, we have an essential interest in critical reflection on our current beliefs about the good, since these beliefs may in fact be mistaken.

However, according to Kymlicka, it doesn't follow that someone else can compel me to live well just because she correctly perceives a mistake in my conception of the good: "On the contrary, no life goes better by being led from the outside according to values the person doesn't endorse… Praying to God may be a valuable activity, but you have to believe that it's a worthwhile thing to do—that it has some worthwhile point and purpose. You can coerce someone into going to church and making the right physical movements, but you won't make someone's life better that way."[26] Kymlicka's view is fallibilist, but not skeptical. Liberals, he claims, are sometimes thought to value individual freedom because they hold that decisions between conceptions of the good are ultimately arbitrary and groundless. Thus, liberals are thought to value individual choice with respect to the good because there is no objective authority that can be invoked against individual discretion. But, according to Kymlicka, liberals hold that we can engage in meaningful and objective deliberation concerning the good, and this is why they place such a high value on freedom. Liberal agents want the ability to inquire into their conceptions of the good in order to understand them better and to check them for possible errors. Thus, when Kymlicka's agents change or revise their current conceptions of the good, they do so in light of what they take to be good reasons, ideas, or revelations concerning the good that have to come to them through experience.[27]

Kymlicka's conception of moral deliberation does not assimilate moral deliberation to some model of scientific inquiry. Rather, it simply asks that people be open to reflection on their commitments in light of the experiences and ideas they may find on the cultural marketplace of a liberal society. Moreover, Kymlicka does not explicitly endorse Raz's notion of value pluralism. He does not deny that there may be a true monist moral ideal, in terms of religion or the good. But his conception of moral autonomy does require that people test their faith in light of new ideas and experiences (and that they let other persons do so as well).

Kymlicka's Autonomy Liberalism and Moral Education

It should be clear that Kymlicka's conception of autonomy and critical reflection does not threaten to impose an over-expansive conception of public education. In the first place, Kymlicka has access to the same limitations that Lively prescribes for "critical reading." As Lively notes, students should not be compelled to endorse specific religious views, and they should not be compelled to act out specific cultural or religious ceremonies. Critical reflection on one's conception of the good does not require one to abandon that conception, much less to abandon it in favour of some specific alternative.

Kymlicka's emphasis on respect for the inner lives of children, and their sense of identification with their religious community, provides strong reason for taking a cautious approach to teaching critical reflection. Mill, of course, indicated that respect for liberty and personal beliefs does not come into play until children approach adulthood. Up until that point, we are entitled to use those forms of mandatory education that best stimulate critical faculties. But autonomy liberals who operate from a Kantian conception of respect for persons, as Kymlicka does, should not ignore concerns about children's personal commitments. Furthermore, Mill himself did not necessarily anticipate the development of large-scale institutions of public education that sometimes pit the state's views of civic education against the moral and religious views that children receive from their parents.

Moreover, as Kymlicka points out in his discussion of state neutrality, we must also consider the history of how state power, including that of educational institutions, has been used against cultural religious minorities.[28] Once we step beyond the "mere" exposure to difference pursued by the Hawkins County school board, it becomes difficult to specify how we would measure or define the promotion of individual autonomy or critical reflection. We cannot expect too much sophistication in the way that elementary students discuss the relevant materials. And we cannot plausibly measure an elementary student's capacity for critical reflection in terms of whether they express doubts or concerns about the veracity of their religious beliefs or those of their parents. Venturing into this territory raises serious concerns of abuse and bias against conceptions of the good or religion that are out favour with teachers or school boards.

Autonomy Liberalism and the Holt Curriculum

Kymlicka's conception of autonomy liberalism does not lead to an expansive version of public education that encourages conflicts with parental authority. In fact, it's not obvious that his autonomy liberalism demands that we go so far as to endorse the Holt curriculum.

First, the autonomy liberal must also consider parents' claims to autonomy. There is no question that the Holt curriculum interferes with the *Mozert* parents' pursuit of their conceptions of the good. So we need to ask whose autonomy should take precedence here, that of the parents or that of the children.

Some autonomy liberals might reject the idea a parent's claim to autonomy or religious freedom includes in its scope a right to indoctrinate their children into their own religious system. Rather, legitimate parental authority in this regard may simply be a by-product of our desire to keep the state from acquiring too much control over moral education (concerns about a threat to diversity or the climate for intellectual dissent are open both to autonomy liberal and political liberals). Likewise, one might argue that parents choose to take on the disruptions and practical problems posed by children's autonomy; presumably, no one forced them to have children in the first place.

William Galston argues that this is an impoverished account of the parent–child relationship. In his view, "the ability of parents to raise their children in a manner consistent with their deepest commitments is an essential element of expressive liberty."[29] Parents do not own their children on Galston's view, but nor can the parent–child relationship be reduced to a merely custodial relationship. I am sympathetic to Galston's view, and I don't think that one can dismiss this view just because she endorses autonomy liberalism rather than political liberalism (see Narveson, in this volume, for a very different account of the parent–child relationship). Moreover, the Holt curriculum may interfere, to some degree at least, with parents' practical control over their households. It is possible that their practical authority would be diminished if their children demanded greater personal autonomy, exemptions from religious practices for instance.

Of course, even if one concedes that there is a genuine conflict between parental autonomy and children's autonomy here, there are plausible reasons for thinking that children's autonomy should win out in this context. From the perspective of autonomy liberalism, the Holt program is intended to help children develop the capacity for making autonomous decisions in the future. If the Holt program really does make an important contribution in this regard, then parents should be expected to bear the burden it imposes. Generally speaking, no one's claim to pursue a particular chosen project should win out over another person's claim to the development of the capacities and skills required for effective choice making.

But how much of a contribution does the Holt program make to children's capacity for autonomous decision-making? A minor contribution might be sufficient if one thinks that the program in no way interferes with parents' legitimate claims to autonomy. But if one thinks that there is a genuine conflict between parental and child autonomy here, then the priority of children's autonomy rests on the idea that the Holt program makes a substantial contribution to their future capacity for autonomous decision-making.

Whether the Holt program makes such a contribution is unclear. Supporters of the program might claim that by exposing children to different ideas and religious systems, we would teach them that these different ideas are legitimate objects of choice and critical reflection. Thus, when children reach the age where they are able to take up their political liberties (regarding religion and lifestyle), the idea of choice and critical reflection will likely be experienced as familiar and welcome rather than alien and intrusive. Without this exposure to diversity, children may be far more likely to follow the dogmatic line set by their parents than to subject their conception of the good to serious criticism.

On the other hand, one might also speculate that too much exposure to diversity (particularly of a sort that parents object to) may interfere with the development of a stable network of values, a coherent conception of the good that can be subjected to critical reflection. As Galston notes, "instructing children within a particular tradition, far from undermining intellectual or religious freedom, may in fact promote it. Knowing what it means to live within a coherent framework of value and belief may well contribute to an informed adult choice between one's tradition of origin and those encountered later in life."[30] This is not to say that children must be protected from any exposure to diversity if they are to be provided with a coherent framework of values. But, as Galston points out, children in public schools are already exposed to significant amounts of social diversity through informal social relationships and the mass media.[31] Additional exposure through academic discussion may not be necessary; moreover it may be confusing and disruptive if students (particularly younger ones) perceive this material as a direct challenge to their parents' religious convictions and moral authority.

Whether autonomy liberals should, at the end of the day, endorse the Holt program is a question that I leave for future discussion (see Wendling, this volume, for further discussion of appropriate standards for civic education in public and private schools). But costs to parental autonomy (particularly costs to their religious commitments) and concerns about possible negative effects to children should incline autonomy liberals to caution regarding the imposition of the Holt series. However, Macedo's politically liberal justification of the Holt Series is intended to smooth over parents' religious objections. He argues that political liberalism can justify the Holt series in a way that limits the conceptual cost to parents' religious beliefs, heading off the confrontation between civic education and parents' religious conception of their children's interests.

In the next section, I argue that Macedo's politically liberal justification of the Holt series fails. The Holt series cannot be justified by a strategy that attempts to avoid or downplay the conflict between the state's educational objectives and parents' religious conception of children's interests. Rather, the Holt series can be justified only if the liberal state is willing to assert that it wields a conception of children's interests (the interest in critical reflection) that is superior to that endorsed by dissenting parents.

Macedo, Political Liberalism, and *Mozert*

Macedo's first line of defence is Lively's claim that mandatory reading and exposure to different ideas do not constitute compelled actions contrary to religious beliefs. Rather, these programs merely make it more likely that children will change their religious beliefs over time. At first, Macedo appears to recognize the problem with this line of argument. He notes Boggs's claim that, within the Christian tradition, reading proscribed books has been recognized as a sinful act. According to Macedo,

> The program could be likened, Judge Boggs suggested, to requiring Catholic students to read items on the Catholic Church's official index of prohibited books, under pain of giving up the right to free public schooling. Public schooling is available to these fundamentalists only on condition that they do things they view as at odds with salvation…Let us concede that the mandatory reading program interferes with these parents' ability to teach their children their particular religious views. Whether this is a violation of moral rights is another question.[32]

The problem with this concession is that it does not come to grips with the issue of compulsion raised by Boggs. Boggs's point is that reading does more than interfere with the teaching of religious beliefs; reading the relevant materials is, by itself, a violation of the parents'—and possibly the children's—religious beliefs. Having mentioned the problem with Lively's argument, Macedo simply trots out Lively's conclusion: the reading program makes changes in beliefs more likely, but it does not require any acts contrary to religious belief. This won't do.

There is no avoiding the fact the reading program requires children to take religiously proscribed actions (at least from their parents' perspective). Any liberal defence of the reading program, be it political or comprehensive, must face up to this conflict. The question is: Can political liberalism defend the reading program in a way that imposes less of a conceptual cost on religious beliefs than that imposed by comprehensive liberalism?

As I pointed out in the previous section, Lively's comments concerning indoctrination are as open to Kymlicka as they are to political liberals. Autonomy liberals would not endorse a form of education that would require students to affirm particular religious views or perform what they regard as objectionable religious ceremonies. On the other hand, there is no question that the reading program encourages the form of critical reflection that Kymlicka endorses.[33] As Lively admits, exposure to different cultural and religious ideas, as objects of legitimate classroom discussion, makes it more likely that children will regard their own views as objects of critical reflection. How, then, can Macedo avoid the implication that the reading program commits us to autonomy liberalism?

Here we come back to the notion of neutrality of aim. For Macedo, the purpose of the reading program is to teach children the forms of civic virtue appropriate to a liberal society. It helps them to develop the thinking skills required for the exercise of democratic citizenship, and it fosters a sense of identification and solidarity with citizens who hold different religious and moral views. That the program also turns out to encourage critical reflection on one's own conception of the good is purely accidental. The purpose of the program is appropriately neutral, so its unintended consequences should be accepted.

But, as Stolzenberg notes, "practices are not wholly defined by their intended purposes."[34] Suppose that Macedo is right about the requirements of public education or, at the very least, the legitimacy of the school board's discretion concerning the disputed requirements. We need to ask how this reflects upon persons whose moral and religious commitments are overridden for the sake of civic virtue.

Proper development of the civic virtues of democratic deliberation and political tolerance apparently requires that children be exposed to a range of different moral religious ideas. Those children who do not receive this education are less likely to make effective and politically tolerant citizens than those who do receive it. Naturally, then, many fundamentalist parents draw the further implication that political liberals such as Macedo see fundamentalist religious commitments as a threat to civil society and political tolerance. Macedo may respond that it is not the commitments themselves that run afoul of political liberalism, but the way some fundamentalists wish to teach them. What seems suspicious to fundamentalists, however, is the fact that even political liberals candidly admit that the preferred educational regime is one that makes their children's retention of fundamentalist beliefs much less likely.

Galston picks up on these concerns, claiming that there is no solid evidence that indicates exposure to difference through public education is required for the promotion of civic virtue and political tolerance (here his concerns are close to Boggs's response to Kennedy). He claims that parents can easily teach their children to be tolerant of rival views, and to respect other people's liberty, without any detailed examination of these rival views or the persons who hold them.[35]

Galston's view makes sense in light of his commitment to political liberalism's detachment from particular comprehensive commitments. Suppose, as political liberals claim, there is a wide variety of different reasonable comprehensive conceptions, all of which are compatible with liberty and political tolerance. If so, then it is reasonable to assume that an educational regime rooted in any one of these conceptions can provide children with adequate reasons for respecting liberty and political tolerance. Thus, if we include monist, faith-based communities among the group of reasonable conceptions, we should think that their preferred educational regimes can promote liberal political values as well. Clearly, many of these communities see exposure to different social views as interfering with their preferred conception of deliberation about the good.

Macedo, however, thinks that exposure to difference is crucial to the development of political virtues. But why? To be fair, there is a significant difference between the theoretical justification of the commitment to liberty and the development of the virtues and dispositions of character that support it in daily life. Fundamentalist education might succeed on the former front but still fail on the latter.

Macedo could argue that in exposing children to the experiences and stories of different cultures and groups, we help to foster a sense of trust between various social factions. Children are able to see people with different views of the good and religion as fellow human beings with common experiences, as people who can be trusted for the purposes of social cooperation. On this view, the point of exposure to different ideas is not think about those ideas so much as to develop a sense of fellow feeling with those who hold them.

Now this is a plausible claim. And relying on this idea would strengthen the claim that the encouragement of critical reflection is merely an accidental by-product of promoting civic virtue. But I doubt that this particular goal could justify the full range of controversial readings within the Holt curriculum, which contains various literary works, including science fiction. In addition to fostering a sense of identity with those who endorse rival conceptions of the good, the Holt curriculum is also designed to foster speculative thought about a wide range of issues.

But if the full Holt curriculum is well designed to promote a sense of solidarity with one's fellow citizens, then the implication is that hostility to critical reflection is closely aligned with hostility to civic virtue. In other words, those who are patently unwilling to reflect on their own conception of the good are expected to have only tenuous commitments to civic virtues such as political tolerance. If that is the case, then for practical purposes, political liberalism's conception of education ends up endorsing Kymlicka's ideal of critical reflection. But whereas Kymlicka can lead with the idea that critical reflection is in people's interests, political liberals must stand firmly on the claim that those who are hostile to critical reflection are untrustworthy.

Avoiding Direct Confrontation with Parents' Beliefs

Political liberalism claims to remain neutral between various reasonable conceptions of the good, but Macedo's endorsement of the *Mozert* result commits him, for all intents and purposes, to a view of reasonableness that favours comprehensive liberalism. Persons who believe that critical reflection or exposure to different views harms their children (in terms of salvation) don't seem to receive any more concessions from political liberals than they do from autonomy liberals.

Is there some additional way in which political liberalism could limit the conceptual cost that civic education imposes on fundamentalist religious beliefs? I consider three alternatives: (1) value pluralism, (2) straightforward concession of truth, and (3) truth "bracketing." I conclude that political liberals, like autonomy liberals, must simply deny the truth of the *Mozert* parents' beliefs.

VALUABLE WAYS OF LIFE   First, consider one of the standard expressions of regret that liberals offer when they endorse policies that offend the commitments of a religious or cultural minority. They say that "the way of life or religion in question is valuable. However, in the context in question, the value of maintaining political virtue is more important." This way of speaking appears to avoid judgments concerning religious beliefs, but the appearance is deceiving. Speaking in this way takes the religious group's beliefs and practices as a whole and judges them valuable. The underlying notion of worth derives from a commitment to value pluralism along Raz's lines. We say that, overall, the religion provides its members with one possible interesting and worthwhile way of life among others (since we are clearly not conceding that their way is the only way).

This is a powerful form of confirmation, but it is also one that cannot be reconciled with fundamentalists' understanding of their commitments. From the perspective of value pluralism, many of their beliefs—ones concerning sin and divine retribution for instance—are instrumentally valuable in that they help to hold a religious culture or way of life together. But in a deeper sense, value pluralism judges these beliefs—as the religious parties themselves understand them—to be false. They are mistaken, just as all monist commitments about the good are mistaken.

CONCESSION OF TRUTH   Political liberals cannot appeal to value pluralism. Nor can they can concede that the *Mozert* parents' beliefs are true but trumped by considerations of civic virtue. The *Mozert* parents claim that, among other things, the reading program requires their children to commit a mortal sin by reading religiously proscribed texts. Conceding the truth of this belief results in a rather odd expectation. Parents should allow their children's salvation to be compromised in order for the state to prepare everyone else's children for damnation as well. Obviously, political liberals don't think parents should see the reading program in these terms. The question is: Can truth bracketing or epistemic abstinence provide them with something better?

TRUTH BRACKETING   Macedo believes that political liberalism offers a way in which parents can retain their religious beliefs (continue to maintain their truth) by limiting the application of these beliefs. As long as religious beliefs are restricted to the private or religious sphere, then public philosophy need not make judgments concerning their truth or falsity.

Fundamentalists resist bracketing the truth of religious claims, Stolzenberg insists, for such a stance lacks religious seriousness. The "essential point" for fundamentalists is that "the objective study of religion, and objective approaches to knowledge in general, are quintessentially secular humanist activities." On Stolzenberg's account, the liberal demand that we not rely upon religious grounds or invoke religious truths in politics gives the *religious* opponents of fundamentalism all that they have sought. Fundamentalists have every reason, therefore, to make holy war against liberalism.

Such a conclusion would be far too hasty because Stolzenberg's analysis does not apply to political liberalism. The political liberal avoids saying anything about how religion is to be studied: that is left to churches and other private groups. The political liberal can live with the notion that fundamentalism may be the truth in the religious sphere—so long as it does not claim political authority.[36] (emphasis in original)

There are two problems with Macedo's description of how truth bracketing works in this context. First, it seems obvious that by using the Holt series a liberal state does, to some degree, make religion an object of study. Whatever pragmatic or political reasons Macedo may offer for this program, he cannot maintain that it leaves religion untouched for the private or religious sphere.

Second, Macedo's division between the religious sphere and the political sphere accommodates only those religious views that are already sympathetic to autonomy liberalism. It is easy to set the truth of one's beliefs aside if those beliefs are readily interpreted in a way that keeps them out of the political realm. But the religious beliefs of the *Mozert* parents are not so easily constrained or reinterpreted.

Political liberals, of course, claim that the bracketing of true beliefs is possible because many persons in our society claim adherence to strong religious views as well as liberal institutions. A familiar example of this bracketing is the idea that we must respect the liberty of those who reject religious truth, even where this rejection comes at the cost of eternal damnation. Although their religious commitments seem to demand that political institutions be geared to saving the souls of those who reject the truth, reasonable fundamentalists are able to set their beliefs aside for the sake of politics. Thus, political liberals expect the *Mozert* parents to accomplish a similar feat of truth bracketing with respect to civic education.

However, political liberals' evidence of successful truth bracketing is inadequate. It is not enough say to say that some self-described fundamentalists claim to have accomplished this task. For it is at least possible that these self-described fundamentalists have retained only the appearance of radical non-liberal religious commitments. The real basis of their commitment to liberalism may have more to do with a move toward Kymlicka's fallibilism or a deeper notion of religious pluralism (even if they do not wish to admit this to themselves).

Political liberals do not wish to investigate this question. As long as fundamentalists do not challenge the liberal conception of politics, political liberals leave the question of how politics and religion are reconciled to the private sphere. This approach might be acceptable were it not for the fact that the *supposed* success of reasonable fundamentalists' truth bracketing is held against fundamentalists such as the *Mozert* parents ("reasonable fundamentalists can do it, so you can too"). Fundamentalists of this stripe do not believe that the truth bracketing is successful; they believe that liberal politics comes at a substantial cost to the content of their beliefs. In the context of this dispute, I see no good reason to privilege the testimony of one self-described fundamentalist group over another.

Moreover, the standard example of successful truth bracketing, even if it is successful, doesn't show that the *Mozert* parents should be able to bracket their beliefs (insofar as these beliefs concern their children). We may reconcile ourselves to the idea that other adult persons, particularly those outside our own family, who refuse to accept religious truth must be left free to suffer eternal damnation. Attempting to force religious truth on such persons could threaten the political institutions that secure our own freedom to live in accordance with religious truth.

But it is far from obvious that one can show the same sense of detachment concerning the eternal damnation of one's own children. Can a parent who takes her religious beliefs seriously bracket those beliefs when she considers what is best for children, regarding education or any other issue? Consider an analogy. I may be able to bracket my beliefs concerning the harmful effects of dangerous physical sports such as boxing in deliberating about the political liberties of my fellow citizens. I may even be able to bracket this belief when thinking about the moral authority that other parents should be afforded regarding their children. Perhaps my fellow citizens should be allowed to box, and perhaps they should even be allowed to encourage their children to do so. But if I genuinely believe that the sport is dangerous and lacking in redeeming social value, I will make great effort to prevent my children from engaging in it or even taking an interest in it. And I would not appreciate it if public educational institutions interfered with my efforts in this regard.[37]

In the context of caring for one's children, it is particularly difficult, if not impossible, to bracket one's comprehensive views about morality and religion. In fact, it's hard to see how the *Mozert* parents could really hold their stated views about damnation, yet be willing to expose their own children to this fate for the purpose of civic education. This would be a sure sign that either they don't really care about their children in the way that parents should or that they don't really hold their stated beliefs about damnation.

One might, of course, be able to accept the idea that her children must eventually be afforded the liberty to damn themselves. It is quite another thing, however, to say that one's children should be forced to take actions— actions that constitute mortal sins—before they reach adulthood. It is not much more plausible to say that one's children should be forced to take actions that will seriously diminish their future chances of eternal salvation. I see no way in which truth bracketing can preserve the content of these beliefs.

So political liberals are caught. They cannot endorse the result in *Mozert* without directly confronting and denying parents' religious conception of children's interests. Contrary to Macedo, truth bracketing doesn't allow political liberals to avoid this confrontation. The only way for liberals to justify the Holt program is for them to assert that autonomy liberalism's conception of children's interests is superior to the religious conception endorsed by dissenting parents.

Conclusion

Political liberalism cannot provide us with an uncontroversial justification of the result in *Mozert*. Instead, we must face up to the conceptual cost that this result imposes on parents' religious beliefs and their account of their children's interests. A liberal state should not pretend to deny the reality of the conflict between the state's conception of children's interests and the rival conception of children's interests held by dissenting parents.

The only plausible moral defence of the outcome in *Mozert* is one that is based on autonomy liberalism and the idea that children have an essential interest in developing their capacity for critical reflection. However, it is far from clear that autonomy liberals should, all things considered, endorse the result in *Mozert*. Once we see that political liberalism's uncontroversial defence of the Holt reading program fails, we are forced to confront the stresses that this program places on the parent–child relationship. Costs to parental autonomy and legitimate questions about the efficacy of the Holt program should give autonomy liberals pause if they are otherwise inclined to impose such programs in the face of serious parental opposition.

Notes

1 406 U.S. 205 (1972).

2 *Mozert v. Hawkins County Board of Education* 827 F.2d 1058 (6th Cir. 1987), 1060; 102 A.L.R. Fed. 497. See Stephen Macedo, *Diversity and Distrust* (Harvard University Press, 2000).

3 Moreover, the historical uniqueness and isolation of the Amish may entitle them to unique exemptions from state authority. Amy Gutmann argues that even autonomy liberals may regard the Amish as, to some degree, a distinct political community that falls outside the authority of the surrounding liberal democratic state. For this reason, *Yoder* is far from ideal as a practical example for discussing the general issue of authority over moral education. Amy Gutmann, "Civic Education and Social Diversity" *Ethics* 105 (1995): 565–72.

4 I thank Rob Noggle for his suggesting that I speak to the differences between *Mozert* and *Yoder*. For additional discussion of these cases, see William A. Galston, "Two Concepts of Liberalism" *Ethics* 105 (1995): 516; Kwame Anthony Appiah, *The Ethics of Identity* (Princeton, NJ: Princeton University Press, 2005), 80, 209–10, 326 n. 69, 327 n. 73. See also the following review of Appiah's book: Alan Ryan, "The Magic of 'I,'" *New York Review of Books* 52 (April 28, 2005): 35–37, 37. With respect to *Mozert*, Appiah laments the Board's refusal to maintain the compromise worked out earlier between local schools and parents. As Appiah notes, Stephen Macedo recognizes the concern that liberal educational policies may drive religious parents to remove their children from the public system. The limited exposure to diversity in an accommodationist public system may be better than the lack of exposure to diversity in highly conservative private religious schools. However, Macedo remains committed to the result in *Mozert*. See Stephen Macedo "Transformative Constitutionalism and the Case of Religion," *Political Theory* 26 (1998): 56, 73.

5 Stephen Macedo, "Liberal Civic Education and Religious Fundamentalism: The Case of God v. John Rawls?" *Ethics* 105 (1995): 475.

6 I thank Rob Noggle for pointing out the importance of recognizing the difficulties that *Mozert* poses from the perspective of autonomy liberalism.

7 *Mozert v. Hawkins*, 1060.

8 Ibid.

9 Ibid., 1062.

10 The list above provides only part of a list of parental complaints compiled by Stolzenberg. There are nineteen items on Stolzenberg's full list. However, the complaints noted above give a clear idea of both the seriousness and religious character of the plaintiffs' objections to the Holt Series. Nomi Maya Stolzenberg, "'He Drew a Circle That Shut Me Out': Assimilation, Indoctrination, and the Paradox of a Liberal Education." *Harvard Law Review* 106 (1993): 596–97.

11 *Mozert v. Hawkins*, 1066.

12 Ibid., 1064. I find some ambiguity in Lively's decision. At some points he seems to regard the idea that reading does not an act contrary to religious belief as a

conceptual truth about the nature of religious beliefs. At other times he seems to reject this claim on the grounds that the plaintiffs offered no evidence that reading the Holt materials was, on their own terms, a religiously proscribed action.

13 Ibid., 1070.

14 Ibid., 1075–76.

15 Ibid., 1077–78.

16 John Rawls, *Political Liberalism* (New York: Columbia University Press, 1996), 199.

17 Amy Gutmann, *Democratic Education* (Princeton, NJ: Princeton University Press, 1987), 30–31.

18 Stephen Macedo, "Liberal Civic Education and Religious Fundamentalism," 473.

19 Ibid., 474.

20 Ibid., 475; Rawls, *Political Liberalism*, 475–76.

21 Stephen Macedo, "Liberal Civic Education and Religious Fundamentalism," 477–78.

22 John Rawls, *Political Liberalism*, 13.

23 I do not think that Macedo's description is particularly fair to Gutmann, but I will not take this issue up in detail here.

24 Joseph Raz, *The Morality of Freedom* (Oxford: Oxford University Press, 1986), 204–206.

25 Will Kymlicka, *Liberalism, Community and Culture* (Oxford: Oxford University Press, 1989), 10.

26 Ibid., 12.

27 Ibid., 17.

28 Will Kymlicka, "Liberalism Individualism and Liberal Neutrality," *Ethics* 99 (1989): 900–901.

29 William Galston, *Liberal Pluralism* (Cambridge: University Press, 2002), 102.

30 Ibid., 228.

31 William Galston, *Liberal Purposes* (Cambridge: Cambridge University Press, 1991), 230–31, 248–56. Galston also points out that social pressures outside the family, including the media, exert a pressure toward conformity. It is naive to think that there is a wide and wonderful diversity of options from which children could freely choose conceptions of the good but for the conformist or illiberal religious beliefs of their parents. William Galston, "Individual Experience and Social Policy: Thinking Practically about Overcoming Racial and Ethnic Prejudice," in Stephen Macedo and Yael Tamir, eds., *Moral and Political Education*, NOMOS *XLIII* (New York: New York University Press, 2001), 425–33.

32 Stephen Macedo, "Liberal Civic Education and Religious Fundamentalism," 472.

33 However, as I note at the end of the second section of this chapter, the Holt program, though it encourages this form of critical reflection, may not turn

out to be the best strategy for making children into effective or successful critical agents.

34 Nomi Maya Stolzenberg, "'He Drew a Circle That Shut Me Out,'" 592.

35 William Galston, *Liberal Purposes*, 248–56.

36 Stephen Macedo, "Liberal Civic Education and Religious Fundamentalism," 479–80.

37 I thank Rob Noggle for pointing out the value of illustrating this point about bracketing through the use of non-religious examples. For what it's worth, while I chose this example, these aren't my personal views about boxing. I'm a fan of the sport.

SEVEN

Education in a Liberal Society:
Implications of *Ross*

KAREN WENDLING

In this chapter, I examine *Ross v. New Brunswick School District No. 15*,[1] a 1996 Supreme Court of Canada decision involving the education of children. In *Ross*, the Supreme Court weighed in on a debate now raging in the philosophical literature. In the past ten years, *Ethics* has devoted a special issue to a "Symposium on Citizenship, Democracy, and Education,"[2] and a spate of books, chapters in books, and articles have been published on this topic.[3] Although most of the literature has been written since the *Ross* ruling,[4] the authors—American, British, and two Canadians—appear unaware of this decision. The literature tends to focus on American cases concerning freedom of religion and education, especially *Wisconsin v. Yoder*[5] and *Mozert v. Hawkins*.[6] The issues raised in *Ross* sharpen the debate, however. What happens when anti-Semitism and other forms of hatred are part and parcel of a teacher's religious and political beliefs? Can the mere presence of a teacher with such beliefs create a "poisoned" educational environment for children, even if the teacher does not profess these beliefs in the classroom? These issues curl around the philosophical debate like the first wisps of smoke from a previously unnoticed fire. We might ask further questions left unaddressed by the Court's decision in *Ross*. Suppose some parents with anti-Semitic or other hate-based views choose to send their children to a private school where such views are part of the curriculum. Should such schools be permitted in a free and democratic society? I will argue that they should not.

The argument takes the following form. In the first section, I briefly summarize the facts in the *Ross* decision, and discuss the court's Canadian Charter of Human Rights–based arguments concerning the political function of education in a free and democratic society. Next, I broaden the application of the *Ross* decision with respect to the complainant. I argue that the fact that the complainant was Jewish, and the fact that he had a child in the Moncton school system, should have been irrelevant to the Court's decision. I then examine the principles underlying education in a liberal society and I justify state-imposed standards on the political content and atmosphere of education. In the following section, I broaden the application of the *Ross* decision with respect to the institution. I argue that the court's reasoning should apply to non-public as well as public schools, and in fact to all institutions and organizations in which children (particularly young children) are educated. Finally, I briefly discuss the implication of the *Ross* decision for parental rights and the public–private distinction.

Ross and the Political Function of Education

Malcolm Ross was a notorious public school teacher at Magnetic Hill School in Moncton, New Brunswick. He believed that an international conspiracy of Jews was attempting to overthrow Christian civilization. Unlike Jim Keegstra, the Eckville, Alberta, high school teacher with similar beliefs who was convicted of promoting hate propaganda,[7] Ross did not teach his views in the classroom. He expressed his views outside the classroom, on television, in letters to the editor, and in four books or pamphlets.

In 1988, David Attis, a Jewish parent of a child enrolled in the Moncton school district (New Brunswick School District No. 15), filed a complaint of discrimination with the New Brunswick Human Rights Commission. Attis alleged that the Moncton school board discriminated against him and his children in the provision of services on the basis of religion and ancestry, in violation of s. 5(1) of the New Brunswick Human Rights Act.[8] The Human Rights Commission's Board of Inquiry found that, by failing to take action against Ross despite repeated complaints, the school board had tacitly endorsed Ross's views and had created a discriminatory environment in that school district for Jewish and other students who were members of visible minorities. Clause 2 of the board of inquiry's order required the school board to

(a) suspend Ross without pay for eighteen months;

(b) appoint Ross to a non-teaching position if one for which he was qualified became available (at which time his suspension would end);

(c) terminate Ross's employment at the end of the suspension if, during that time, he had not been offered and accepted a non-teaching position;

(d) terminate Ross's employment immediately if, at any time, he:

  (i) published, or wrote for publication, anything mentioning a Jewish or Zionist conspiracy, or attacking Jews, or

  (ii) published, sold or distributed any of his four books or pamphlets.[9]

Ross appealed the Human Rights Commission's decision. He argued, first, that the board of inquiry exceeded its jurisdiction in the finding of discrimination and the order to the school board. Second, he argued that the order violated his freedoms of religion and expression, which are protected by ss. 2(a) and 2(b) of the Canadian Charter of Rights and Freedoms.[10] The appeal ultimately was heard by the Supreme Court of Canada. On the jurisdictional issue, the Supreme Court ruled that the Moncton school board's failure to discipline Ross did indeed constitute discrimination under s. 5(1) of the New Brunswick Human Rights Act, and that the Human Rights Commission had not exceeded its jurisdiction in so finding. On the constitutional issues, the court ruled that, while the Commission's order did violate the freedom of religion and expression protections of ss. 2(a) and 2(b) of the Charter, clauses 2(a)–(c) of the board of inquiry's order satisfied the *Oakes* requirements for a s. 1 exception to those constitutional protections.[11] That is, the Supreme Court found that the Human Rights Commission's objective, remedying the discrimination caused by the school board's inaction, was of pressing and substantial concern in a free and democratic society, and that the first three of its remedies were proportional to the objective. Hence, clauses 2(a)–(c) of the board of inquiry's order met the *Oakes* requirements for a s. 1 exception to Ross's freedoms of religion and expression. The Court ruled that clause 2(d) of the order failed the "minimal impairment" criterion of the proportionality portion of the *Oakes* test, however, and so was unconstitutional.

Ross was not charged with the criminal offence of promoting hatred against members of an identifiable group or with any other criminal or civil offence. This was a human rights case involving the provision of services available to the public—in this case, education. The New Brunswick Human Rights Commission had ordered the Moncton school board to remove Ross from his teaching position because his out-of-classroom activities had created a "poisoned educational environment" at the school, which violated s. 5(1) of the New Brunswick Human Rights Act. The case required the Court to discuss in some depth the purpose of education in a free and democratic society and the role of teachers in education. This discussion occurs primarily in two parts of the *Ross* decision: in the section on discrimination which begins the examination of the constitutional issues, and in the section on the application of s. 1 of the Charter.

The first discussion in the section on discrimination sketches the political purpose of education, and examines the role of teachers as "the medium for the educational message" (para. 44).[12] Writing for the Court, Justice La Forest stated, "A school is a communication centre for a whole range of values and aspirations of a society. In part, it defines the values that transcend society through the educational medium. The school is an arena for the exchange of ideas and must, therefore, be premised upon principles of tolerance and impartiality so that all persons within the school environment feel equally free to participate."[13] Teachers are crucial here. They "are inextricably linked to the integrity of the school system. Teachers occupy positions of trust and confidence, and exert considerable influence over their students as a result of their positions."[14] Not only must they actually model the appropriate political values, they also must be perceived to do so. Even their conduct out of the classroom and away from school may be relevant in some circumstances: "[W]here a 'poisoned' environment within the school system is traceable to the off-duty conduct of a teacher that is likely to produce a corresponding loss of confidence in the teacher and the system as a whole, then the off-duty conduct of the teacher is relevant."[15]

The Court makes a distinction between political and non-political values here. It is careful to focus on the roles of schools and teachers in modelling appropriate *political* values, and not particular or controversial moral, religious, aesthetic, or other sorts of values. La Forest explicitly states that teachers should not be held to "more onerous moral standards of behaviour," nor should their private lives or beliefs suddenly be put under the public's microscope.[16] A teacher's on- or off-the-job conduct can be subject to legitimate scrutiny only when it contributes to a poisoned environment that undermines the political values of equal citizenship on which the Charter is grounded. Notice that this is not a s. 15 case, based on the equality provision of the Charter, however.[17] This is a s. 1 case: according to La Forest, the political values referred to here are those without which freedom and democracy, and thus the Charter, cannot exist. La Forest cites the words of Justice Dickson from a previous Supreme Court decision: "A free society is one which aims at equality with respect to the enjoyment of fundamental freedoms and I say this without any reliance upon s. 15 of the Charter. Freedom must surely be founded in respect for the inherent dignity and the inviolable rights of the human person."[18] Because of the trust and responsibility vested in teachers, if a teacher's conduct contributes to a poisoned educational environment that undermines public confidence in "the inherent dignity and the inviolable rights of the human person," that conduct falls within the public's (and the Court's) legitimate purview.

The second discussion of education focuses on schools' influence on the political development of young children. La Forest cites a previous Supreme Court decision in which he wrote, "Whether one views it from an economic, social, cultural or civic point of view, the education of the young is critically important in our society."[19] He also quoted from the US Supreme Court's decision in *Brown v. Board of Education*: "Today, education is perhaps the most important function of state and local governments.... It is the very foundation of good citizenship. Today it is a principal instrument in awakening the child to cultural values, in preparing him for later professional training, and in helping him to adjust normally to his environment."[20] Schools teach more than just employment-related skills such as reading, writing, and mathematics; they also teach the political values of citizenship and of participation in society. In a free and democratic society grounded by the Charter, schools must inculcate—or, at a minimum, model—liberal democratic values.

The fact that Ross taught in a grade school was particularly relevant. Young children are extremely impressionable; they "are especially vulnerable to the messages conveyed by their teachers."[21] The foundations of the political values upholding "the inherent dignity and the inviolable rights of the human person" are laid during the grade school years. Undermining those foundations can have a serious impact on children's future citizenship, as well as on their current and future self-respect and self-esteem. "The importance of ensuring an equal and discrimination-free educational environment, and the perception of fairness and tolerance in the classroom are paramount in the education of young children. This helps foster self-respect and acceptance by others," La Forest wrote.[22] Grade school teachers who model inegalitarian values damage children's political prospects, and this undermines the political foundations of Canadian society.

Broadening the Application of *Ross*, Part 1:
The Complainant

In *Ross v. New Brunswick School District No. 15*, the Supreme Court upheld a specific order by the Human Rights Commission's Board of Inquiry. A Jewish parent alleged that his daughter, who attended the Moncton public school system in which Ross taught, was subject to a poisoned educational environment. In this section, I argue that the facts that the complainant was Jewish and that his daughter was a student in the school district in which Ross was employed are irrelevant.

A Jewish Complainant

The New Brunswick Human Rights Commission's Board of Inquiry found evidence of "a poisoned educational environment in which Jewish children perceive the potential for misconduct and are likely to feel isolated and suffer a loss of self-esteem on the basis of their Judaism" in the Moncton school system.[23] They concluded that Ross's out-of-classroom conduct contributed to the poisoned environment, and the Supreme Court upheld that conclusion. According to the Court, "education awakens children to the values a society hopes to foster and to nurture."[24] These values include but are not limited to "respect for the inherent dignity of the human person, commitment to social justice and equality, accommodation of a wide variety of beliefs, respect for cultural and group identity, and faith in social and political institutions which enhance the participation of individuals and groups in society."[25] Ross's presence as a teacher in the school undermined these values and lessened the likelihood that the children attending the school would come to accept these values as their own.

Should it matter that the complainant, David Attis, was Jewish? No. Suppose that something like this situation occurred elsewhere, and, for whatever reason, no parent of a child subject to intimidation and discrimination based on group membership complained. Unfortunately, it is not hard to imagine that the atmosphere in a community could be so poisoned that no parent from the targeted group(s) would dare complain. Even so, parents of non-targeted children might object to the existence of a poisoned educational environment in which children are exposed to such inegalitarian values, despite the fact that their own children are unlikely to be the victims of inegalitarian intimidation and discrimination. Parents might well object to their children being taught to be bigots. Indeed, if parents take seriously the values underlying the Charter, they should so object. The values underlying the Charter ought to matter to all Canadians, not just to those who are, who have been, or who are likely to be subject to discrimination. A complaint from a non-Jewish parent in the Ross case might have been supported on slightly different grounds under the New Brunswick Human Rights Act, but it should have been supported. All citizens have a stake in children developing political values that support "respect for the inherent dignity and the inviolable rights of the human person."

A Child in the School System

David Attis's daughter Yona was a student in the Moncton public school system; she was one of the students who gave evidence of the poisoned educational environment in the school. But should it matter that the complainant had a child in the school system? No. Indeed, if the educational environment was so poisoned that all the Jewish parents chose either to move or to send their children to other school districts rather than subject them to the intimidation and discrimination in the Moncton system, the parents of those children would have had clear grounds for a human rights complaint. There might have been other reasons that no Jewish students attended public school in Moncton, though there might still have been Jews living in the city. Suppose these Jewish children were taunted and harassed by children from the Moncton public school board. The board of inquiry might well have concluded that the teacher's behaviour had contributed to a poisoned environment not for Jewish students attending the school district but for Jewish children living in the city. The board could have applied a broad interpretation to the phrase "accommodation, services or facilities available to the public" in s. 5(1)(b) of the Human Rights Act, or it could have relied on a different section of the act.[26]

The fact that those for whom the environment is poisoned might not be students of the Moncton school board is irrelevant to the obligations of both Ross and the Moncton school board. Ross's and the school board's obligations to model and not to undermine the political values of Canadian society, including but not limited to respect for all people, still apply to them in their educational roles. Students must learn that these values apply not only to their interactions with other students in the school district but also to all those with whom they come into contact. (This applies especially to their contact with other children, who are particularly vulnerable to the effects of discrimination.) Certainly that is the point of schools' and teachers' responsibilities to inculcate political values in their students in the first place. "Extracurricular" discrimination would be evidence of greater, not lesser, failures on the parts of teachers and the school board. It would constitute evidence that teachers' influence extends beyond the school or even beyond the school system.

Education and Children's Interests

The *Ross* decision has wider implications for the education of children than those discussed by the Supreme Court. The case intersects with the growing debate in the literature on education for citizenship because it highlights children's needs and interests, rather than only parents' and the state's. Most of the philosophical literature focuses on the conflict between the demands of liberal citizenship, on one hand, and the wishes of parents to educate their children according to their non-liberal or non-democratic beliefs, on the other hand. That is, the literature focuses on the conflict between parents and the state over who should control the education of children. Generally, the clashes concern parents' claims that they are being denied religious freedom, as was the case in *Wisconsin v. Yoder* and *Mozert v. Hawkins*. In *Yoder*, Amish parents were successful in their request to remove their children from school at fourteen rather than sixteen on the grounds that the extra schooling tended to undermine the Amish way of life. In *Mozert*, fundamentalist Christian parents were denied their request to exempt their children from a reading program in a public school that presented a diversity of viewpoints with which the parents disagreed. (See Ramsay, in this volume, for further discussion of the *Mozert* case.)

What tends to get lost in these discussions is consideration of the independent interests of children, separate from those of their parents or the state.[27] (See Macleod, in this volume, for a discussion of children's entitlements.) Children's interests were paramount in the *Ross* decision, however. The Supreme Court discusses the sort of educational environment required for children to develop into equal citizens of a free and democratic society. The Court does cite an American decision, but it is one in which children's interests took priority: *Brown v. Board of Education*, not *Yoder* or *Mozert*. In *Brown*, the US Supreme Court argued that segregated schools harmed the developing self-respect of African-American schoolchildren: "To separate them [African-American children] from others of similar age and qualifications solely because of their race generates a feeling of inferiority as to their status in the community that may affect their hearts and minds in a way unlikely ever to be undone."[28] Since self-respect is necessary for equal citizenship, and since equal citizenship is a requirement of democracy, this cannot be allowed.[29] Any interests of white parents in keeping the schools segregated were outweighed by the requirements of equal citizenship for African-American children.

Someone might object that this merely assumes the state's case for priority over parents' interests in cases of conflict; it doesn't argue for it. And why should the state's claims trump parents'? After all, parents bear the primary physical, moral, and financial responsibility for children. No one argues that children are better off if they are raised by the state rather than by parents. So it is parents, not the state, who should retain the ultimate control over what their children are taught, the objector might conclude.

Do children have any independent claims here? Some writers acknowledge that parents' claims can be justified only against a background conception of normal human development. For example, parents may not starve or beat their children and must raise them to be contributing members of the society[30] (assuming this is compatible with the child's inborn physical and mental capacities, of course). But notice that such a background conception is not normatively neutral. What counts as "normal human development," and to whom it applies, varies widely from society to society. A slave society has very different standards for slaves than for free people. A strongly gender-divided society has different standards for women and men, and in some cases these standards are so different that female children receive less education and even less food and medical care than male children.[31] States have different standards for citizens than for non-citizens, or at least for residents and non-residents.

We might wonder whether a society is justified in imposing its conception of normal human development on parents. In particular, may a liberal society impose a normatively liberal conception of normal human development on non-consenting, non-liberal parents? The answer here must be yes. This is because background conceptions, such as what counts as "normal human development," must be political and not individual. Otherwise, the state would lack justification for punishing any law-breakers who do not accept society's rules—especially psychopaths and sociopaths, who accept no rules other than their own. Shared political background conceptions ground the authority of the state, not only to punish transgressors but to make the rules that determine what counts as a transgression in the first place.

Notice that I am not arguing that the state's interests in education trump parents' interests. Rather, I am arguing that children's independent claims to normal human development trump any contrary claims and that the correct normative standard for "normal human development" is political

and not individual. Unless children have independent claims, there are
no grounds to object even to parents who murder their children, much
less to anything else parents do to children. (See Brennan and White, in this
volume, for a discussion of restrictions on parents' behaviour based on
children's rights. See also Purdy, in this volume, for a discussion of parents' responsibilities and children's rights.)

But, someone might object, some religions do not accept the basic tenets
of liberalism; imposing a liberal background conception of normal human
development violates the freedoms of expression and religion guaranteed
by s. 2 of the Charter. The correct standard for what is permitted by freedom of expression and freedom of religion must be political, however. The
state rightly forbids murder and assault, even if committed in the name of
religion. No one can claim religious freedom as grounds for refusing to
provide services available to the public; that is, businesses may not refuse
to serve Jews or members of certain ethnic or racial groups because their
religion frowns on such people. The state forbids polygamy, even though
some religions permit it. And the state forbids forcible conversion of non-
believers. Section 1 guarantees all the rights and freedoms set out in the
Charter, "subject only to such reasonable limits prescribed by law as can be
demonstrably justified in a free and democratic society." Practices or policies that undermine the very grounds of a free and democratic society
must be restricted. Thus schools may inculcate any beliefs consistent with
liberal requirements (as most religious beliefs are), but they may not inculcate beliefs at odds with such requirements. Even the mere presence of
a teacher such as Malcolm Ross violated this requirement, despite the fact
that Ross did not profess his beliefs in the classroom. His notoriety created a poisoned educational environment for Jewish and other minority
children incompatible with the requirements of equal citizenship in a free
and democratic society, the Supreme Court ruled. The Court correctly
applied a political standard to the interests of children in becoming equal
citizens.

The Institution

In this section, I argue that the facts that Ross taught in a public school
and that the discriminatory atmosphere occurred in a school are also irrelevant. Children's developing capacities for equal citizenship must be
protected in all educational environments, whether these be religious or
secular, whether schools or other organizations.

A Public School

Ross taught in a public school district, and so his behaviour and the school board's inaction clearly fell under the purview of the New Brunswick Human Rights Act, which deals with property, employment, accommodation, goods, services, or facilities "available to the public." Should it matter that the Moncton school board was public, though? No. The act applies not only to public services and facilities but to any services, facilities, accommodation, etc., to which the public has access. This includes private and other non-public services, facilities, accommodation, etc., including private schools.

According to the Supreme Court, education instills political values in children. This includes especially "equality with respect to the enjoyment of fundamental freedoms," which is an analytic requirement of political freedom.[32] The political values should not be considered important only for students in public schools, however. Since they are "essential to a free and democratic society,"[33] they must be taught to all children, regardless of the sorts of schools they attend. Provinces set requirements for curricula for children who are educated in private schools or who are home-schooled. Certainly if the provinces have the power to mandate which skills ought to be taught to children, they also have the power to require that these skills include learning and practising the values that underlie Canadian society. If a province does not currently require this, the relevant legislation should be changed. Ideally, these changes should be made by legislatures. However, if legislatures do not make appropriate changes to their education acts, perhaps because the issue is perceived to be too controversial, the courts ought to "read in" the same political requirements for public, denominational, and private schools. Canadians have a stake in *all* children developing the appropriate political values, not just those who attend public schools.

What about s. 29 of the Charter, which states that "Nothing in the Charter abrogates or derogates from any rights or privileges guaranteed by or under the Constitution of Canada in respect of denominational, separate or dissentient schools"? Should this section protect actions similar to Ross's in a non-public school? Moreover, all human rights acts in Canada leave room for legitimate exceptions to their requirements. For example, s. 5(2) of the New Brunswick Human Rights Act states, "Notwithstanding subsection (1), a limitation, specification, exclusion, denial or preference because of sex, physical disability, mental disability, marital status or sexual orientation shall be permitted if such limitation, specification, exclusion, denial or preference is based upon a bona fide qualification as determined by the Commission." Suppose Ross had taught in a private religious school that shared his beliefs and that admitted only children of practising members of the religion to the school. Would this constitute grounds for a s. 29 Charter exception, or a "bona fide qualification" for a human rights code exception, to a requirement that political values be taught to students? No. It might be permissible for such a school to restrict its admissions to children of practising members, but it would be no more justified for such a school to teach political values at odds with the values underlying the Charter than it would be for it to omit teaching children to read. This is especially true of schools that accept public funding, whether directly or in the form of tax credits for parents of children attending the schools, or that have tax-exempt status; if they benefit from public monies, they ought to be subject to public requirements. A requirement that schools teach the values of the system that funds them, directly or indirectly, is surely reasonable.[34]

But no "poisoned educational atmosphere" would be created by such a school, an objector might argue, since only the children of people who agreed with such beliefs would be admitted to the school. As I argued above, however, this still could create a discriminatory environment for children living in the neighbourhood or the city. Furthermore, a free and democratic society requires that citizens see each other as moral and political equals. If it is wrong to view some citizens as less worthy than others, then it must also be wrong for some citizens to view themselves as more worthy than others. A free and democratic society will allow adult citizens to adopt such views about themselves or others; the freedoms of expression and religion allow people to adopt illiberal as well as liberal views.[35] But these freedoms should not allow adults to teach such views to children, who are not yet capable of making free and informed decisions about the sorts of people they wish to be. The background political conception of "normal human development" as development for the requirements of equal citizenship, not the views of dissenting parents, must guide the education of all children.

Other Institutions

Schools certainly are a primary site for the education of children, but they are not the only institution engaged in education.[36] (See Mullin, in this volume, for a discussion of the ways that non-parents are involved in childrearing and education.) Daycare centres, religious organizations, Girl Guides, Boy Scouts, and many other organizations also are "communication centre[s] for a whole range of values and aspirations of a society."[37] Should schools be the *only* such "communication centre" subject to political requirements? No. Any organization that communicates values to children—in particular young children, who are very impressionable, as the court emphasized—ought to be required to foster, or at the very least ought to be forbidden to hinder, development of the appropriate political values. The off-duty conduct of the adults in those organizations who have teacher-like roles also may be subject to public scrutiny under certain circumstances, as is the case with teachers in schools. Poisoned educational environments fall within the ambit of legitimate public scrutiny, no matter in which institution they occur because, once again, citizens have a stake in all children developing the political values that allow a free and democratic society to flourish.

Privacy and Parents' Rights

In *Ross*, as in several other Supreme Court decisions,[38] the court has distinguished between public behaviour on one hand and private beliefs and attitudes on the other. While individuals' private beliefs and attitudes must be given the widest possible constitutional protection, their public behaviours based on those beliefs and attitudes may be subject to publicly defined limits. (Private behaviours are subject only to the requirement that they not infringe the rights of others.) This implies that all educational institutions, including but not limited to schools, must teach children to make appropriate public–private distinctions. Individuals may believe whatever they want in private, and their behaviours as private individuals are subject only to the limitations of the harm principle plus whatever contracts, bargains, or promises they have made. But in their public roles, such as teacher or citizen, individuals' behaviours must meet a higher standard: the behaviours must be consistent with the political values that undergird the Charter. In particular, they must act in ways that demonstrate respect for "the inherent dignity and the inviolable rights of the human person"[39]—that is, the rights and dignity of their fellow citizens. (Not only their fellow citizens, but citizens first and foremost, because these are fundamentally political values.)

Some critics might question whether people either can or should make such public–private distinctions. They might argue that requiring that citizens be able to make these distinctions is a violation of the freedoms of conscience and religion, because some belief systems deny such distinctions. But, as La Forest argued in *Ross* with respect to freedom of religion:

> This Court has affirmed that freedom of religion ensures that every in-
> dividual must be free to hold and to manifest without State interference
> those beliefs and opinions dictated by one's conscience. This freedom is
> not unlimited, however, and is restricted by the right of others to hold and
> to manifest beliefs and opinions of their own, and to be free from injury
> from the exercise of the freedom of religion of others. Freedom of religion
> is subject to such limitations as are necessary to protect public safety,
> order, health or morals and the fundamental rights and freedoms of
> others.[40]

Freedom of religion and freedom of expression must be limited to protect
children's developing capacities for equal citizenship. These limitations
in no way prevent religious education and practice, however. The Charter
proscribes only religious *discrimination*, no matter how deeply or sin-
cerely held the religious beliefs. Most religious education in Canada will be
left untouched by these limits.[41]

Other critics might claim that these requirements violate parents' rights.
Parents' rights are grounded in their responsibilities for their children, and
they require that parents' actions be insulated from public scrutiny, they
might say.[42] (For more on parents' responsibilities, see Narveson and Vopat, in this volume.) No one fully supports a private sphere completely
insulated from the public, however; such a private sphere would, in principle, license child slavery and even child murder. Any view that prohibits
child slavery or murder contains a private sphere with permeable boundaries. This is an analytic truth: the possibility of public intervention for any
reason implies that the private sphere is not inviolable. Parents' rights, like
the freedoms of religion and expression, must be limited by others' rights,
including children's rights—as independent individuals and as future citizens—to normatively liberal human development. Parents' rights to believe
as they wish do not include the right to determine all the content of their
children's education.[43] Children must be educated to become equal citizens,
even if this conflicts with their parents' beliefs.

While this might appear to subject families to the same political requirements as schools, it need not do so. By promoting the values of pluralism
and equal citizenship, schools and other educational institutions can coun-
terbalance beliefs inculcated by parents that are incompatible with respect
for the equal dignity and rights of others. This leaves families the widest
plausible sphere of privacy, without allowing parents to determine irrevo-
cably their children's future beliefs and prospects.

Pluralism is a fact of life in any well-functioning democracy. People will
always disagree about political, religious, and other matters, and these dis-

agreements will sometimes touch on the deepest possible issues of meaning and human purposes. Political respect for the dignity and rights of others requires public tolerance of all views, but it does not require private acceptance. Indeed, the very concept of tolerance, as opposed to acceptance, implies the ability to make distinctions between public and private beliefs and behaviours. Children must be taught that they and all others are equal as citizens. Schools and any other institutions and organizations that deal with the education of children, especially young children, must create an atmosphere in which the values of equal citizenship can flourish.

Notes

1 *Ross v. New Brunswick School District No. 15*, [1996] 1 S.C.R. 825. All references to this decision will be given in the text, citing the appropriate paragraph number from the decision.

2 *Ethics* 105, no. 3 (1995).

3 See, for example, David William Archard, *Children, Family and the State* (Hampshire: Ashgate, 2003); Harry Brighouse, *School Choice and Social Justice* (Oxford: Oxford University Press, 2000); Eamonn Callan, *Creating Citizens: Political Education and Liberal Democracy* (Oxford: Clarendon Press, 1997); William A. Galston, *Liberal Pluralism: The Implications of Value Pluralism for Political Theory and Practice* (Cambridge: Cambridge University Press, 2002); Will Kymlicka, *Politics in the Vernacular: Nationalism, Multiculturalism, and Citizenship* (Oxford: Oxford University Press, 2001); Stephen Macedo, *Diversity and Distrust: Civic Education in a Multicultural Democracy* (Cambridge, MA: Harvard University Press, 2000); Stephen Macedo and Iris Marion Young, eds., *NOMOS XLIV: Child, Family, and State* (New York: New York University Press, 2003).

4 But see Amy Gutmann's important book, *Democratic Education* (Princeton, NJ: Princeton University Press, 1987), as well as Hugh LaFollette, "Freedom of Religion and Children," *Public Affairs Quarterly* 3, no. 1 (1989): 75–87; Stephen Macedo, *Liberal Virtues: Citizenship, Virtue, and Community in Liberal Constitutionalism* (Oxford: Clarendon Press, 1990); and William Galston, *Liberal Purposes: Goods, Virtues, and Diversity in the Liberal State* (Cambridge: Cambridge University Press, 1991).

5 *Wisconsin v. Yoder*, 406 U.S. 205 (1972).

6 *Mozert v. Hawkins County Board of Education*, 827 F.2d 1058 (6th Cir. 1987).

7 *R. v. Keegstra*, [1990] 3 S.C.R. 697. Section 319 of the Criminal Code prohibits promoting hatred against members of groups identifiable on the basis of race or religion.

8 Section 5(1) of the New Brunswick Human Rights Act states:
   No person, directly or indirectly, alone or with another, by himself or by the interposition of another, shall...

(b) discriminate against any person or class of persons with respect to any accommodation, services or facilities available to the public, because of race, colour, religion, national origin, ancestry, place of origin, age, physical disability, mental disability, marital status, sexual orientation or sex.

9 Cited in *Ross*, para. 7.

10 Section 2 of the Charter states:

Everyone has the following freedoms:
   (i) freedom of conscience and religion;
   (ii) freedom of thought, belief, opinion and expression…

11 Section 1 of the Charter states, "The Canadian Charter of Rights and Freedoms guarantees the rights and freedoms set out in it subject only to such reasonable limits prescribed by law as can be demonstrably justified in a free and democratic society." This section both enables the rights and freedoms in the Charter and sketches the grounds for their limitation: they must be "reasonable," "prescribed by law" and "demonstrably justified in a free and democratic society."

In *R. v. Oakes* ([1986] 1 S.C.R. 103) the Court laid out grounds for a s. 1 exception to one of the Charter rights and freedoms. First, the objective of the state action under consideration must be "of pressing concern in a free and democratic society," and second, there must be proportionality between that objective and any measure for achieving it. The proportionality part of the Oakes test has three parts: rational connection (the measure adopted must be rationally connected to the objective), minimal impairment (it must impair the right or freedom in question as little as possible), and proportionality (there must be proportionality between the effects of the measure and the objective).

12 *Ross v. New Brunswick School District 15*, para. 44. Citing Allison Reyes, "Freedom of Expression and Public School Teachers," *Dalhousie Journal of Legal Studies* 4 (1995): 35–72.

13 *Ross*, para. 42.

14 Ibid., para. 43.

15 Ibid., para. 45.

16 Ibid.

17 Section 15 (1) of the Charter states, "Every individual is equal before and under the law and has the right to the equal protection and equal benefit of the law without discrimination and, in particular, without discrimination based on race, national or ethnic origin, colour, religion, sex, age or mental or physical disability."

18 *Ross*, para. 72. Quoting from *R. v. Big M Drug Mart Ltd.*, [1985] 1 S.C.R. 295, at p. 336.

19 Ibid., para. 81. citing *R. v. Jones*, [1986] 2 S.C.R. 284, at p. 296.

20 Ibid., citing *Brown v. Board of Education of Topeka*, 347 U.S. 483 (1954), at p. 493.

21 *Ross*, para. 82.

22 Ibid., citing *Brown*.

23 *Ross*, para. 40.

24 *Ross*, para. 82.

25 *Ross*, para. 77. Quoting *Oakes* (see note 11), at p. 136.

26 S. 4(1) of the act might have applied. It states,

> No person directly or indirectly, alone or with another, by himself or by the interposition of another, shall…
>
> > (b) discriminate against any person or class of persons with respect to any term or condition of occupancy of any…dwelling unit, because of race, colour, religion, national origin, ancestry, place of origin, age, physical disability, mental disability, marital status, sexual orientation or sex.

27 The dissenting opinion in *Yoder* did consider children's independent interests, but it did not carry the day.

28 Quoted in *Removing a Badge of Slavery: The Record of Brown v. Board of Education*, ed. Mark Whitman (Princeton & New York: Markus Wiener Publishing, 1993), 308.

29 Rawls says self-respect is the most important primary good in a just society. See *A Theory of Justice* (Cambridge, MA: Belknap Press of Harvard University Press, 1971), 396, 440ff.

30 See, for example, William Galston, *Liberal Purposes*, 252, and *Liberal Pluralism*, 93.

31 See Martha C. Nussbaum, *Sex and Social Justice* (Oxford: Oxford University Press, 1999), 32, and *Women and Human Development* (Cambridge: Cambridge University Press, 2000), 255ff.

32 *Ross*, para. 72. Quoting *R. v. Big M Drug Mart Ltd.*, [1985] 1 S.C.R. 295, at p. 336.

33 Ibid., para. 77. Citing *Oakes* at p. 136.

34 In *Multicultural Citizenship: A Liberal Theory of Minority Rights* (New York: Oxford University Press, 1995), Will Kymlicka argues in favour of making some exceptions for small groups like the Amish that do not participate in political society. I cannot agree in the case of teaching the political values that underlie a society (nor perhaps would Kymlicka). To permit these sort of exceptions would undermine the very foundations of the society.

35 For a defence of such a view, see Nancy Rosenblum, *Membership and Morals* (Princeton, NJ: Princeton University Press, 1998). Rosenblum explicitly excludes children from her analysis, though.

36 Don Hubin suggested (personal communication) that my conclusions should not be limited to schools.

37 *Ross*, para. 42.

38 For example, *Keegstra* (see note 7) and *Vriend v. Alberta*, [1998] 1 S.C.R. 493.

39 *Ross*, para. 72. Quoting *R. v. Big M Drug Mart Ltd.* at p. 336.

40 Ibid.

41 For a nice argument tying the goals of multicultural education to basic liberal
    principles, see J.S. Andrews, "Liberal Equality and the Justification of Multicul-
    tural, Civic Education," *Canadian Journal of Law and Jurisprudence* 7 (1994):
    111–26. See also the references in notes 2–4.

42 The classic statement of this position remains Ferdinand Schoeman, "Rights of
    Children, Rights of Parents, and the Moral Basis of the Family," *Ethics* 91, no. 1
    (1980): 6–19.

43 For a similar argument, see Michael David Jordan, "Parents' Rights and Child-
    ren's Interests," *Canadian Journal of Law and Jurisprudence* 10 (1997): 363–85.

EIGHT

Could There Be a Right Not to Be Born an Octuplet?

LAURA M. PURDY

Twice in the last few years the bioethics sensation of the week has been the arrival of high-order multiple births (or "supertwins"), first the McCaughey septuplets in Des Moines, Iowa, then the Chukwu octuplets in Houston, Texas. The media commentary on the cases tended to focus, as usual, on short-term issues—the need for hundreds of diapers, the images of babies on ventilators, and the expense. But little scholarly work has yet appeared on the subject, perhaps because of media formats that inhibit in-depth exploration and, also, the peculiar lack of sustained interest in children's issues.

The Context

There has been a spectacular increase in the number of multiple births: since 1971, such births have quadrupled in the United States because of treatment for infertility.[1] Powerful new drugs can cause many eggs to ripen and, if the woman has intercourse, be fertilized simultaneously. If she is undertaking in vitro fertilization (IVF), as many as seven or eight embryos might be placed in her uterus to increase the chances of a successful pregnancy.

Women's bodies are designed for singleton pregnancies. The greater the number of fetuses, the greater the strain on her body,[2] and the greater the risk of disability or death for the fetuses. Babies born of supertwin pregnancies are always seriously premature and require intensive medical care to survive. For example, Mrs. Chukwu delivered thirteen weeks early, and none of her babies weighed even two pounds.[3]

There are several interesting perspectives on the supertwin phenomenon that cry out for critical analysis. Among them is the glorification of motherhood (one is reminded of the old Soviet heroines of the republic, women who had had ten or more children), the implication that no sacrifice is too great in the production of such births (Mrs. Chukwu spent weeks in the hospital, head down to reduce the pressure on her cervix[4]), the inconsistency in the McCaugheys's and Chukwu's expecting God to help them cope with what high-tech medicine created, and more. But here I want to focus on the outcome for children.

Health Risks

Premature infants born weighing less than two pounds often have breathing difficulties and brain damage. Many infants die, and those who survive may suffer from long-term problems:

> Studies of low-birth-weight children (not from multifetal pregnancies but from premature births) have shown that approximately 20 percent have severe disabilities; among those weighing less than 750 grams (1.7 pounds) at birth, 50 percent have functional impairments. A recent study that followed these very small infants to school showed that up to 50 percent of them scored low on standardized intelligence tests, including 21 percent who were mentally retarded. In addition, nine percent had cerebral palsy, and 25 percent had severe vision problems. As a result, 45 percent ended up enrolling in special-education programs.[5]

These statistics tend to be obscured in the media flurries attending the births, and follow-up bulletins are sparse. For example, the Chukwu babies have pretty much disappeared from the scene except for a terse announcement several months after their birth that three of them were released, in good health, from the hospital.[6] The others remained in hospital, three of them critically ill.[7] I picked up another story about the harsh reality facing a family with quintuplets on an e-mail discussion list: "All of Aymond's 6-year-old quints have medical problems. One is blind. Four of them are in speech therapy, three in occupational therapy and three in physical therapy."[8]

Given such outcomes, it seems reasonable to raise the question whether it is morally permissible to take such risks to have babies. Notice that this chapter considers only the moral issue, as there is an enormously greater burden of proof needed to support any legal regulation of reproductive behaviour.

Other Risks

Most of the criticism of parents who knowingly go forward with higher order multiple pregnancies has focused on the risk of death or disability such pregnancies involve for the resulting babies. Morally serious though I believe this risk to be, few have commented on other problems facing these children. In fact, the only somewhat detailed discussion I have found is by Ezekiel Emanuel, who writes:

> Equally important, but rarely articulated, are the emotional health risks children in multiple births face. Loving and raising children through the normal developmental milestones is enormously wonderful and rewarding. But it is also hard work. Raising children is not a sprint to a healthy birth but a marathon through variable terrain until the goal of independent adulthood. The real way to assess these miraculous pregnancies—indeed, any pregnancy—is whether they are ultimately good for children. Quite clearly, they are not.[9]

Emanuel goes on to point out that children's needs change over time, and that shepherding them through the various stages of growth is physically, emotionally, intellectually, and socially demanding. Most parents have their hands full dealing with one or two children of different ages, and, he argues, "it is simply not physically possible for two parents to do this successfully for seven children of the same age."[10] Although many children from average-sized families spend significant amounts of time with paid caregivers, they are much more likely than supertwins to get quality time with their parents. He points out that it would take two and a half hours a day if parents of septuplets were to attempt to spend a mere twenty minutes a day focusing on each child. Most busy parents have trouble finding twenty minutes a day for each of two kids.

So it's hard to see how a couple could meet the needs of such a brood well unless one parent stays home with them. Maureen Boyle, president of Mothers of Supertwins, a support group for mothers of three or more children born at the same time, points out that couples often decide that the parent with the best health insurance will continue working.[11]

Finding resources to meet the needs of a large family is doubly difficult when all the children are born at the same time. Most families would have trouble paying for a couple of nannies or eight rounds of daycare on two

salaries, let alone one. Tolson writes, "for parents, the emotional and physical toll is overwhelming. And the expense is an uphill climb with no end.
When an item is needed for a child, it's needed for four, five or six at once.
There are no hand-me-downs, no making do." Most insurance plans have
gaps, and "because the children usually have greater medical needs, that
adds to the financial burden." The insurance paperwork alone could be
staggering. "The working parent often takes a second job. Emotional stress
on the family is constant. Depression is common."[12] Families under these
pressures are unlikely to be able to meet their children's needs well.

These concerns are consonant with my own views about parental
responsibility. I have argued that children need substantial, consistent love
and attention from parents or other adults to develop character traits and
habits necessary to flourish and become ethical persons. If this need is not
met, children are seriously at risk. They are less likely to do well at school,
and may adopt as models peers who are into drugs and criminal behaviour.
These adolescent choices may have permanent consequences, leaving
them with much reduced prospects for satisfying lives.

Thus it seems as if a realistic view of the problems created for children
(and their parents) by being supertwins might suggest that it could be
wrong to have them at all under anything like the circumstances now faced
by most couples. I will call this view the "wrongness thesis with respect to
supertwin pregnancies" ("WS" hereafter).

Objections

The WS depends first of all on the premise that these pregnancies can be
prevented, given that "ought implies can." Most such pregnancies can be
avoided. Ultrasound can show when fertility drugs have caused many eggs
to ripen at once, and women can be warned against having unprotected
intercourse during that cycle. In addition, the standard of care for IVF could
require that no more than two or three embryos are implanted after fertilization. Most problematically, perhaps, both women naturally pregnant
with supertwins and those pregnant with them as a result of technology
could be encouraged to consider reduction of the pregnancy to twins or a
singleton. So there are ways to prevent the birth supertwins.

What other objections might be raised against the WS?

Arguments Focused on Disease and Disability

I have been arguing for years that it can be wrong to bring children into this world that are especially likely to suffer. A few more brave souls have written in this vein (Bonnie Steinbock, Dena Davis, Cynthia Cohen) recently. However, I suspect that most philosophers are persuaded not to accept it by the Parfit/Robertson view. That is, it is okay knowingly to bring people to life in a harmed condition unless they are so miserable they wish they were dead, because the harm that was done to them is a condition of their very existence.[13]

I have argued against this view at some length elsewhere and will just briefly sketch the main lines of my objections here.[14] First, my general approach is utilitarian, and so I see rights as derivative of duties flowing from judgments about overall utilities; this avoids the pitfalls of attributing rights to beings that may not yet exist. Second, I believe that the Parfit/ Robertson view derives a good deal of its plausibility from the desire to stick with a minimalist and libertarian moral framework. This desire is understandable in a secular, pluralistic world where a more demanding moral outlook may well be rejected on a variety of grounds. Nonetheless, a minimalist/libertarian framework both undermines the kind of welfare rights necessary for equal opportunity (let alone any more demanding conception of a good society) and emotional concern for others upon which a decent society ultimately depends. Furthermore, this approach relies too heavily on abstract principles that are compatible with permitting a great deal of preventable suffering, when a richer contextual analysis would not do so.

More compatible (apparently) with a progressive moral and political position is the recent disability rights argument that attempting to prevent the birth of children with serious health problems promotes callous judgments about the worth of human life. According to this view, it also fails to respect the lives of those now living with disabilities and ignores the fact that a great deal of the suffering on the part of those with disabilities is caused by social factors, not disability itself. These arguments tend to assume that the underlying premise really is that the birth of "imperfect" children should be prevented because of the burdens they impose on parents and society, not that the suffering inherent in some impairments should be prevented. Even where such potential suffering is acknowledged, this disability rights position tends to fail to take account of the vast range of different kinds and degrees of impairment. Downplaying such suffering seems to me to undermine the case for broad social and political action to change environments to minimize its impact, provide help for people with impairments, and wide-ranging public health measures to prevent impairing accidents or diseases. So I still believe that we as parents have a loving duty to try to avoid the birth of children who are likely to have serious health problems.

Arguments Focused on Children's Emotional and Intellectual Needs

Objections to the WS when children's emotional and/or intellectual needs are unlikely to be met fall into four general categories. First, it may be argued that the WS presupposes middle-class values centring on the production of "successful" children. Second, it may be argued that the WS is predicated on the existence (and superiority of) the nuclear family. Third, the WS may be taken as reinforcement for some noxious constellation of "family values." Fourth, WS raises important questions about privacy and the family.

"SUCCESSFUL" CHILDREN   Implicit in this objection to the WS is the premise that the only reason one would argue for the importance of such intense parental "investment" in children is concern for their ability to compete for scarce positions of power and prestige in society. Even were this true, it would be unreasonable to discount it entirely. Good parents are justifiably anxious about their children's future welfare in societies where the gap between rich and poor continues to grow and where the basic resources necessary for a decent life (like good education or access to good health care) are slipping from the grasp of an ever-larger proportion of the population.

But it is false, in any case, that the only reason for taking the time for good parenting is the pursuit of such a narrow and inadequate version of the "successful" child. I believe that many parents would be delighted to produce children who find life activities that are a source of satisfaction to them, and that, with the help of social resources if they are impaired, render them at least modestly independent. Successful individuals must also be good citizens who are genuinely concerned about—and act on behalf of—the welfare of others. This much broader conception of success is based on the premise that having choices about how to live, engaging in intrinsically appealing activities, and caring about others are key elements of a good life. Achieving this goal without intense involvement—consistent, individual, loving attention—in one's child's life is improbable, especially in contemporary societies where they are exposed to many destructive and conflicting pressures.

NUCLEAR FAMILIES   The second objection to the WS related to the impossibility of parenting them well presupposes that the nuclear family is necessary or desirable.

Neither claim is true. Many people are aware of the problems inherent in contemporary versions of the nuclear family. In particular, the belief that it should be self-sufficient means that many families, especially those headed by single women, are struggling to balance work and children's needs with little or no social support. So the nuclear family is often an obstacle to the kind of parenting necessary to grow successful children rather than a prerequisite for it.

Moreover, I suspect that most of us who grew up in nuclear families can point to numerous other difficulties with them, difficulties that underscore the need for further exploration of alternative approaches involving more communal responsibility for children. Children who grow up in such systems might, naturally, develop somewhat differently from those who grow up in nuclear families, and we would need to get very clear about what we consider a desirable outcome. But if our aim continues to be individuals capable of living the sort of good life described above, loving guidance will still be necessary, even if not necessarily provided by genetically related individuals.

"FAMILY VALUES"   The "family values" objection takes for granted that any objection to the WS is based on admiration for the patriarchal family and the gendered division of labour that relegates women to the home nurturing children.

It is true that theories that emphasize children's physical welfare and the need for consistent adult love and attention have tended to presuppose that only mothers can provide these things to children and that children have a right to this kind of undivided care. The clearest critiques of this position can be found in Shulamith Firestone,[15] Ann Oakley,[16] Jessie Bernard,[17] and Dorothy Dinnerstein.[18] Firestone argues that this view of children was concocted to tie women to the home, and that children's liberation would also liberate women. But her theory of children's liberation fails to take account of the empirical literature on child rearing. Still at issue is the crucial question whether the gender of the caregiver matters. Despite the conservative insistence that it does, in my view this remains to be shown.

Ironically for those who worry about the reinforcement of patriarchy, the birth of supertwins is quite likely to force women back into the home, for reasons mentioned earlier. Caring for so many same-aged children means that a parent will be needed at home even where a smaller family or one with children of a range of ages could manage without that. If couples tend to keep the job that provides health insurance, it will generally be the woman who returns home, given that fewer jobs held by woman come with health insurance. Stereotyped views of womens' nature reinforces this trend.

Arguments Related to Privacy and Control

The more difficult issue involves the extent to which public concern about childbearing and child rearing invades family privacy, a genuinely conflicted issue.[19] Traditionalists have wanted to shield the family from observation or judgment, but concern about the abuse of women and children shows how morally untenable is any such shield. Feminists have good reasons of their own, however, for wanting reproductive decisions shielded from prying eyes.[20]

First, some thoughts about different strands of mainstream views. One strand continues to see children as parents' property, and so society has no business interfering with parents' decisions about children. This position is represented, for example, by those who believe that school systems have no right to expose their children to ideas they disapprove of. A different strand of mainstream thought believes that state intervention could be justifiable but that the burden of proof is on the state's shoulders.

Perhaps the most interesting (and meaningful) split is between those who oppose government spending, even in the service of values they approve, and those who support such spending. The first would relinquish attempts to guide or control childbearing or rearing decisions whenever they require state spending. The second would "invest" in such spending where it advances their principles. Some such principles might be shared by progressives, such as the importance of spending to promote high-quality education, although the two constituencies would have quite different visions of it. However, the willingness to spend might also be in the service of an antithetical goal. Who could forget the plans of the newly Republican 1994 Congress as it floated the idea of eradicating welfare payments for single mothers, sending their children instead to orphanages, despite the enormous expense of any such program.

Feminists and other progressives have fought hard to open up the family to moral and legal scrutiny to protect women's and children's rights as humans and equal citizens. In the absence of such scrutiny, for instance, women had to live with the marital rape exclusion and other threats and indignities. Moreover, it is sometimes reasonable to take action to protect children from their parents, even to the extent of removing them from their homes.

Because of women's special relationship with fetuses, babies, and children, however, fully opening up family relationships also threatens their still fragile status as equal citizens. Thus, feminists are rightly wary of proposals to intrude in reproductive decisions and child-rearing, despite the occasional need to protect children. A look at the history of such intrusion shows that authorities have often ignored women's rights, interests, and desires because of unfounded stereotypical assumptions about their intelligence or judgment. In particular, pregnant women have been jailed or threatened with forced medical care, even where widely accepted legal principles of autonomy are violated.[21] Some feminists believe, then, that reproduction should be a completely private matter, not subject to any moral or legal scrutiny. A more plausible position would be, in my view, that the burden of proof is against any such scrutiny, but that the public interest does require us to develop and adopt some moral framework for reproductive decisions, even though it should not be enacted into law.

There is no comfortable ground here. But ensuring that any proposals remain in the realm of ethics (but not law) may help society achieve the goal of respecting women's decisions while minimizing harm to children. In addition, a general strategy relying on prevention and support, rather than the more usual punitive and coercive approach focusing on symptoms (not causes) should allay fears. Thus, society could do many things to help couples prevent the birth of supertwins. It could, for example, make research on the causes of infertility a higher priority. Or it could counteract the motivations for undertaking supertwin pregnancies by paying for fertility treatments so that couples are not so desperate for success no matter what the price, and by funding research to find treatments that are not so hard on women. It would also be helpful for professional societies to adopt guidelines that restrict the number of embryos that are placed in women's uteruses after IVF.[22] Such moves would encourage couples to resist the suggestion that multiple embryos be placed in the woman's uterus. At the same time, work arrangements need to be changed to permit people to plan pregnancies before fertility diminishes, and workplaces and environments that expose individuals to substances that lower fertility should be cleaned up. Last but not least, the cultural and institutional sources of pronatalism should be eradicated so that individuals are encouraged to make more reasoned and realistic choices about childbearing.[23]

Notes

1 Arlene Judith Klotzko, "Medical Miracle or Medical Mischief? The Saga of the McCaughey Septuplets," *Hastings Center Report*, May–June 1998, p. 6. In Canada, the incidence of twins rose 35% from 1974 to 1990, that of triplets, 300%, and that of quadruplets, 400% (http://www.multiplebirthscanada.org/english/incidencesmb.php, accessed January 29, 2003).

2 Robert Blank writes that multiple pregnancies ("MP") are "associated with increased incidence of preeclampsia, placenta previa, placental disruption, premature rupture of the membranes, postpartum hemorrhage, and Cesarean sections, all of which increase morbidity. Moreover, particularly for older women undergoing IVF, multifetal pregnancy may produce an unbearable overload for the cardiovascular and renal functions, among other body systems...." (Robert Blank, "Assisted Reproduction and Reproductive Rights: The Case of In Vitro Fertilization," *Politics and the Life Sciences* 16, no. 2: 279–88).

3 Claudia Kalb, "Families: The Octuplet Question," *Newsweek*, January 11, 1999, p. 33.

4 Ezekiel J. Emanuel, "The Case against Octuplets. Eight Is Too Many," *The New Republic*, January 25, 1999, p. 8.

5 *New York Times*, March 4, 1999, Thursday, late edition, Section A, p. 19, column 3.

6 Reported by CNN, March 3, 1999; accessible at http://www.cnn.com/US/9903/03/octuplets/.

7 Mike Tolson, "Eventually Reality Bites Parents in Multiple Births," *Houston Chronicle*, January 10, 1999, p. 1.

8 Laura Purdy, *In Their Best Interest? The Case against Equal Rights for Children* (Ithaca, NY: Cornell University Press, 1992).

9 Emmanuel, "The Case against Octuplets," 8.

10 Ibid.

11 Tolson, "Eventually Reality Bites," 1.

12 Ibid.

13 Laura Purdy, "Loving Future People," *Reproducing Persons: Issues in Feminist Bioethics* (Ithaca, NY: Cornell University Press, 1996).

14 Ibid.

15 Firestone, *The Dialectic of Sex*.

16 Ann Oakley, *Women's Work: The Housewife, Past and Present* (New York, NY: Vintage, 1976).

17 Jessie Bernard, *The Future of Motherhood* (New York, NY: Penguin, 1975).

18 Dorothy Dinnerstein, *The Mermaid and the Minotaur: Sexual Arrangements and Human Malaise* (New York: Harper and Row, 1976).

19 For recent writing that touches on this general subject, see Uma Narayan and Julia J. Bartkowiak, *Having and Raising Children: Unconventional Families,*

Hard Choices, and the Social Good (University Park: Pennsylvania State Press, 1999; Geoffrey Scarre, *Children, Parents and Politics* (Cambridge: Cambridge University Press, 1989); David Archard, *Children: Rights & Childhood* (London: Routledge, 1993); Susan M. Turner and Gareth B. Mathews, *The Philosopher's Child: Critical Essays in the Western Tradition* (Rochester, NY: Rochester University Press, 1998); Laurence D. Houlgate, *Family and State: The Philosophy of Family Law* (Totowa, NJ: Rowman and Littlefield, 1988); and Rosalind Ekman Ladd, *Children's Rights Re-Visioned* (Belmont, CA: Wadsworth, 1996).

20 For discussion of this issue, see, for example, Judith Wagner DeCew, *In Pursuit of Privacy: Law, Ethics, and the Rise of Technology* (Ithaca, NY: Cornell University Press, 1997), chap. 5, and Patricia Boling, *Privacy and the Politics of Intimate Life* (Ithaca, NY: Cornell University Press, 1996).

21 See, for example, Cynthia R. Daniels, *At Women's Expense: State Power and the Politics of Fetal Rights* (Cambridge, MA: Harvard University Press, 1993).

22 See, for instance, the consensus-based Committee Reports of the American Society for Reproductive Medicine and the Society for Assisted Reproductive Medicine, such as "Guidelines on Number of Embryos Transferred" (http://www.asrm.org/Media/Practice/blastocyst.pdf, November 1999, accessed February 7, 2003). However, this report suggests that it could be reasonable to transfer up to four embryos in some cases.

23 See Diana T. Meyers, "The Rush to Motherhood-Pronatalist Discourse and Women's Autonomy," *Signs: Journal of Women in Culture and Society* 26, no. 3 (2001): 735–73.

BIBLIOGRAPHY

Addiction Research Foundation. 1993. "Smokers Rejected as Adoptive Parents." *The Journal—Addiction Research Foundation*, Centre for Addiction and Mental Health. May 22. 7.

Alleyne, George A.O. 2001. "Second-hand Smoke Kills. Let's Clean the Air." Message from the director of the Pan American Health Organization, World No Tobacco Day, May 2001. http://www.paho.org/English/AD/SDE/RA/wntd-DirectorMessage.pdf.

American Academy of Pediatrics. 2000. "What Is Environmental Tobacco Smoke (ETS)?" http://www.medem.com.

American Society for Reproductive Medicine and the Society for Assisted Reproductive Medicine. 1999. "Guidelines on Number of Embryos Transferred." http://www.asrm.org/Media/Practice/blastocyst.pdf.

Andrews, J.S. 1994. "Liberal Equality and the Justification of Multicultural, Civic Education." *Canadian Journal of Law and Jurisprudence* 7: 111–26.

Appiah, Kwame Anthony. 2005. *The Ethics of Identity*. Princeton, NJ: Princeton University Press.

Archard, David. 1993. *Children: Rights and Childhood*. London: Routledge.

———. 1996. "Child Abuse: Parental Rights and the Interest of the Child." In Rosalind Ekman Ladd, ed., *Children's Rights Re-Visioned: Philosophical Readings*. Albany: Wadsworth, 107–20. Originally published 1990 in the *Journal of Applied Philosophy* 7 (1): 183–94.

———. 2003. *Children, Family and the State*. Aldershot, Hampshire, UK: Ashgate.

Archard, David, and Macleod, Colin M., eds. 2002. *The Moral and Political Status of Children*. Oxford: Oxford University Press.

Aronson, Jane. 1998. "Lesbians Giving and Receiving Care: Stretching Conceptual-
    izations of Caring and Community." *Women's Studies International Forum*
    21: 505–19.
Bailey, Alison. 1994. "Mothering, Diversity, and Peace Politics." *Hypatia* 9: 188–98.
Bailey, Ronald, ed., 1996. *The True State of the Planet.* New York: Free Press.
Bartky, Sandra Lee. 1990. "Feeding Egos and Tending Wounds: Deference and Dis-
    affection in Women's Emotional Labor." In Bartky, *Femininity and Domi-
    nation: Studies in the Phenomenology of Oppression.* New York: Routledge.
Bell, Linda A. 1993. *Rethinking Ethics in the Midst of Violence: A Feminist Approach
    to Freedom.* Lanham, MD: Rowman & Littlefield.
Bernard, Jessie. 1975. *The Future of Motherhood.* New York: Penguin.
Blank, Robert. 1997. "Assisted Reproduction and Reproductive Rights: The Case of
    In Vitro Fertilization." *Politics and the Life Sciences* 16, no. 2: 279–88.
Blustein, J. 1982. *Parents and Children: The Ethics of the Family.* Oxford: Oxford
    University Press.
Boling, Patricia. 1991. "The Democratic Potential of Mothering." *Political Theory* 19:
    606–25.
———. 1996. *Privacy and the Politics of Intimate Life.* Ithaca, NY: Cornell Univer-
    sity Press.
Brennan, Samantha, and Noggle, Robert. 1997. "The Moral Status of Children: Chil-
    dren's Rights, Parents' Rights, and Family Justice." *Social Theory and Prac-
    tice* 23: 1–26.
Brighouse, Harry. 2000. *School Choice and Social Justice.* Oxford: Oxford Univer-
    sity Press.
British Columbia Adoption Act, B.C. Reg. 291/96, Part 2, c. 7.
Callan, Eamonn. 1997. *Creating Citizens: Political Education and Liberal Democracy.*
    Oxford: Clarendon Press.
Canadian Health Network. 2001. "Second-Hand Smoke Kills: Let's Clear the Air."
    http://www.canadian-health-network.ca.
Card, Claudia. 1990. "Gender and Moral Luck." In Owen Flanagan and Amelie O.
    Rorty, eds., *Identity, Character and Morality: Essays in Moral Psychology.*
    Cambridge, MA: MIT Press, 199–218.
———. 1996. "Against Marriage and Motherhood." *Hypatia* 11: 1–23.
Carey v. Population Services International, 431 U.S. 678 (1977).
Casal, Paula, and Williams, Andrew. 1995. "Rights, Equality and Procreation," *Ana-
    lyse & Kritik* 17: 93–116.
Code, Lorraine. 1991. *What Can She Know? Feminist Theory and the Construction
    of Knowledge.* Ithaca, NY: Cornell University Press.
Collins, Patricia Hill. 1994. "Shifting the Center: Race, Class, and Feminist Theoriz-
    ing about Motherhood." In Donna Bassin, Margaret Honey, and Meryle
    Mahrer Kaplan, eds., *Representations of Motherhood.* New Haven, CT: Yale
    University Press.
Daniels, Cynthia R. 1993. *At Women's Expense: State Power and the Politics of Fetal
    Rights.* Cambridge, MA: Harvard University Press.

DeCew, Judith Wagner. 1997. *In Pursuit of Privacy: Law, Ethics, and the Rise of Technology*. Ithaca, NY: Cornell University Press.

Dietz, Mary. 1985. "Citizenship with a Feminist Face: The Problem with Maternal Thinking." *Political Theory* 13: 19–37.

Dinnerstein, Dorothy. 1976. *The Mermaid and the Minotaur: Sexual Arrangements and Human Malaise*. New York: Harper & Row.

DiQuinzio, Patrice. 1999. *The Impossibility of Motherhood: Feminism, Individualism, and the Problem of Mothering*. New York: Routledge.

Dixon, Nicholas. 1995. "The Friendship Model of Filial Obligations." *Journal of Applied Philosophy* 12: 77–87.

Dworkin, Ronald. 2000. *Sovereign Virtue: The Theory and Practice of Equality*. Cambridge, MA: Harvard University Press.

Emanuel, Ezekiel J. 1999. "The Case against Octuplets: Eight Is Too Many." *New Republic*, January 25, 1999, 8–11.

Feinberg, Joel. 1992. "The Child's Right to an Open Future." In Feinberg, *Freedom and Fulfillment*. Princeton, NJ: Princeton University Press, 76–97.

Ferrence, Roberta, and Ashley, Mary Jane. 2000. "Protecting Children from Passive Smoking: The Risks Are Clear and a Comprehensive Strategy Is Now Needed." *British Medical Journal* 321 (August 5): 310–11.

Firestone, Shulamith. 1970. *The Dialectic of Sex: The Case for Feminist Revolution*. New York: William Morrow.

Fishkin, James S. 1983. *Justice, Equal Opportunity and the Family*. New Haven, CT: Yale University Press.

Friedman, Marilyn. 1989. "Friendship and Moral Growth." *Journal of Value Inquiry* 23: 3–13.

———. 1993. *What Are Friends For? Feminist Perspectives on Personal Relationships and Moral Theory*. Ithaca, NY: Cornell University Press.

Frisch, Lawrence. 1982. "On Licentious Licensing: A Reply to Hugh LaFollette." *Philosophy and Public Affairs* 11: 173–80.

Fromm, Suzette. 2004. "Total Estimated Cost of Child Abuse and Neglect in the United States." http://www.perspectivesonyouth.org/Pages_Articles/Summer-Fall-2004.

———. 2004. "Total Estimated Cost of Child Abuse and Neglect in the United States." http://www.perspectivesonyouth.org/Pages-Articles/summer-Fall-2004.

Galston, William. 1991. *Liberal Purposes: Goods, Virtues, and Diversity in the Liberal State*. Cambridge: Cambridge University Press.

———. 1995. "Two Concepts of Liberalism." *Ethics* 105: 516–34.

———. 2001. "Individual Experience and Social Policy: Thinking Practically about Overcoming Racial and Ethnic Prejudice." In Stephen Macedo and Yael Tamir, eds., *Moral and Political Education, NOMOS XLIII*. New York University Press, 425–33.

———. 2002. *Liberal Pluralism: The Implications of Value Pluralism for Political Theory and Practice*. Cambridge, MA: Cambridge University Press.

Grimshaw, Jean. 1986. *Philosophy and Feminist Thinking*. Minneapolis: University of Minnesota Press.

Gudorf, Christine. 1985. "Parenting, Mutual Love and Sacrifice." In C. Gudorf and M. Pellauer, eds., *Women's Conscience: A Reader in Feminist Ethics*. Minneapolis: Winston Press, 175–91.

Gutmann, Amy. 1987. *Democratic Education*. Princeton, NJ: Princeton University Press.

———. 1995. "Civic Education and Social Diversity." *Ethics* 105: 565–67.

Hampton, Jean. 1995. "Feminist Contractarianism." In Louise M. Antony and Charlotte Witt, eds., *A Mind of One's Own: Feminist Essays on Reason and Objectivity*. Boulder, CO: Westview Press, 227–55.

Held, Virginia. 1993. *Feminist Morality*. Chicago: University of Chicago Press.

Hoagland, Sarah Lucia. 1991. "Some Thoughts about 'Caring.'" In Claudia Card, ed., *Feminist Ethics*. Lawrence: University Press of Kansas, 246–63.

hooks, bell. 1984. *Feminist Theory from Margin to Center*. Boston: South End Press.

Houlgate, Laurence D. 1988. *Family and State: The Philosophy of Family Law*. Totowa, NJ: Rowman & Littlefield.

Houston, Barbara. 1987. "Rescuing Womanly Virtues: Some Dangers of Moral Reclamation." *Canadian Journal of Philosophy* Suppl. Vol. 13: 237–62.

Irvine, William. 2001. *Doing Right by Children*. St. Paul, MN: Paragon House.

———. 2003. *The Politics of Parenting*. St. Paul, MN: Paragon House.

Jordan, Michael David. 1997. "Parents' Rights and Children's Interests." *Canadian Journal of Law and Jurisprudence* 10: 363–85.

Kalb, Claudia. 1999. "Families: The Octuplet Question." *Newsweek*, January 11, 1999, 33.

Klotzko, Arlene Judith. 1998. "Medical Miracle or Medical Mischief? The Saga of the McCaughey Septuplets," *Hastings Center Report*, May–June 1998: 5–8.

Kupfer, Joseph. 1990. "Can Parents and Children Be Friends?" *American Philosophical Quarterly* 27: 15–26.

Kymlicka, Will. 1988. "Liberal Individualism and Liberal Neutrality." *Ethics* 99: 883–905.

———. 1989. *Liberalism, Community and Culture*. Oxford: Oxford University Press.

———. 1995. *Multicultural Citizenship: A Liberal Theory of Minority Rights*. New York: Oxford University Press.

———. 2001. *Politics in the Vernacular: Nationalism, Multiculturalism, and Citizenship*. Oxford: Oxford University Press.

Ladd, Rosalind Ekman, ed. 1996. *Children's Rights Re-Visioned: Philosophical Readings*. Albany, NY: Wadsworth.

LaFollette, Hugh. 1980. "Licensing Parents." *Philosophy and Public Affairs* 9: 182–97.

———. 1989. "Freedom of Religion and Children." *Public Affairs Quarterly* 3: 75–87.

LaFollette, Hugh, and Aiken, William, eds. 1980. *Whose Child? Children's Rights, Parental Authority, and State Power*. Totawa, NJ: Rowman & Littlefield.

Lauritzen, Paul. 1989. "A Feminist Ethic and the New Romanticism: Mothering as a Model of Moral Relations." *Hypatia* 4: 40–42.

Macedo, Stephen. 1990. *Liberal Virtues: Citizenship, Virtue, and Community in Liberal Constitutionalism*. Oxford: Clarendon Press.

———. 1995. "Liberal Civic Education and Religious Fundamentalism: The Case of God v. John Rawls?" *Ethics* 105: 468–96.

———. 1998. "Transformative Constitutionalism and the Case of Religion." *Political Theory* 26: 56–80.

———. 2000. *Diversity and Distrust*. Cambridge, MA: Harvard University Press.

Macedo, Stephen, and Young, Iris Marion, eds. 2003. *NOMOS XLIV: Child, Family, and State*. New York: New York University Press.

Macleod, Colin. 1997. "Conceptions of Parental Autonomy." *Politics & Society* 25: 117–40.

Mahood, Garfield. 2003. "Smoking in the Home: Social and Legal Implications." Non-smokers' Rights Association. http://www.nsra-adnf.ca/cms/index.cfm ?group_id=1209.

Meyers, Diana T. 2001. "The Rush to Motherhood: Pronatalist Discourse and Women's Autonomy." *Signs: Journal of Women in Culture and Society* 26: 735–73.

Mills, Claudia. 2003. "The Child's Right to an Open Future?" *Journal of Social Philosophy* 34 (4): 499–509.

Mozert v. Hawkins County Board of Education, 827 F.2d 1058 (6th Cir. 1987), 1060; 102 A.L.R. Fed. 497.

Nagel, Thomas. 1991. *Equality and Partiality*. Oxford: Oxford University Press.

Narayan, Uma, and Bartkowiak, Julia J. 1999. *Having and Raising Children: Unconventional Families, Hard Choices, and the Social Good*. University Park, PA: Pennsylvania State Press.

Narveson, Jan. 1986. "Abortion and Infanticide: A Contractarian Defense of the Right to Abortion and the Wrongness of Infanticide." *Bowling Green Studies in Philosophy VIII*. Bowling Green, OH: Bowling Green State University Press.

———. 1999. *Moral Matters*. Peterborough, ON: Broadview Press.

———. 2002. *Respecting Persons in Theory and Practice*. Lanham, MD: Rowman & Littlefield.

National Clearinghouse on Child Abuse and Neglect Information. "Child Maltreatment 2003." US Department of Health and Human Services Administration for Children and Families. http://www.acf.hhs.gov/programs/cb/pubs/cm03.

National Foster Parent Association Information and Services Office, 226 Kilts Drive, Houston, TX 77024. http://www.nfpainc.org/content/index.asp?page=628 &nmenu=3.

Noddings, Nel. 1984. *Caring: A Feminine Approach to Ethics and Moral Education*. Berkeley: University of California Press.

Noggle, Robert. 2003. "Special Agents: Children's Autonomy and Parental Authority." In David Archard and Colin Macleod, eds., *The Moral and Political Status of Children*. Oxford: Oxford University Press, 97–118.

Nussbaum, Martha. 1999. *Sex and Social Justice*. Oxford: Oxford University Press.

———. 2000. *Women and Human Development*. Cambridge, MA: Cambridge University Press.

NYS DSS Standards of Practice for Adoption Services (State of NY, Title 18-DSS, Part 421), Section 421.16 Adoption Study Criteria.

Oakley, Ann. 1976. *Women's Work: The Housewife, Past and Present*. New York: Vintage.

OMA Committee on Population Health. 1996. "Cigarette Smoke and Kids' Health." http://www.oma.org/Health/tobacco/2ndsmoke.asp, accessed June 1, 2007.

Ontario Association of Children's Aid Societies. 2006. "What Is a CAS?" and "How and When to Report Abuse or Neglect." http://www.oacas.org/resources.

Physicians for a Smoke-Free Canada. n.d. "Cigarette Smoke and Kids' Health." http://www.smoke-free.ca/Second-Hand-Smoke/health_kids.htm.

Planned Parenthood of Central Missouri v. Danforth, 428 U.S. 52 (1976).

Purdy, Laura. 1992. *In Their Best Interest? The Case against Equal Rights for Children*. Ithaca, NY: Cornell University Press.

———. 1996. "Loving Future People." In *Reproducing Persons: Issues in Feminist Bioethics*. Ithaca, NY: Cornell University Press.

R. v. Keegstra, [1990] 3 S.C.R. 697.

R. v. Oakes, [1986] 1 S.C.R. 103.

Rakowski, Eric. 1991. *Equal Justice*. New York: Oxford University Press.

Rawls, John. 1971. *A Theory of Justice*. Cambridge, MA: Harvard University Press.

———. 1993. *Political Liberalism*. New York: Columbia University Press.

Raz, Joseph. 1986. *The Morality of Freedom*. Oxford: Oxford University Press.

Ritchie, Karen. 1995. "The Little Woman Meets Son of DSM-III." In Françoise Baylis et al., eds., *Health Care Ethics in Canada*. Toronto: Harcourt Brace Canada, 237–47.

Robertson, John. 1994. *Children of Choice: Freedom and the New Reproductive Genetics*. Princeton, NJ: Princeton University Press.

Rosenblum, Nancy. 1998. *Membership and Morals*. Princeton, NJ: Princeton University Press.

Ross v. New Brunswick School District No. 15, [1996] 1 S.C.R. 825.

Ruddick, Sara. 1989. *Maternal Thinking: Toward a Politics of Peace*. Boston: Beacon.

Ryan, Alan. 2005. "The Magic of 'I.'" *New York Review of Books*, April 28, 35–37.

Scarre, Geoffrey. 1989. *Children, Parents and Politics*. Cambridge: Cambridge University Press.

Schoeman, Ferdinand. 1980. "Rights of Children, Rights of Parents, and the Moral Basis of the Family." *Ethics* 91: 6–19.

Stolzenberg, Nomi Maya. 1993. "'He Drew a Circle That Shut Me Out': Assimilation, Indoctrination, and the Paradox of a Liberal Education." *Harvard Law Review* 106.

Thomas, Laurence. 1987. "Friendship." *Synthese* 72: 217–36.

Thompson, Audrey. 1989. "Friendship and Moral Character." *Philosophy of Education* 45: 61–75.

Thomson, Judith. 1990. *The Realm of Rights*. Cambridge, MA: Harvard University Press.

Tinker v. Des Moines Independent Community School District, 393 U.S. 503 (1969).

Tolson, Mike. 1999. "Eventually Reality Bites Parents in Multiple Births." *Houston Chronicle*, January 10, 1999, A1.

Tronto, Joan. 1993. *Moral Boundaries: A Political Argument for an Ethic of Care*. London: Routledge.

Turner, Susan M., and Matthews, Gareth B., eds. 1998. *The Philosopher's Child: Critical Essays in the Western Tradition*. Rochester, NY: University of Rochester Press.

Unger, P. 1996. *Living High and Letting Die: Our Illusions of Innocence*. Oxford: Oxford University Press.

UNICEF. *The State of the World's Children 2006*. http://www.unicef.org.sowco6/index.php.

United States Department of Health and Human Services. Child Abuse and Neglect Data. http://www.childwelfare.gov/can/index.cfm.

Uttal, Lynet. 1996. "Custodial Care, Surrogate Care, and Coordinated Care: Employed Mothers and the Meaning of Child Care." *Gender and Society* 10: 291–311.

Vallentyne, Peter, and Lipson, Morry. 1989. "Equal Opportunity and the Family." *Public Affairs Quarterly* 3: 29–47.

Volunteer Court Appointed Special Advocates (CASA). 2000. NCASAA Staff, Statistics on Child Abuse and Neglect, Foster Care, Adoption and CASA Programs. February.

Vopat, Mark. 2003. "Contractarianism and Children." *Public Affairs Quarterly*: 49–65.

Westman, Jack. 1994. *Licensing Parents: Can We Prevent Child Abuse?* New York: Insight Books.

Willett, Cynthia. 1995. *Maternal Ethics and Other Slave Moralities*. New York: Routledge.

Wilson, James Q., and Hernstein, Richard J. 1985. *Crime and Human Nature*. New York: Simon & Schuster.

Winning Kids. 2006. "Foster Care Frequently Asked Questions." http://www.fosteradoptwinningkids.com/website/eng/index.php.

Wisconsin v. Yoder, 406 U.S. 205 (1972).

NOTES ON CONTRIBUTORS

COLIN M. MACLEOD is Associate Professor in the Department of Philosophy and the Faculty of Law at the University of Victoria. He is the author *Liberalism, Justice and Markets* (OUP 1998) and co-editor with David Archard of *The Moral and Political Status of Children* (OUP 2002).

AMY MULLIN is Professor of Philosophy at the University of Toronto. She is the author of *Reconceiving Pregnancy and Childcare* (Cambridge 2005), along with articles in feminist philosophy, the history of philosophy, and aesthetics. She has three children.

JAN NARVESON is Distinguished Professor Emeritus of the University of Waterloo, after teaching there for more than forty years. He is the author of *The Libertarian Idea, Respecting Persons in Theory and Practice, Moral Matters,* and various others. He is the father of three and devotes a lot of his life to organizing chamber music concerts.

LAURA M. PURDY received a PhD from Stanford University and is Professor of Philosophy and Ruth and Albert Koch Professor of Humanities at Wells College, where she has been based since 1979. Her areas of specialization are applied ethics, primarily bioethics, reproductive ethics, family issues, and feminism. She is author of *In Their Best Interest? The Case against Equal Rights for Children* and *Reproducing Persons: Issues in Feminist Bioethics* and co-editor of *Feminist Perspectives in Medical Ethics* (with Helen B. Holmes), *Violence against Women: Philosophical Perspectives* (with Stanley French and Wanda Teays), *Embodying Bioethics: Recent Feminist Advances* (with Anne Donchin), and *Bioethics, Justice, and Health Care* (with Wanda Teays), as well as many articles.

MARC RAMSAY is Assistant Professor in the Department of Philosophy at Acadia University. In addition to children's rights, his current research interests include the role of the harm principle in constitutional law and the relevance of religious beliefs to the law of torts.

MARK C. VOPAT is Assistant Professor of Philosophy at Youngstown State University in Youngstown, Ohio. His research interests are in moral and political philosophy, particularly in the areas of children's rights, education, distributive justice, and justice and technology. He has written recently on issues of justice, religion, and a child's right to an education, as well as on issues in professional ethics. His homepage can be found at www.as.ysu.edu/~philrel/faculty/vopat/Vopat.html.

KAREN WENDLING is Associate Professor of Philosophy at the University of Guelph in Guelph, Ontario. Most of her publications are on egalitarianism, broadly conceived. She also has a long-standing interest in the political development of children from unfree and unequal subjects into free and equal citizens.

ANGELA WHITE is a doctoral student in Philosophy at the University of Western Ontario. Her research interests are in political philosophy and social justice, health care ethics, and feminist ethics. She has published and presented work on ethical issues related to reproductive technologies, particularly in vitro fertilization and human embryo stem cell research. Her homepage is at http://publish.uwo.ca/~awhite33/.

INDEX